Commer

"Tommy Bibey keeps his feet and his heart in three different worlds: bluegrass music, family medicine, and golf. In 'The Mandolin Case' he conflates these three worlds into an arresting story that sheds humane light and his gentle humor on his world and the folks who inhabit it."

— *Ted Lehmann, Bluegrass Photojournalist*

"Dr. Bibey honors the truth and simplicity of rural southern life and traditional music. Finally, an author resists the hackneyed stereotype to accurately portray the integrity of bluegrass music and the people that love it."

— *Kristin Scott Benson, member of Grascals,*
IBMA Banjo Player of Year 2008 and 2009

"Ranger Dog knew the truth all along."

— *Cindy Carter, long time Dr. Bibey Blog reader from N.C.*

"There is something you can learn from every mandolin player you hear."

— *Sam Bush, King of Newgrass and the right-hand rocking,*
reggae ruler of the Mandolin Universe.

"Dr B – I have really enjoyed reading your work. It appears you have captured the essence of what we strive to do in the legal profession with your portrayal of Martin Taylor. He has the requisite qualities and attributes of a true Southern lawyer and what I consider the ultimate qualification—a seeker of truth. Perhaps one day you could introduce me to him. I would love to get to know him better. You should continue your writing efforts, as you have a unique talent."

— *Bill Elam -prominent Charlotte, N.C. attorney and medical malpractice specialist*

"If the mandolin stands for the truth, I'm all for it."

— *Ronnie McCoury of the Del McCoury band and the Traveling McCoury's*

"I introduced Dr. B to bluegrass music and helped with his medical education. He has blended both of these disciplines into a metaphor for his story telling and view of life in general. My congrats on the publishing of his book. It will be well received."

— Dr. Peter Temple, Retired rural Family Physician and Community Medicine preceptor for East Carolina University School of Medicine

"I was raised in a valley town between the Cumberland Mountains, I know the characters in 'The Mandolin Case.' Dr Bibey shows them as they are; fun loving musicians, card players and sportsman. These are the people I grew up with. Mix them with a bunch of lawyers and you've got one hell of a read. I didn't want it to end.'

— Don Sterchi, Newspaper columnist and free lance writer

"The secret is in the mandolins."

— Tony Williamson, Merlefest Mandomania moderator and mandolin master.

"I meet a great many characters and untangle a lot of plot lines in my job as a book editor. I meet a great many authors, too. Tom Bibey is certainly up at the top level with those, because both his characters and his plot in 'The Mandolin Case' match his philosophy on life: You cannot get through it by cheating your family, neighbors, or friends. Love and loyalty make up his life and his novel. The book is a little gem that I'm sure you will all enjoy, but it's his underlying message that gives it its luster."

— Dorrie O'Brien, professional editor, Dallas

"Dr. B captures the personality and traditions of Bluegrass in a new millennium setting. However, this book is not only for lovers of mandolins, but also for readers who love a good mystery."

— Mary Weber, Weber Fine Acoustic Instruments

"The 'The Mandolin Case' provides more twists and curls than the grain in a piece of birds-eye maple. Like a master fiddler weaving notes through the melody of a song, Bibey holds forth simplicity as the most complex asset when prejudice and greed place honor and integrity on trial."

— Dan Hays, International Bluegrass Music Association

"With the right education even a doctor can write fiction."

– *Peggy Turner, Mississippi English teacher and graduate of the Bread Loaf School of English, has led numerous creative internet exchanges between diverse classrooms to foster authentic writing experiences*

"The Mandolin Case has more twists and turns than the stock market on a volatile day."

– *Jay D. Westmoreland, CFP® Charlotte, NC*

"A yarn that spins music and medicine spiced with down home Southern cooking and values. You are in for quite a read."

– *Therese Zink, MD, editor of The Country Doctor Revisited: A 21st Century Reader*

"We have known Dr. B for years. He is a good doctor, a serious amateur mandolinist, and a writer. Most of all though, 'The Mandolin Case' shows, he is a man who cares about his people."

– *Darin and Brooke Aldridge, the Bluegrass Sweethearts*

"Midwestern bluegrassers will recognize their own stories in the doc's tale. Around the world, those who listen for the ancient tones, are a family and we know the real thing when we read it."

– *Carmen Claypool, member Summit Grass, Jefferson City MO*

"Thanks for a wonderfull vivid description of golf in 'The Mandolin Case'! As Bones and Martin were playing their match, it seemed that I was on the course with them enjoying their company and conversations."

– *Phil Wallace, N.C. PGA golf professional*

Comments on Dr. Tom Bibey's Blog
http://drtombibey.wordpress.com

"Dr Bibey is Australia's favourite American import. Who else combines country doctoring, mandolin picking and writing like he does? What a story, what characters, what a rip-roaring tale, Dr. B."

— *Karen Collum, Australian Author*

"Folks in Texas find a bluegrass brother just one beat away in Dr. B. - We believe we will understand the mysteries of "The Mandolin Case" and await its release."

— *Adam Rekerdres (Rekx)*

"Dr Bibey, I loved your story. Sounds like a place I would love to work."

— *Carolyn*

"I will miss Indie too. Hope that his passing is not too painful. He deserves to get some rest…."

— *Newt221*

"Love to hear you weigh in sometime on how supporting live music is a better investment of a person's time than veging around the house on weekends."

— *mandogrin*

"Dr. B sure is a pretty good picker for a doctor. We're all looking forward to his new book, 'The Mandolin Case.'"

— *Woody Platt, the Steep Canyon Rangers*

"When a man writes like that, there has to be a reason."

— *Irene Lehmann*

"The visions you put in my mind, dance. A photo would squelch my dreams".

— *Billy Watson*

"I live in a city with almost 2 million other souls… If I ever come to the south I'll definitely go to a bluegrass festival."

— *Susan Egan*

The Mandolin Case

A Novel about Country Doctors, Honest Lawyers and True Music

—◆•◆•◆—

DR. TOM BIBEY

Ford, Falcon & McNeil Publishers

Chattanooga

The Mandolin Case

Copyright © 2009-2010 Tom Bibey

Designed by Aimee Roberts of Luna Graphic Design
Cover & Back Cover Photographs by Jesse Guardiani
Cover Mandolin courtesy of Levi Jackson Wiggins.
Editor: Dorrie O'Brien

ISBN 978-0-9827252-0-7

Library of Congress Subject Headings
          Southern States - Fiction
          Mystery - Fiction
          Appalachia - Fiction
          Bluegrass music - Fiction
          Medical - Fiction
          Country Doctor - Fiction
          Legal - Fiction

Author's Note

My name is Dr. Tom Bibey. I teach at Sandhills University, a medical center fifty miles from Harvey County. After residency I practiced medicine in Harvey County, and shared call with Dr. Jenkins, or 'Indie' as everyone called him. He drank too much and smoked a pack a day but always put his patients first and would not lie if you tortured him. He played a bluegrass fiddle so well that everyone in Harvey County said he had the talent to go pro but enough sense not to. I think the fact was he simply could not leave his people.

I am convinced Dr. Henry 'Indie' Jenkins was one of the wisest doctors I have ever known. He knew all the secrets of Harvey County. The deepest one was what happened when Blinky Wilson died. Blinky was Indie's patient and best friend. His death brought on a lot of trouble, and in the doctor world that means lawyers.

When it happened, Indie worked with a young doctor named James 'Bones' Robertson. As the troubles wore on, Bones began to realize Indie possessed wisdom uncommon to ordinary men. The young doctor felt he was a witness to events no one should forget, and began to take notes.

When Indie's wife died and he wound up in the nursing home, Bones got up the nerve to ask Indie's permission to write the story. Indie chuckled. He knew all along Bones had kept a journal, and encouraged him to continue his pursuit of the truth.

I love rural medicine, and have all respect for doctors like Indie Jenkins. But when Sandhills offered me a teaching position I couldn't turn it down. It was in my wife's hometown, and promised us security and a tranquil life.

We moved away after only four years and I didn't know of Indie's trial for years.

I first got to know James Robertson when he became a medical student at Sandhills. Indie was the one who later nicknamed him "Bones." He was a good student, though not brilliant. We both loved bluegrass music. I played a little guitar, and James picked the mandolin. Over the years we would run into each other at a medical conference or bluegrass festival.

A year before Indie died, James saw one of my articles and called. He had trouble writing Indie's story and insisted we visit. At first I resisted. It sounded like a project that could consume a man. After many phone calls, I agreed to meet him at MerleFest behind the Americana stage. There he spilled out the story as fast as he could sputter the words.

He had an army surplus backpack full of notes. It was a hopeless jumble of file cards, spiral notebooks, and two shoe boxes of memos. I could not see how anyone could organize it and create a readable story. He had tried to get publishers interested and showed me a file of sixty-three rejection letters. "Bibey, take these notes and write it," he begged.

I understood why Indie's story had failed to attract any interest; it was a mess. My specialty was logical medical articles. The trial had intrigue, but I was skeptical and unsure I had the emotional energy to write a whole book. I tried to brush him off and said I was a busy professor with obligations at Sandhills.

The boy had no give up in him. He continued to call to see if I had made up my mind. I finally told him I would consider it. When Indie's health started to fail, James begged me to visit him. Indie didn't have children. I feared his story would be lost once he was gone, and couldn't say no.

We spent a full afternoon with Indie at the nursing home. He was dying, but his mind was clear. Barney the skeleton stood watch at bedside with a stethoscope strung around his neck. A worn "Harrison's Text of Medicine" was open on the table next to his fiddle. We talked about the case and life, and then Indie lent me the keys to his cabin. "Take some time off," he said, "relax and give writing the story some thought."

I told him I would but went back to work and tried to forget the promise, but I could not get the old man off my mind. I began to have trouble with concentration and my golf game was in shambles. I decided I had to take him up on the offer to use his cabin.

It was isolated, and as the river rolled across the rocks and a fire crackled in the fireplace, I could see how Indie found strength there. I began to write that night and soon had a rough draft.

Still, I needed to learn the craft of a story. I placed a few non-medical articles in regional magazines and through those, found an agent. He suggested I start a blog to develop a non-medical voice. I also started a FaceBook page to get in touch with real bluegrass people.

Readers of my blog became endeared to Indie, and suggestions came in from all over the world. I am convinced some of them must have personally known him. The details they forwarded could only have come from someone who did.

On weekends I went back to Harvey County and interviewed everyone who had been connected to the case. Many said they learned truth from Indie, and could not let his memory die. As I studied his life, I also began to learn.

Near the end of Indie's life, I asked him what he wanted us to remember. He lay there in bed and struggled to sit up a bit. He opened his eyes, smiled, and then raised his left hand as if he cradled a fiddle. He began to bow a slow shuffle. "Show what 'Bones' learned. When he came back home, 'Bones' was a good boy, and smart too, but he was naïve. People make life too complicated, and it's really simple. All he needed was experience and a little music."

I asked Indie what his secret was. "Ain't nothing to it," he said. "It doesn't take any special talent to be wicked. Anyone can do that. But to be a decent person requires creativity that borders on art. Simple as that."

It did not seem that simple to me and Indie knew I wasn't convinced. "Son, by the time you finish your book, you'll understand."

"The Mandolin Case" is his story. After you have read it, if you would like to email me, I would love to hear from you. If you know a story from Indie's life please send it along. I'll try to incorporate it in a future edition.

I hope you enjoy. I did my best to pass Indie on to you.

Dr. Tom Bibey, MD

http://drtombibey.wordpress.com

CHAPTER ONE

How "Bones" Met "Indie"

DR. JAMES F. ROBERTSON STOPPED BY the nurse's station. "Where's the doctor's lounge?"

The clerk smiled. "You must be Dr. Robertson." She glanced to her right and nodded. "Down the hall; second door on the left."

"Thanks." He looked up at the wall clock. 4:15, then opened the door to the lounge and saw a thin, stoop-shouldered elderly man hunched over a banjo, intent on his music. A Stetson hat obscured his features.

"Do you know where I can find Henry Jenkins?"

"Nope."

James scratched his head. "Mr. Olden told me he would be here at four."

The old fellow's stained cowboy boots tapped in perfect time with the music. "Starting to sound like Ralph Stanley, huh?"

James looked at his watch. "But Mr. Olden said he'd be here."

"You know how doctors are, always damn late."

The man stood up, set the banjo down, took off his Stetson, and peered into Robertson's blue eyes. He grasped the younger man's hand with a firm shake.

Robertson was struck by the man's leathered face, weary and etched with a road map of wrinkles.

"Doctor Jenkins! I didn't recognize you."

"Son, you don't need to call me doctor."

"Well, I don't know. Somehow Henry doesn't seem right."

"It's Indie to my friends."

"Uh, okay, Indie. So you play the banjo?"

"Ah, I'm just messing. I'm still a fiddle man." He tugged on his ear, "Now, your name again?"

"James. James Fitzgerald Robertson."

"James? Sounds like a butler. Didn't you play baseball at Harvey High?"

"That's me."

"He smiled. "Residency put a few gray hairs on you didn't it, son?"

"Yes, sir."

"Better to turn gray than turn loose." He looked at James again. "You've put on weight since those days."

"Yes sir. Got married."

"Yeah, you were skinny back then." He smiled. "Still lanky, though." He rubbed his bald head as he thought. "From here on you're 'Bones.' James Fitzgerald is too formal for me."

"Yes, sir."

CHAPTER TWO

First Signs of Trouble

HARVEY COUNTY DIDN'T HAVE MANY DOCTORS in those days. All the family doctors were in solo practice, but Indie and Bones shared office space and night call with Dr. Sanjay Sharma.

Dr. Mike Blake was the other family doctor in town. He didn't have to take hospital call, and for a long time no one knew why. He told his patients it was because they deserved the best, and he preferred an internist take care of them in the hospital.

"One year my cousin in Chicago was sick with cancer and I took my Boards up there." Indie said. "I ran into Blake."

"What was he doing all the way up there?"

"Counting on anonymity."

"I bet he was surprised to see you."

"Surprised? Sumbitch Blake saw me from across the room after the test, turned white and left."

"So?"

"Blake never showed up on the recertification list. I know he took the exam. I saw him in the test room."

"So he flunked?"

"Worse than that, he's never been certified."

"Damn." Bones paused for a moment. "I thought we had to have our boards to be on the staff."

Indie laughed. "We do. But our red-haired CEO put him on the Board of Trustees because he gets things done. When Blake's cousin paved the hospital parking lot, a new road was put in at Olden's farm. Blake did a lot for Olden like that. When payback time came, Olden made our internists cover Blake's calls. He had 'em over a barrel 'bout something."

"Good Lord."

"You shoulda seen Olden's face when I told him I knew." Indie leaned in closer. "I stood over him at his desk and said, Indians know the truth and never tell lies. Made him mad as hell."

Indie played cards every Friday with Blinky Wilson at the Billiard-&-Bowl. They also went on motorcycle road trips every fall, and hunted and fished together. They'd been tight for years.

Blinky got his nickname from a nervous twitch in his right eye. Indie said it was just a tic and nothing to worry about, but Blinky's wife Betty made him go to a neurologist at Sandhills University, the medical center about fifty miles down the road.

When Betty saw Indie at the grocery store she said, "I wish you'd be more careful, Henry. The specialist said he had a neuro-ophthalmologic spasm."

"Hell, Betty, it's still a tic; just a high dollar one." He looked around to be sure no one was within earshot, and then whispered, "Betty, it's caused by lack-a-nooky syndrome."

Betty took a swing at Indie but he dodged, then she stormed out of the store. Later he realized Betty took it out on Blinky, and he never brought it up again.

One Friday at the card game Indie handed Blinky a prescription for Vicodin. Bones pulled Indie aside, "You can't do that. You gotta see him in the office and put it in the chart. Somebody from the Board's gonna get after you."

"You worry too much. He needs the damn medicine. What's wrong with it? It's the same stuff the Pain Clinic gives him, but they charge him four hundred bucks. Blink can't afford that. Besides, we're like brothers. We've both got some Choctaw blood, you know."

One time at his cabin, Indie had a few drinks and told Bones about his baseball days. He'd played Legion ball in a little town called Waynesville, and Olden had been a bat boy for Charlotte. He said they all called Olden "Bloomer" 'cause his pants fell down on the ball field in the semi-finals. When Indie told the story, he laughed until his eyes watered. The next day, he came in early and asked Bones not to repeat it.

Blinky Wilson's health began to deteriorate but he and Indie never missed a Friday poker game. One night Blinky missed a play.

Indie put down his cards. "What the hell's up with you? You never miss."

"Awh, this hyena hernie's acting up. You got any of them 'Tagemets' out in the Jeep?"

"You're getting too many illnesses. I'm gonna send you to a specialist."

"You ain't gonna make me go to Blake are you?" Blink asked.

Indie laughed out loud. "Nah, Blink. Love ya too much for that." He put on his Stetson, and the two got up to go out to Indie's Jeep.

Indie pulled on the door handle of his Jeep. It creaked open.

"What happened to your door?" Blinky asked.

"Ah hell, I hit a telephone pole in the ice storm. I'll get around to fixing it. Besides, it's a '75," he said. "Depreciated out anyway."

Indie sorted through a pile of cassettes and journal articles in the front seat. "I don't see any Tagamet. I don't know if it'd help you or not anyway. You short of breath?"

"You treat me for emphysema, you know."

"Yeah, but you're worse."

"I guess so."

"I never did see a report on that treadmill I ordered. Didja get it done?"

"I meant to."

"You tight in the chest at all?" Indie asked.

"You just want me in that hospital."

Indie shook his head. "Damn it, I've been worried about you for a month. Park your ass over there and let me write an order to put you on the treadmill tomorrow morning. And you better be there."

Indie fished around in the glove box and found an admission sheet, and wrote the orders. At first Blinky protested, but agreed to check in and stuffed the paper in his back pocket.

On the way home, Blinky stopped at the Seven-Eleven to get his Friday night beef jerky. He picked up a Goody Powder and some Tums. He talked to the clerk a while, began to feel better, and went home.

The next morning on rounds Indie looked for Blinky. "Did Blinky not show up?" he asked the charge nurse.

"Afraid not, sir."

"Good Lord." Indie shook his head.

"Doc, are you surprised?"

"I guess not. He's probably okay. He can't help it."

After rounds Indie rode by Blink's house, but Betty said Blink had gone out to breakfast. He assumed it was a false alarm, turned the Chief down Marion Street, and went for a ride in the country. Indie loved his Chief. It was a '47 vintage Nevada Highway Patrol Indian Motorsports bike that Indie and Blink found on a hunting trip to Missouri. It sat in his garage two years before they restored it.

Indie was halfway to the cabin when he realized he'd left his helmet behind. The sun beat down on his bald head and the wind whistled by. Indie thought, *Doctors worry too much, I guess Blink's okay. I'll catch up with him come first of the week.*

CHAPTER THREE

Curb Service

MONDAY MORNING BLINKY CHECKED IN with Indie to get an EKG.

As it rolled off, Indie began to pace. "Heart attack," he mumbled. "Good Lord, Blinky. Why didn't you come in on Friday like I told ya?"

"I got to feeling better. Hell, it ain't *your* fault."

Indie studied the EKG again. "Let me send you down to the medical center. They've got a new cardiologist at Sandhills I really like."

"I gotta?"

"Yep. We don't have a cardiologist."

Indie handed the EKG to his nurse. "How 'bout copying this, Trina? Blink needs to take it with him." He looked at it one last time. "I don't know if they can change much. Damn."

Blinky winced. "This'll foul up Betty's bridge game."

"She'll have to get over it. You better not change your mind this time."

"I won't, I promise."

Indie phoned. "Betty, Blink's had a heart attack. I'm gonna ship him over to Sandhills. He probably had it Friday night."

"Friday night? Why didn't you do something then?"

"I gave him orders, but—"

"Damn it, Indie, I've told you a thousand times. You have to make Blinky. You can't leave it up to him."

"Whatever. He's okay, though."

"How's he going to get there?"

"I've already called the ambulance."

"Well, tell him I need the car. I have my bridge game today. He should know that."

"Bridge game?! Betty! Don't worry about the car. I'll have Trina bring it to you. Damn." *God-all-mighty*, Indie thought. *You'd think a heart attack would trump bridge.*

Betty complained to CEO Jim Olden, who called the hospital attorney, Jackson Leggett. Leggett tracked down Pete Bowen who verified Indie had recommended admission on Friday night. Leggett advised against any intervention.

Blinky stayed in Sandhills Heart Unit two days, and then was sent home. When the records came in from the Medical Center it was clear the damage was minimal. A med student did the discharge, and dictated a note that Blinky would have been just as well off at home.

Betty was furious. "What does that kid know? Hell, he's not even out of medical school yet."

Blinky's problems began to add up. His arthritis was worse. He'd had a motorcycle wreck the summer before, and his back flared up so bad that Fentanyl patches were all that would keep his pain under control. Now he'd had a heart attack.

Betty read in the *Ladies Home Journal* how Fentanyl was addictive. She despised the patches, but Blinky said it worked. She arranged a second opinion at Grey Pain Clinic in Durham after she saw the ads on T.V. but Blinky wouldn't take Dr. Grey's medicines.

"Damn dope doctor," Blinky told Indie. "Hell, he's on the Medical Board black list."

"How'd you know that?"

"I read it."

"I didn't see it in the Harvey Herald."

"It warn't. It was in that Bulletin you get from the Board. I read 'em when I'm in your office waiting on you to go to lunch."

"Damn, Blinky. I'm gonna have to take away your key."

Betty Wilson tried to one-up Indie, and sent Blinky to a doctor the Board had on the ropes. Indie laughed every time he thought of Blinky rummaging through his trash for the doctor dirt.

Indie gave Blinky samples and wrote off most of his office visits. Several times Betty tried to line up Blinky with another doc, but no one would take on the case. Of course, she wouldn't call on Bones or Dr. Sharma; they were too tight with Indie. The Internists knew not to take on Indie's problems; his were never easy cases. When Dr. Blake said no, Betty knew she was stuck with Indie.

Blinky put away his motorcycle early that fall. Indie went along. "Too cold this year, brother. We'll get 'em back out come spring."

By mid-winter Blinky seemed to stabilize. He wasn't healthy, and always short of breath, but he stayed out of the hospital. Every so often, he'd go to Pete's Friday night card game, but other than that kept close to home. Indie talked about getting the bikes out next spring and Blinky said he didn't care. Once Blinky lost interest in his bike, Indie knew he was in trouble.

Indie finished up early one Friday and propped up his feet on the desk. He lit a cigarette, blew some smoke rings, and then got out his fiddle.

Strains of *Lonesome Road Blues* drifted down the hallway. Up front, Trina laughed. "Ole doc's done got out the fiddle. I don't think we'll get any more work out of him today."

A few minutes later, Betty Wilson arrived unannounced. "Where is Dr. Jenkins?

"I'm sorry, Betty, do you have an appointment?" Trina asked.

"Tell him Blinky's sick."

Trina went to Indie's office. Indie had slid his fiddle behind his desk. "Don't have to tell me; I hear her."

Indie put out his cigarette and walked to the front desk.

"Henry, something is terribly wrong with Blinky." Betty stood with one hand on her hip and motioned toward the parking lot. "Something has to be done."

"What's wrong?"

"You're the doctor. He has a fever; I know that."

"Where is he?"

"Out in the ambulance. I told him he needed to go to the hospital, but he won't listen."

"Hell, Betty, don't you know about curb service?"

"Curb service?"

"Yeah. Blink knows if I check him here, he won't have to wait four hours in the ER. What happened?"

"He's been out of his head all day."

Indie picked up his stethoscope. "If Blinky gets out of that ambulance he'll get stuck for a second ride; I'll see him outside. We call it Curb Service. Blink just wants to save money. You should be thankful."

Betty Wilson didn't comment.

Indie went out to the ambulance.

CHAPTER FOUR

Perked Up

INDIE CLASPED THE GRAB BARS on the back of the ambulance, ducked his head, and climbed in. Blinky heard his voice and tried to sit up, but couldn't. He took Blinky's hand and noted his tremor was worse.

"Indie ... I think ... I'm at the end ... of the road ... pal. 'Preciate you."

"Where are you, Blink?" Indie asked.

Blinky ventured a guess. "We at the cabin?"

Indie smoothed out Blinky's hair and tucked his covers under his chin. "Yeah, you look cold. I'll start us up a fire. Nothing can be wrong at the cabin, you know."

Blink grasped Indie by the elbow and held tight. "The cabin? Damn. Good, Indie . . -the---the –the… cabin ... Let's go for a swim ... we can cool off ... I got a fever, Indie."

A song flashed by Indie—*'a fever in my head.'* What was the tune? *Blinky has delirium and probably infection. We'll sort it out,* he thought.

"Okay, Blink, tell ya what. I'm gonna hold off on your Fentanyl for now, and get you in the hospital. Fluids, antibiotics; you should be okay in a day or two. I ain't done you wrong yet, huh?"

Blink smiled.

Indie ducked his head to climb back out of the ambulance. Betty waited in the car.

The Wilson's battered '76 Pinto was more worn out than Blinky. The factory paint was Emerald Green, but Blinky called it "emesis green" after he read the word in one of Indie's doctor books. The rear quarter panel had a big dent Blink hadn't gotten around to fixing. It crossed Indie's mind that the next time he and Ms. Jenkins got ready to trade, maybe they could just give their car to Blinky. The man needed a better ride.

Ms. Wilson rolled down the window. Indie leaned over to speak to her. "I think he'll perk up in a day or two."

"Well, I hope so. The man is sick all the time."

"I'll call Admitting and get him a room. I'll be over in an hour or so."

"Call me when he's good enough to come home. I have a busy weekend. I've got the Sunday School lesson, so I wish you wouldn't bother me during church."

"Well, I'm going be gone this weekend, but I'll get him covered before I go."

"Very well." She drove off.

Bitch, Indie thought. He instructed the driver to take Blink to the hospital.

Indie finished up the paperwork in his office, then dropped by the house to pick up a few items. At the hospital he reviewed Blinky's chart. No blood clot, no heart attack. Urinary infection, no doubt, but his temperature was down. He was still confused, but not as bad. Maybe he'd turn around.

"Blink, I think you're better."

Blinky grunted. "Yup."

Indie tucked him in.

When Indie walked into the doctor's break room, Bones was there and called out to him. "Hey, Indie. Moose Dooley picked up a gig in Raleigh tomorrow night. Gonna play for the Boy Scout Winter Jamboree."

"Damn, it'll be cold."

"Naw, it's gonna be in the Scout Hut. You wanta go? Sharma's on call."

"I'd love to, but I gotta be in Asheville. Mama's going into hospice."

Bones shook his head, "I hate that."

"Yeah, but at ninety-eight ... Hmm. I wish you were gonna be here. Blinky's in two-two-one. Sharma'll take good care of him, but I hate for both of us to be gone when he's sick."

"What's up with Blink?"

"Don't know yet, but I think he's septic. He looks better than he did earlier. Betty brought him by right when the office was closing up."

"Dropped him off so you could babysit for the weekend, huh?"

"Yep. Hell, she went home. She won't be back until it's time for him to leave, and she'll gripe about having to come get him then."

"What is it with her? How come she hates Blinky so bad?"

"That's a long story." He went over to the counter and put on some coffee. "We all go back a ways." Indie rummaged through the cabinets. "They don't keep any snacks worth a damn in here." He pulled out some potato chips. "Me and Blink played against each other in Legion ball. He was a one hell of a third baseman."

"Blinky?"

"Yep. Blink met Betty in Tupelo when he played in the old Southern Series. And let me tell you, that girl was hotter than a two-dollar pistol."

"Hard to believe."

"No kidding. Well, like I say, Blink was a star, and well, uh ... Look, Bones, I ain't told anyone this stuff in years."

"It's okay; you don't have to go there." Bones poured a cup of coffee.

"Nah, you need to know. If anything ever happened to me, Blink would want you to be his doc. Anyway, Betty didn't hide the fact she was willing, and Blinky got her pregnant."

"Dang."

"Yeah, well, I was at the Legion game when her folks showed up. Her father, Mr. Langhorne, didn't say much in front of me, but you could tell he was pissed. Anyway, Blink said her father went on about they'd disgraced the family. Well, Betty was gonna show them, so she and Blink got married."

"How'd the old man take it?"

"Disowned her. She and Blink moved to North Carolina. At first it went okay. Blinky was a great prospect. The Braves wanted to sign him."

"Blinky played pro ball?"

"He didn't. He got hit in the head by a wild pitch and was laid up at University Hospital for two weeks. After that, he was good, but never quite the same. He went into the service and became a mechanic."

"How'd Betty take all that?"

"Good for a little while. Then she got selective memory. All I heard was about how Blinky got her pregnant and ruined her life. I reminded her it took two, and she didn't like it."

"Uh, hey, you don't have to answer this, but have you heard that Olden and Betty, uh...?"

Indie looked around the corner. "Might not mention that. One time I told Betty I knew she had a thing for ballplayers and Olden and I went back to Legion days. She got pissed, and cut Blinky off for two months."

"God, she's mean. Poor Blink. He's had a hard road."

"When he went on disability after his back surgery, it was over. She never had any more to do with him after that."

"I'll believe I'll go speak to him before I go home."

"He'd love to see you. But, not a word about all this, okay?"

"No problem. Hey, you need to get out of here to check on your mom? I can cover you tonight."

"Well, mama doesn't like for me to drive much after dark. Says I'm too old and my vision isn't any good. Can you believe that woman?"

"She's a jewel. You going over to the Billiard-&-Bowl?"

"Nah. I'm gonna skip. I believe I'll stay close to the phone. If I can get Blink squared away by morning I think he'll be okay. Y'all have a good gig if I don't see you. I'm gonna check on him around dark-thirty. I'll tell him you asked about him."

"Thanks."

At home, Indie called to check on Blinky one more time. His lab reports were good, and the nurse reported no new problems. He sat by the phone in his Lazy Boy and soon drifted off to sleep. His wife woke him up after the evening news, and they went to bed.

On his way out of town, Indie went by the hospital to check on Blinky. He was already up. The Saturday cartoons blared away.

Indie turned down the TV. "Here's your percolator. I brought it last night."

"Were you here?"

"Yeah, you were in a fog."

"I musta got hold of some bad liquor."

"Maybe so, Blink. I put your Jim Beam under the sink in case you need him."

Indie put on a pot of coffee and chatted a while. "You sure look better; I think you're gonna make it." He chuckled and handed Blinky a cup of coffee.

"Jeez, I hope so, Indie. What the hell happened yesterday?"

"I believe it was just infection and dehydration. I thought at first the pain patch might have gone against you, but now I'm not so sure."

"My back's killing me. These beds ain't worth a fart in a whirlwind." Blink repositioned and sat up. "How 'bout restarting my patches?"

"Sure thing. I don't want you to hurt. Pain's against my doctor's rule book."

"Hey, I'm better anyway. Can't I go home?"

"No. You better soak up another couple days of antibiotics. Look, man, I hate to tell you, but I gotta be gone. They're putting mama in hospice in Asheville."

"That's too bad, Indie. She's a sweetheart. Damn if you didn't pick good ancestors."

"It's my secret to longevity; it sure ain't my habits."

"I believe I'd rather go with you. That woman made the best pecan pie in the South."

"Didn't she? All the Brashear women could cook up a storm."

"Maybe Bones can check on me."

"He's out of town. Sharma's here."

"Well, okay. Sanjay's good; just don't send Blake. I heard he didn't pass his Boards."

"How do you find out all this stuff, Blink?"

"I don't know."

Indie laughed. "Tell you what. When you get better, we'll take a road trip." He patted Blinky on the shoulder. "Well, if they don't take good care of you, let me know. Come Monday I'll give Olden hell."

Blinky laughed. "Hey, I don't want the damn DTs again. You remember the night I was in here and Olden's nephew snuck in and swiped my Jim Beam?"

"Yeah. God-a-mighty, Blink, that was the worst I've ever seen you."

"Yeah, boy. DTs are a hellava lot worse than being drunk."

"It's a damn shame to 'bout let a man die for lack of a drink." Indie rubbed his chin and chuckled. "If I'm in here, you see to it they don't treat me that way."

"I'll always look out for you, Indie. Whenever I got the DTs they sent a man from PR to talk to me, I told him it was Mr. Olden's nephew what caused me to go bad. I said I was gonna tell the paper, and that sumbitch Olden knocked ten grand off my bill."

"I thought he let the whole thing go."

"He didn't do that until I said I was gonna tell the reporter they used to call him Bloomer."

Indie slapped his side and laughed so loud the nurse came to see what was wrong. "Everything okay in here, Dr. Jenkins?"

"We're fine, Carol. Blinky's just funny, that's all."

"I'm glad you're better, Mr. Wilson."

"Thanks, ma'am."

She closed the door.

"Well Blink, I sure hate to be gone today." Indie poured the last of the coffee.

"I'm all right, man. You go check on your mama."

"Sure you're okay?"

"Hell, Indie, check my chart—you're the damn doctor." Blink laughed. "I'll be at the house before you get back to town."

"Okay." Indie straightened up Blink's covers. "I'll see you Monday." He closed the door and walked down to the nurses' station. "You know, Carol, I think Blink is better."

"Yeah, he's more like himself, Dr. Jenkins. Telling all kind of old war stories."

"If he tells one on me, it ain't true."

"Yes, sir."

Indie walked down the hall and punched the button to wait on the elevator. Good old Blink. He'd be okay.

CHAPTER FIVE

Cheetos and Cheerwine

AS SATURDAY WORE ON, BLINKY GREW MORE restless. He'd left his cigarettes at home, and he missed them. He went to his stash of Jim Beam and took a drink every so often to calm his nerves. Maria Diosas gave him an injection of Haldol, and it helped. Blinky watched as she walked away with that hypnotic wiggle. *God, what a set of legs,* he thought.

At dark, he felt weak and shaky. He curled up under his covers and called Betty. "Please come get me, sweetie. I promise I'll be good. I'm scared."

"For God's sake, you are such a child. I can't take care of you here. Get them to give you a pill and go to sleep."

"Could you at least bring me my cigarettes?"

"Damn, Blinky, you're in there to get well. You need to give them up anyway."

"Yes, ma'am."

He wanted some help to get to the bathroom, but no one would answer the call bell. When he got up he saw a bedpan and used it instead. He set it all in the hall, and then went back to bed. Someone scurried down the hallway to get it. Blinky chuckled.

The charge nurse went off duty at seven, and checked in before she left. "Are you okay Blinky?"

"Yes, ma'am. Sure wish you could stay."

"You'll be fine."

Shift change was without incident. Nights were short-staffed, but everyone in the rooms seemed stable.

Blinky called to complain he didn't have any soda. Molly Tenbrooks, the nurse assistant on the floor, soon brought him some Cheerwine and several bags of Cheetos. "Don't you worry, Mr. Wilson. When you get out of here, me and Johnny'll take you for a ride on the Harley just as soon as Dr. Indie says it's okay."

"You're a sweetie, Miss Molly." He settled down again.

Dr. Sharma checked in on him before he went home. He surveyed the snack supply in the corner. He laughed and told Molly it looked like Blinky had opened a canteen annex.

Blinky ran out of Cheerwine, which irritated him. There was a commotion down the hall. A code blue was called, but then cancelled right away; a false alarm but still hard on the nerves. He got back into his stash, and called home a second time.

"Betty, honest to God something ain't right. Come get me outta here."

"Are you drinking again? You leave before you're well and it'll be hell to pay."

He stayed.

He began to sweat, and mopped his brow. Maria brought him another injection. Chills set in. He got up, wandered around the room and found an extra blanket in the closet. The lullaby song played overhead—there was a new baby in the nursery.

He called Betty again. "Sweetie I ain't kidding; it's them heebie-jebbi…."

"Good God, will you please let me rest? You've got the damn DTs again. Tell then to give you a shot and leave me the hell alone." She slammed the phone down.

Toward midnight, the fever came back. Someone brought a couple Tylenols. The nausea was worse. Phenergan didn't help and he threw up.

His fever spiked again. The night nurse called Sanjay Sharma, and he ordered two blood cultures and added a second antibiotic.

The tech came up from the lab to get the cultures. "Can I get you anything? You look like you feel bad."

"Nah, but I appreciate it. Hey, take you a bag of them Cheetos. They're good."

"Thanks."

His temperature went up again. Someone brought another injection. Blinky was groggy, and not sure who it was. Calm set in.

Then his temperature spiked to 102.4.

The nurse at the monitor station jumped to her feet when the alarm went off. "God-a-mighty! It's Blinky. Cardiac arrest. V-fib. Code 99. Room 238. Molly, call the team STAT! And get hold of Sanjay right away."

Molly called the ER to set the code team into motion. She hung up and called Sharma at home.

"Damn," he said. "I can't believe it. I'll be right there."

Molly began to cry. After a minute, she remembered to call Ms. Wilson.

Ron Kirk was up from the ER inside of two minutes. Sharma arrived to assist. They put in an all-out effort, but Blinky was gone.

Sanjay paced around the room. "Man, he seemed fine. I mean, he had some fever, but he was okay, I swear he was. What do you think happened?" he asked Kirk.

"Ah, hell. Blink was worn out." Kirk knew Blinky well; he was a regular visitor to the E.R. "He ain't been right since he wrecked the cycle. Chronic pain will wear you down. His lungs were shot too. I bet he had another heart attack."

Betty Wilson arrived at 2:00 AM. She'd thrown on a sweater and house-coat, but still had on her flannel pajama bottoms and pink fluffy house slippers. The secretary put her in the family waiting room, and went to get the doctors. Kirk walked in first. Betty recognized him from the ER. She got right up in his face and wagged her finger under his nose.

"By God, I demand some answers. Blinky was fine. I just talked to him before I went to bed." She waved her arms around and knocked off one of her hair curlers. It bounced along the floor and came to rest under one of the Queen Anne chairs they had for the visitors. Sharma retrieved it, and tried to hand it back to her.

"Oh, go to hell." She threw it across the room. "Where is he? I want to see him."

The doctors took her to Blinky's room. She surveyed the body, and latched onto the Fentanyl patch that still was stuck on his chest. "It's that patch. I know it is. I told Blinky not to use them. Damn that Jenkins. Someone's going to pay big time. I want an autopsy!"

Sanjay Sharma stepped back and let Ron Kirk try to deal with her.

"Betty, I'm sorry he's gone," Kirk said. Everyone loved Blinky. I agree; an autopsy is in order. We'll be sure to get it done first thing in the morning."

"Damn right you will." Betty went to the desk. "My Blinky's gone—dead. That stupid Henry Jenkins. I'm going to call Mr. Olden."

"Ma'am, it's two-thirty in the morning. Don't wake him up," Molly said.

Betty pushed her aside. "Hand me that phone. I'll call him myself." She jerked the phone out of Molly's hand.

"Ms. Wilson, please. He won't take it any good at all if you call him now."

Betty dialed a couple numbers, and then slammed the phone down. It fell to the floor, banged the tile, bounced a couple times, and came to rest. The busy signal buzzed.

"Well, then, I'll find him in the morning, but by God, it'll be first thing, you can count on that."

Molly cradled the phone back into place.

As Betty Wilson stomped down the hall, she almost ran into Elisa Reyes, the night housekeeper. Elisa glared at her a moment. Mrs. Wilson was well known around town. A lot of folks thought all of Ms. Wilson's demands were a big part of Blinky's troubles, but Elisa kept her thoughts to herself. She needed her job.

"What are you staring at?" Betty demanded. "Do I have to do your job for you?" She started to leave, and then turned around. "That room is filthy. You clean it up or I'll talk to Jimmy about you, too." Then she was gone.

Jeff, the orderly from the morgue, pulled the covers up over Blinky. He and the night nurse placed him on the stretcher. Elisa tidied up the room.

Jeff stopped at the door. "Lordy, lordy, Mr. Indie he isn't going to be happy when he hears about this."

Elisa stopped sweeping. "No, sir, he sure ain't. Mr. Indie he loved Blinky like one of his own. He not gonna be happy at all."

Jeffery wheeled Blinky by the nurse's station and began the slow procession down the hall to the morgue.

CHAPTER SIX

I Hear That Train A-Coming

AFTER BLINK DIED, INDIE DIDN'T LEAVE the house for a week. Bones went over to visit, and Ms. Jenkins met him at the door. She held the screen door so it wouldn't slam shut, and stepped out on the porch.

"Bones, I'm so glad you're here. Why, he won't even go to the cabin."

"Hm. That isn't like Indie at all." Bones put an arm around her shoulder. "I knew he'd take it hard. Okay for me to check on him?"

"By all means, please. Maybe he'll talk to you."

Indie sat in his Lazy Boy and stared out the window. A bottle of Jim Beam sat on the floor by a pile of newspapers.

"Indie?"

"Oh, hey. Bones. Come on in."

"Come on, brother. It isn't your fault." Bones sat down on the couch.

"Maybe if I hadn't left ..." Indie turned on the TV.

"Man, I've been over it with Sharma a dozen times. He can't figure out what happened either, and he was there."

"Where did all that fever come from?" Indie asked.

"I don't know. Sharma ordered two blood cultures right at the end, but they were negative. He said to tell you he's sorry as hell."

"God, I bet Blink was lonely."

"C'mon, Indie. You had to go check on your mom. If you hadn't stuck by Blink, he'd been out of here a long time ago. Honest to God, man, I know you've been over it and over it in your head. I have, too. I just don't see what else you could have done. He had a bad heart, you know. I'll bet it was an arrhythmia."

"I should have had him on telemetry, maybe if I hadn't left—"

"Shoot fire, Indie. He had negative enzymes, and a zip D-dimer. Are you going to have everyone who needs fluids and antibiotics on Telemetry?" Bones got up and turned down the television. "Try to go tell that to Olden and the trustees. We'd have a country hospital with ninety-eight cardiac monitor beds. I don't think so."

"Still, it's hard as hell."

"Yeah, ole Blink was a good drop thumb banjo man, huh?"

"Yeah, boy. No one around here could frail a banjer like Blink. Hell of a card player, too. At least Betty got her way. He ain't at Pete's every Friday, huh?" Indie's forehead scrunched up. "You know, Bones, that's one mean-ass woman." He picked up the paper, and pulled out the sports section. "The Braves ain't worth a damn this year, are they?" He tossed it back in the floor. "I bet she and Olden are studying that autopsy as we speak."

"Well, he won't have the first notion as to how to interpret it."

"That's what worries me. He has political connections. If there is any way to make me look bad, Olden would do it."

"C'mon, Indie, Olden's ABCDA."

Indie smiled. "A Board Certified Dumb Ass. At least the State guys won't fudge for him. I worry about Betty. You know she's gonna go to him."

"I'm sure you're right, Indie, but you'll get your chance, too. I'll help you any way I can, and I'll be glad to go over it with Betty if you want me to. I won't abandon you, bud. I don't think Sharma will, either."

Indie frowned. "You'll be the only ones. Olden's been out to get me for a long time. I'm afraid I hear that train '-a—comin'."

Indie didn't give a damn about his paperwork, never gave up smoking, and sometimes would drink too much, though never on the job. He had his flaws, but Indie understood people. Bones knew he was right, and could hear the coming train, too. "Don't worry, Indie. I'll ride with you no matter what."

Indie rubbed his eyes. "I'm gonna have to crash. Hey, I appreciate you coming by."

"No problem. We'll get through it."

Indie fell asleep and began to snore. Bones covered him with one of Ms. Jenkins' coverlets off the couch, and made his way to the door.

Ms. Jenkins followed him to the porch. "Thank you, James. Your mother is right. You're such a good boy." She kissed him on the cheek. "Indie isn't going to talk to any of the other doctors. He needs you. Thank you so much." Her eyes were moist, but she held back the tears.

"Yes, ma'am. I love Indie like a second dad. Don't worry 'til Bones says to worry."

"I'll try, James. I'll try."

CHAPTER SEVEN

Autopsy

JIM OLDEN HAD NEVER BEEN TO visit Pathology. If it hadn't been for his monologues at the Medical Staff meetings, and his picture in the last Annual Report, no one could have picked him out of a lineup.

Olden breezed in. "Gentlemen, how's the autopsy coming along on poor Blinky Wilson? God rest his soul."

Seymour Anselm, chief of pathology, stirred his coffee. "I didn't know you cared so much for Blinky, Prez."

"Well, Dr. Anselm, you can be sure Betty Wilson does."

"I have no doubt."

"So, when will it be completed?" Olden handed Seymour Mrs. Wilson's signed and notarized disclosure consent form. "She wants me to go over the report with her in detail."

"God Almighty, Jim," Anselm countered. "Can't help you, anyway. We had to send him out to the State due to the circumstances. Should have it back Wednesday."

"As soon as you have it, notify me."

"Aye, aye, sir." Seymour gave him a sarcastic salute.

Olden went out the door and down the hall. Anselm looked at the notarized form and put it on his desk.

Jeannie, the chief tech, watched as Olden left, and then went in Anselm's office. "Olden's not got much use for Indie, huh?"

"Of course not."

"Well, I think Indie's an okay guy and Olden's a jerk."

"Ha. You told Olden that?" Anselm asked.

"Are you kidding? He signs my paycheck. I'm no fool. How come Olden hates him so bad?"

"I don't know," Anselm said, recalling those days. Olden was hired as CEO when Indie was Chief of Staff. Indie recommended the Board not hire Olden; he remembered too much from their days in Legion ball. Anselm suspected Indie didn't tell all he knew by a long shot.

Dr. Blake got wind of it and took the trustees to dinner at the Country Club. Olden got the job. Indie's tenure as Chief of Staff was up in a month, and he never got so much as a committee chair position after that, not that he cared.

Anselm debated whether to tell her but decided against it. No use to stir things up now. He let it rest.

"Well, I hear it goes back a ways," she said. "It's probably got something to do with a woman. No one should trust a middle-aged skirt-chaser," Jeannie said.

Amselm laughed.

She went on. "I'd love a shot at Olden. My cousin was a nurse assistant on three-west. He tried to sleep with her. She turned him down, and the next thing you know she was out a job." She scowled. "At least Jenkins is faithful."

Wednesday morning a letter arrived at the Pathology Lab from the State Coroner's Office. Anselm opened the envelope and peeked inside, much like the day his State Boards had arrived in the mail. He didn't have to read far. CAUSE OF DEATH: FENTANYL TOXICITY. The Fentanyl level was ten times normal.

Anselm went into his study, closed the door, and placed the phone call. "Maria? Dr. Anslem here. I need to speak to Mr. Olden."

"He busy, cannot talk."

"Tell him it's important. It's about an autopsy."

Anselm heard her call out to Olden in her broken English and soon he came to the phone. "Dr. Anselm, so good to hear from you, sir. I trust you have good news?"

"The cause of death is Fentanyl toxicity."

"I'm a layman, so you'll have to interpret for me, but I assume there is only one way this could be the cause of death? He was given too much Fentanyl correct?" Olden's voice went squeaky like a child's. "And only one doctor prescribed this medicine, correct?"

"On the surface it would seem that way, but I haven't studied the entire record, so, Jimmy, try not to wet your pants yet."

"I'll be down at once, Doctor. Please have your staff copy the report in its entirety. Mrs. Wilson is beside herself with grief. I need to report to her as soon as possible." He hung up.

Anselm slammed down the phone, angry that Blinky was dead, and all Olden could think about was how to nail Indie.

Seymour put a copy of the autopsy in a manila envelope, marked it as confidential, and put it in Jenkins' box at the hospital. Then he called Indie. It was the least he could do.

CHAPTER EIGHT

Sense of Dread

INDIE KNEW IT WAS COMING, so it was no surprise when Jim Olden summoned him to his office. He went to hear the verdict.

"Well, hey, Maria. I thought you were a nurse now."

"Yes, Dr. Indie. I got my two-year L.P.N. But nights very hard. Jimmy, he got me job here during the day. He so sweet. Jimmy say he love the springtime, and we can't wait ..."

Olden came to the door. "Enough, Miss Diosas. Dr. Jenkins doesn't have time to hear your life history." He motioned Indie inside. "Hold my calls." Olden closed the door. "Have a seat, Henry." Olden flopped the report on his desk, and opened it to his point of interest. "This does not look good. Fentanyl overdose."

"Now wait a damn minute, Jim. He was only on twenty-five micrograms. Hell, I had my aunt on that much after her hip surgery, and she only weighed eighty-four pounds. That ain't right."

Olden pointed out the highlighted section on page six. "I'm sorry, Henry, but it is correct. Ten times the normal level. Here it is in bold letters: Cause of Death: Fentanyl Toxicity." He slid the report across the table for Jenkins to review.

Indie could not respond.

Olden enjoyed Indie's distress. "This is the catastrophe Betty Wilson has predicted for years." Olden shook his head. "We will try to help however we can, Henry, but we have no choice but to take action. Perhaps if you turn in your license we can help you with some sort of plea bargain. I do have good contacts, you know." Olden penciled some notes. "I think incarceration can be avoided. However, the truth speaks for itself."

"Yeah, res ipsa loquitur-" Indie replied.

"Huh?"

"Never mind. Let me talk it over with my lawyer. I'll need a day or two."

"Sure, sure, Henry. I have all the time in the world. We want to keep you in the family, and there's no sense in going to Atlanta." Olden looked out his window at the Cancer Center which now bore his name. The corner of his lip turned up in a smile. "You know, Henry, you doctors fail to understand one thing about hospitals."

"What's that?"

"We own them, you just work here." Olden laughed out loud.

"But, a good landlord should never abuse the tenant. You gotta have 'em."

"Well, we will be fair, but this must be dealt with."

"Whatever." Indie got up to leave and managed a handshake.

When he left, he went by his mailbox in the doctor's lounge and picked up the copy of the autopsy. His Parkinson's disease always seemed worse when he was tired. Damn, he thought. Where did I leave my cane? He looked over the report again. How could it be? It was such a low dose. Maybe there was a drug interaction. It didn't add up.

He trudged out to the Jeep. His cane was on the floorboard. He picked it up, tucked it by his side, and then drove home. *What a way to end my career, doing in my best buddy.*

Ms. Jenkins called Bones after dark. "What's going on with Indie?"

"What do you mean?"

"He had a meeting with Jim Olden today and now he's talking doctor jibberish, all about metabolism and pharmacodynamics and he won't quit pacing. I know he's trying not to worry me, but ..."

"I'll be over, Ms. Jenkins."

By the time Bones got there, Indie was slumped in the Lazy Boy, his feet sprawled out. His eyes hadn't been that red since his Daddy died.

"Hey, you got a hole in your sock."

"Humphf." He gave it a disinterested glance.

Ms. Jenkins asked, "Bones, can I fix you a Co-Cola?"

"Yes, ma'am."

She went to the kitchen.

"So what's Olden selling?"

"He says Blinky died from his Fentanyl patch, and it's my fault."

"How much was he on?"

"Just twenty-five micrograms."

"Twenty-five? It's impossible to die from that."

"That's not what the State says."

"Then something's tangled up there."

Ms. Jenkins brought Bones' Coca-Cola, and a glass of tea for Indie. "Now, can I get you boys anything else?"

"No, ma'am, I'm fine."

Indie smiled. "How about a Jimmy Beam for me, Mama?"

"Now, Henry, you know three is your limit."

"Yes, ma'am."

Ms. Jenkins tweaked the patch of hair on the back of his head. "I'm going to go on to bed, Chief. Don't stay up too late."

Indie turned red around the ears. "Yes, dear."

She kissed him on the cheek and went upstairs.

"Ms. Jenkins is a sweetheart."

"Yeah, I'd rather not bother her, but that woman knows everything anyway."

"There's not much she can do but ride out the storm. So what did Olden say?"

"Aw, he went on with all this crap about how I killed Blinky, and how

Betty said it was gonna happen and how he'd try to keep me out of the pen in Atlanta."

"He's crazy."

"I know. But he does hold good cards on this one. I can't understand it, but that's what the autopsy shows." Indie reached over to the coffee table and handed the report to Bones. "Look at page six."

Bones read page six. "Damn. Ten times the amount?"

"What should I do?"

"You better call Brad Keith in Atlanta."

"Atlanta! Don't mention that city right now. The Federal Pen is down there, you know."

"Awh, Indie you aren't going there and you know it."

"Who was Keith? The name's familiar."

"Brad Keith. You remember. He's the consultant we took fishing in the Bonfield case."

"Didn't his boy play ball for Georgia Tech?"

"That's the one. He's our broker for the insurance carrier nowadays."

"Hmn. Maybe I'll wait and see if they file the suit."

"Hell, no. This is Betty's lottery ticket, and Olden can't wait to help her cash it in. You better call Brad in the morning."

"I guess."

"No guess. You have to. He'll understand. Better get him in early rather than late. He'll want a game plan before Olden gets too far ahead."

"I hope Keith has a damn good imagination, Bones."

"He does. Try not to worry."

"I'll try."

"Look, man, in the Bonfield case they extricated me like a sardine out of a tin can."

"Yeah, but everyone knew you were going to be okay from the start."

"Hm. I wish they'd told me."

"It wasn't even close. Besides, you're a damn Boy Scout. I've got a few skeletons in my closet."

"Yeah, well, Barney's all for you, pal."

Indie smiled. "I guess so, Bones."

CHAPTER NINE

Rambling Wreck

"TRINA, HOW MANY PATIENTS DO I HAVE THIS MORNING?"

"You're pretty solid, Dr. Jenkins. Booked 'til eleven-thirty."

"Well, if any more call, put them in the afternoon or send 'em to the ER."

"Are you okay, Doc?"

"Yeah, I'm fine. I gotta line up a fishing trip. Gonna go to Hatteras with a guy named Brad Keith. I've got a call in to him; come get me as soon as you hear from him."

"Yes, sir."

Indie was in exam room three with Ezzie Watkins when Trina cracked the door and peeked in. "Excuse me, Dr. Jenkins, but Mr. Keith in Atlanta returned your call."

"Thanks, Trina. If you would, help Ms. Watkins down here. Her rheumatism is acting up."

Indie went to his office and closed the door. "Hey, Brad, Indie Jenkins here. We need to get out to Hatteras again."

"Man, that was a good trip. The Bonfield case, as I recall."

"Uh, yeah, uh ... Brad, uh ... I need to talk."

"It's okay, Indie. I'm a regular Ann Landers. What's up?"

"Well, I'm afraid I'm in trouble. I swear, though, it makes no sense."

"Tell me about it."

Indie poured out the story all the way up to the autopsy report. "I tell you, Brad, the stakes are high on this one. Olden said he'd try to keep me out of the pen in Atlanta, but that bastard will hang his mama to save a dime."

Keith laughed. "God, Indie, no way he's got that kind of leverage. The only way you're coming to Atlanta is to watch a Braves game with me."

"I hope you're right."

"I wouldn't worry about Olden. Little weasel. The only one of these I ever saw go for a manslaughter charge was when that doc in Fayetteville stole morphine from a hospice patient and did in his wife's boyfriend."

"He deserved it."

"You don't need to worry about criminal charges, but the case does have exposure. You need to report it to Physician's Liability ASAP."

"How 'bout running interference for me? Last time they had to deal with me, I thought they were gonna cut me loose. They said I was more headstrong than Bones."

"I'm not so sure about that, but yeah, I'll talk to them for you. You'll need someone in town on the team. Bones is a good man. You run it by him yet?"

"Yeah, I talked to him last night. He said I'd better call you today."

"What does he think?"

"He said it didn't make any sense, but I could tell he was worried. Hell, if he's thinking that way, I figure I'm in deep."

"Yeah, don't forget, he went through one. I'm sure he'd rather you didn't have to."

"Yeah, I thought that poor boy's heart was gonna break before he got released."

"You make it sound like he was in jail."

"Trust me, for a doc it's like a prison sentence when you know you didn't do the crime. It was a happy day for Bones when it was over." Indie thought back to the day. "You know, old Bones ain't in the data bank, so for the history book it never happened, but ..."

Keith had not forgotten. "I'm sure he knows how you feel."

"I'm afraid this is a different game."

Keith paused. "It may be, but we go through these all the time. Most of them never go to trial. And as far as the criminal charges, Olden is just blowing smoke."

"You know what? When Bones went through his, he didn't talk much. He bottled it all up inside for the most part."

"Yeah, maybe too much so. He's quiet. He'll hold your cards close. Better to rely on him than that Jim Beam of yours. Hold on. Let me check my calendar. Hm. Let's see. I'm going to be in Raleigh on Wednesday. I'll make an appointment with Lucille Taggert and go over it with her. I guess I had better do it in person instead of over the phone. How bout faxing me that autopsy report?"

"Sure thing."

"After I talk to her, I'll give you a buzz. Keep the faith."

"I'll try. Damn, I dread the whole thing. I'm gonna be a Rambling Wreck."

"Nah, we'll be eating cheeseburgers at the Varsity before you know it."

"You save my ass and I'll never forget you."

"Well, save me a spot on the boat, and some of that Jim Beam, too."

Keith hung up, sat for a minute, and then buzzed his secretary. "Linda, you remember the Hamilton case?"

"La Grange?"

"Yep."

"How could I forget? Three mil."

"Wasn't that the Fentanyl case?"

"Yes, sir."

"How about pulling the record for me? I need to go over it again."

"Will do, boss."

CHAPTER TEN

The Loyalty List

AFTER HE HUNG UP WITH BRAD KEITH, INDIE called Bones. "So how'd it go?"

"Brad's seen so many of these it's just another day's work. I think he's concerned, though."

"I'm sure he is."

"He's gonna be in Raleigh on Wednesday. Said he'd talk to a Lucille Taggert."

"That's good. She's the best."

"How 'bout meeting me at the Billiard-&-Bowl? Brad cleared it for me and you to talk."

"Get a table in the back. I'll be there."

"Six o'clock okay?"

"Sure."

The Harvey Billiard-&-Bowl, or the B-&-B, was on the east side of town. It was a hangout for all sorts of card players, bluegrass boys, some of the golf choose-up crowd, and an assortment of other ne're-do-wells. Most of the clientele were middle-aged men who stopped in after work to play cards and drink a few beers before going home. Lou Bedford owned the place and made his living several ways. For one, he owned the B-&-B, which was a grill and pool hall with a couple of duck pin bowling lanes. Out behind was a trailer park with thirty units. A front-end loader sat in the gravel parking lot. And it was one of the few places in town where the local bluegrass pickers could play and make a little money.

One year Bedford put up a handwritten sign out front that read HARVEY BILLIARD & BOWL, TRAILER PARK, AND TRIDITIONAL BLUE-GRASS MUSIC. Bones pointed out to Lou that he'd misspelled "tradi-tional." Lou looked at the sign. "Ah, hell, Doc, I'll have to wait 'til it wears out to change it. It's done paid for."

The Neuse River Band was Bedford's only regular act, and they did a show one Saturday night a month. They played for a collection. The hat they passed was a popcorn basket; Lou had the best buttered popcorn in town. He had bought the machine when the local movie house closed down.

He didn't charge admission except when a big name came in. Lou hosted III Tyme Out once a year and they packed the house. They were popular right from the first time they showed up. Russell, the lead singer, wailed the lonesome blues, and the mandolin man worked the stage like a bluegrass Mick Jagger. It was the middle of winter, but by the end of the show, the sweat poured off the band members like construction workers on a summer day.

They sat down in the office after the show. "How'd we do, Lou?" Dilling, the banjo player, asked.

"Great show boys, great show." Lou thumbed through some bills, and handed a stack to Dilling. "See if I counted yours right. I cleared three hun-dred for me after expenses."

"Good. We'll be back next year right after Kinston. How 'bout one of them cheeseburgers?"

The B-&-B was a good place to meet—Jim Olden would not be caught dead there.

Lou had a myna bird named Minnie. She stayed up front. The bird could mimic anything, and had a whistle as shrill an ambulance siren. Bones & Indie would be safe at the B-&B, at least as long as they met in the back-room.

They took a small table in the south dining room.

Lou took their order, Bones' first. "Whadda you have, Doc, the usual?"

"Sure, Lou."

"Okay. Bacon Swiss CB, hold the onions, and a chocolate shake." Lou jotted it down.

Bones confirmed.

"How 'bout you, Indie?"

"The same 'cept bring me some fries and some extra ketchup. Taters and 'maters are in the four food groups, you know." Indie had a unique interpretation of the literature. "Bring me a Pabst, too." He pulled out some extra coins for the beer. It was a dry county, but Lou kept Pabst in a rigged Coke machine. All you had to do was put in a couple extra quarters, push the Tab button, and it'd spit out a PBR. The law knew about it, but they were regulars, too.

"Hey, Indie," Lou said, "I'm sorry 'bout Blink. Hell, if he was still alive he wouldn't hold it against you."

Indie paused for a second. "Yeah, well, Blink's dead, Lou, and I hate I was out of town when he died."

"Well, it ain't your fault." Lou left to go cook up the order.

"So, what did Brad have to say?"

"He's gonna talk to Physician's Liability. I'm sure they'll say to settle."

"Yeah, it might be best. That Betty will be hard to fight with."

"Ever since Blinky got her pregnant she's had some kinda thing against me and him both."

"What is it with that?"

"I don't know, but if you want to see her riled up just tell her me and Blinky both got a bit of Choctaw in us. Makes her mad as hell."

"The woman hates everyone who doesn't drink their liquor at the country club. So, tell me about that Fentanyl."

"There's not much to say. Twenty-five micrograms is a baby dose."

"It is, Indie. I had a case somewhat like that right after Fentanyl came on the market. I need to go look it up."

"Only twenty-five micrograms. What happened?"

"I don't know. Let me go look at that chart. I remember they first thought my man died from Fentanyl, but it turned out not so. The lawyers looked over the record, but no one was named. I guess they did not see much in that one. I'm not sure how similar the stories are."

"I don't think it killed Blinky, but the problem is I don't know what the heck did."

"Too early to say. What I learned when I went through the Bonfield case was if you don't know everything, you don't know nothing. I couldn't believe they included me. Bo had his heart attack on Friday night. Heck, it was over Saturday. I was out of town that weekend. I don't know what anyone thought I could do about it come Monday. Still, you can count on the fact they're gonna include everyone 'til they can sort it out. They call it 'empty chair syndrome.' They won't miss anyone they might see a return on. At first the company thought I might have some exposure, but once experts testified, I was okay."

"Yeah, well, this one ain't gonna go that way."

"I'm afraid you're right, but you gotta remember they'll do their best to settle. No one wants to go to court." Bones wanted to be optimistic, but couldn't find the words. "Let's hope for the best. You need to make you a loyalty list right off."

"A loyalty list? What's that?"

"You're doing it without realizing it. As the case wears on, I would revise it on a regular basis. As you learn about the integrity of the parties involved, you rearrange your order. The changes give you a road map of how to proceed. You figure the whole thing based on who you believe tells you the truth, and who deserves the truth, too."

"God-a-Mighty Bones, you're an obsessive little S.O.B."

"It was the only way I got though med school. I am not as smart as you."

"Go to hell." Indie laughed.

Lou came back in and started to wipe down the next table. "Anything else, guys?"

"Nah, Lou. We're good," Bones said.

"Snookers is gonna be by in a while."

"Okay. We're about to finish up."

After Lou left, Bones had to ask. "Lou said Snookers was coming by. Who all knows about this?"

"I've got a feeling Lou knows, but I haven't said anything to him."

"You haven't told Snookers, have you?"

Indie shifted in his chair. "Hey, can you give me a lift home? Ms. Jenkins needed the car."

"Sure. What did you tell Snook?"

"Uh, not much. But I had to tell him some. He's too valuable in the hospital to not be on the look-out for me."

"I don't know. You gotta keep these things close to the vest."

"You said make a loyalty list. Who's more loyal than Snook?"

"Well, I know, but the fewer the better. Look man, Brad cleared me, but I can promise you Lucille Taggert would ax me off the list in a heartbeat if she thought I'd work the case with a hospital maintenance man. I meddled in mine something awful. They like to run their own deal. If I hadn't gotten out with a goose egg it mighta been different. I've often thought if I'd been nailed they might have dropped me. Doctors get emotional about these things. To them it's a business; just a matter of money."

"I don't even know her."

"Well, you will. And you have to. You need that lady on your team a lot more than you need me." Bones poured the last of his beer. "Look, you better put Taggert on your list before you meet her. And you have to be loyal to yourself, so keep looking for the truth. If you think you tangled up the case, I would own up to it in some diplomatic way and settle. After all, Blink was your patient and your friend. Make your list."

Indie pulled out a napkin from the holder and took out a pen. He wrote Blink's name. "You're right. Blinky has to be right up at the top. I owe it to him to find out what happened. He ain't here to defend himself. Sharma is up there, too. Without him, we'da been worked to death by now."

"I don't think Sharma did anything wrong. I would not want him to get hurt. Besides, Olden will see to it that doesn't happen. Wallace Walton pulled the political strings to get Sharma here; Olden won't touch him."

"Hell, Sharma's a damned sacred cow. He could go by Olden in the hall and moo." Indie got quiet again. He got up, looked around the corner, and came back to the table. "So, Bones, who's at the bottom?"

"Olden. He'd tie a cinder block around your leg and throw you in the Neuse if he thought he could get away with it."

"I'm glad I'm not paying you for that advice. I've known that for years. Who else? The attorney who'll be against me?"

"Not necessarily. I had to go up against Martin Taylor, but he proceeded with integrity. Believe it or not, by the end of the case he managed to crack my top ten."

"Dream on, kid."

"Well, okay. He only made it to nine. Still, I thought that was pretty good for a plaintiff attorney."

"Hell, Bones, you'd try to make peace with Attila the Hun."

"Only if he fought by the rules."

Indie looked at his list. "Blink, Bones, Sharma, Snookers ... I don't know how many folks I can count on in this thing."

"Taggert, Taggert, don't forget."

"Okay." Indie scratched down the name on the napkin. He reached in his pocket for a few spare coins, got up and went to the door. "Hey, Lou, how 'bout another Pabst?"

"Indie wanna Pabst. AWWK. Pabst Blue Ribbon beer. AWWWKK." Minnie the myna bird broke into the TV commercial theme song.

"Damn, Bones. Don't say anything in front of that bird. She's not one bit discreet." Indie sat back down.

Lou brought Indie another beer. "You take care of Mr. Indie, Bones, and I take care of you. I need my doctors."

"Sure enough, Lou. Thanks." After Lou left, Bones offered a toast. "Here's to Betty Wilson."

"Are you trying to ruin our meeting?"

Bones laughed. "Hey, don't worry. If it does not work out, I'll come visit you in Atlanta. They allow music and conjugal visits on Sunday. I can only help with the bluegrass, though. Now Betty, that's a different matter ..."

"Shut the hell up, Bones." Indie had a wry smile.

"Snookie wanna beer, Snookie wanna beer. AWWK."

Indie went to the door.

"Indie, what's cookin'?" Snook shook Indie's hand, and grasped his shoulder.

"Lou, how 'bout a cheeseburger for Snookers? Put it on my tab," Indie said.

"Come on in and have a seat, Snook. How's the hospital?"

"Sucks, man. Olden is a damn wuss."

"Olden's a wuss. Olden's a wuss. AWWWK."

"Dang it, guys. Y'all be careful. Come on in here." Bones got up and shut the door behind them. They all took a seat at the table.

"So what's Olden got to say about it?" Indie asked.

Bones could not believe it. "Wait a minute! I'm telling you right now Ms. Lucille Taggert is going to pitch a fit, y'all talking about this thing. You can't do it, I tell ya. Hell, Snook, those guys will have you on the stand and ask about your sex life if it'll help 'em win."

"There ain't nothing there to talk about."

"That's not the hospital talk. Trust me, Snook, they will try to twist you around and make it look like you were trying to rig something for Indie. It can't help and it might hurt.'

"Bones, you're such a damn Boy Scout." Snook went to the door to yell for his beer, and then came back to the table. "Olden's yakking all over the hospital about how he's gonna kick Indie's ass. When I was sweeping up after the Board meeting he was going on about how mad he was, and he'd see to it Indie was kicked out. Hell, it ain't gonna happen. I ain't going to no other doc ... well, except you Bones. You're okay."

"Lord, God." Bones slumped in his chair.

Indie folded his napkin list and placed it in his wallet. "I appreciate the intelligence, Snook. Keep me informed. Don't talk to anyone but me or Bones. He's right. You gotta keep these things quiet. They can get out of hand. Still, I'm gonna have my people in the loop."

"Sure 'nuff. Hey, Bones, you gonna play the choose-up Wednesday?"

"I don't know, Snook. I don't feel so good."

Other than the radio, the drive home was in silence. Bones pulled into the driveway. "Taggert will never let me help you if she knows Snook is a spy. They don't want anyone to interfere. It's their game and their rules, pal."

"She don't have to know, Bones. I ain't gonna tell her. You're higher on my loyalty list than her. I ain't never even met her."

"Loyalty list? Okay, yeah, yeah. I did say that. Okay. Well, you better put Taggert up there, I tell you."

Indie opened the door to get out. "Let me know what she has to say."

"Will do, brother."

CHAPTER ELEVEN

The Beauty Operator

CARMEN CLARY WAS A SEMI-RETIRED hairdresser in town. She used to have a saying: "Never underestimate a beauty operator." She saw it like the power structure of a school. When her son became a teacher, she told him not to worry about the principal. The folks who wielded the most influence were the janitor and the school secretary. "Don't ever cross them if you want to get along, son. Same way with a beauty operator; they know too much."

So, it came as no surprise to Carmen that Betty Wilson turned to Janie Johnson, her Beauty Operator, for advice when Blinky died.

Carmen watched and listened from where she was working in the back room when Betty sat in the chair and spilled out her story.

Janie got right to the point. "Why, Betty, honey, I wouldn't hesitate, not for a minute. I never did care for Henry Jenkins ever since he ran around on Immogene with that little French girl when he was in his thirties."

Carmen nodded her head in agreement. Beauty Operators were known for their long memories.

"If it was me, I'd sue his ass off," Janie finished.

"Who would you get? How about Roy Davidson?" Betty suggested. "He did a fine job for Blinky when he had his D.U.I."

"Nope, won't work. For one thing, he done some of that kind of lawyering for Indie. It's what they call a conflict of interest. Besides, they say for this kind of stuff you need a specialist. I heard there are some in Raleigh."

"Well, let's look them up." Betty went to get the Yellow Pages.

Janie thumbed through the pages. "Here they are. Malpractice attorneys.

That's whatcha want. There are three of 'em in Raleigh, plus one here from Norfolk." Janie picked up the phone. "Which one you want me to call?"

"I don't know. Might as well go in alphabetical order, I guess. Try the ones in Raleigh. I don't know if one would come all the way from Norfolk or not."

Janie dialed up the first, an Albright. The secretary asked too many questions and made her mad. The second one was out for the day. She connected with the third, but got put on hold. She put her hand over the receiver and whispered to Betty. "William Franklin Howell the Third," she said. "Sounds real official."

The secretary came back to the phone. "He says he'll happy to return your call. May I take your number?"

"Now, ma'am, you tell him this is Janie Johnson from Harvey County. We got us a case down here that's a damn keeper, and if he don't want it we'll just send it right over to Mr. Albright." The secretary put her on hold. Janie again cupped the receiver in her palm. "That's how you gotta talk to these folks, Betty. Heard it on TV. This whole law thing runs on fear, you know."

Mr. Howell came to the phone and heard out a brief description, then interrupted. "Yes, Ms. Johnson. I do think your case may have some merit. However, our corporate policy is to accept only those cases which have been screened by a referral firm. We would be glad to have one of these associates contact you."

"Hell, if we ain't good enough for you, forget it." Janie slammed the phone back into the cradle. She was undeterred. "Look at this one from Norfolk, Betty. He's kinda cute."

"Hm. Well, he sure is young. Wonder why he lives in Norfolk?"

"Dunno." Janie studied the photos.

"You think he's any good?" Betty asked.

"Well, he can afford to advertise way down here. He must have some money. I reckon he's won a few cases. It can't hurt to call." Janie picked up the phone and began to dial.

"Now be nice, Janie," Betty admonished.

"I'll try, but these people are starting to piss me off ... Oh, hello, this is Janie Johnson from Harvey County. I would like to discuss a case with Mr. Gibson Taylor. Is he in this afternoon?"

"Yes, ma'am, would you like to speak to him?"

"Yes, it won't take but a minute."

Gibson Taylor came to the phone. He listened for a few minutes.

"So, Mr. Taylor, what do you think?"

"Well, ma'am, first of all, I'm sorry to hear about your husband," Taylor said.

"Oh, he warn't mine, he belonged to Betty here, but she's too tore down to talk."

"I understand. Let's see. I'm going to be in Raleigh on Wednesday the twenty-second, right after we get through tax season. My father is testifying on the Senate floor. I could come back through Harvey County on my way home around supper. Would that be acceptable?"

Janie again covered the phone with her hand. "Damn, Betty, his Daddy's in the Senate, and the boy's gonna come see us!" She calmed down and spoke to Taylor again. "Let's see, Mr. Taylor. The twenty-second. Yes sir, I think that would work. One thing, though; we better meet across the County Line. Everyone knows everyone's business 'round here. My client is nodding, so we should be good."

"'My client'?" Betty asked.

Janie again placed her hand over the phone. "Shush, girl. I cut your hair, don't I? Damn." Janie rolled her eyes. "I'm sorry for the interruption, sir. You were saying?"

"Yes, ma'am. No problem. I'll see you on the twenty-second," Taylor said. "If you would, I need a written summary of the case forwarded to me. I will be better prepared with that information in hand prior to the visit. Let me get your phone number." The two exchanged contact information.

"Yes, sir. See ya then." Janie hung up. "Dang, Betty. We got us a lawyer. He sounds good- lookin' too."

"You didn't ask him what all he's won."

"Didn't have to; I can tell. He's so nice. That Howell fellow talked fast like someone from New York. I couldn't understand a word he said. And he just cut me right off, too. I ain't stupid." She tossed the phone book on the couch. "Now this Taylor, he sounds like a Southern boy. If someone's gonna kick Henry Jenkin's ass here in Harvey County, they better be a polite sort or they'll never get it done."

Janie had taken stenography in high school, so she and Betty Wilson set out to write down Ms. Wilson's grievances. They only got one first impression, and she was determined it would be a good one.

Every afternoon the pair would tune into the soaps to get up to speed on legal lingo, and then write. Janie would take a look at the draft and exclaim, "Ain't no fancy big city lawyer gonna look at no such crap as that!" Then they would tear it up, and start all over. It was slow progress, but a satisfactory statement began to emerge.

When they finished, Janie held the letter with pride, then handed it to Betty. She read it over one last time. Janie insisted on a light spray of her finest perfume, and they sealed it with some little flower stickers.

When it arrived at the Taylor suite of offices, it made an impression. The legal assistant screener only read a paragraph before she went to find Gibson Taylor.

"Boss, I believe we've got a winner."

Taylor knew a disgruntled client was not sufficient. There had to be legal malpractice, too, and the more clear-cut the better. Cases could be hard to prove, and if it was the least bit muddy, it'd often die on the vine. For it to be worth his time, it needed to be significant damage, a very poor outcome, and little chance of improvement. Otherwise, they could not justify the expense of a two- or three-year fight.

Like his father before him, Gibson Taylor had honed his medical/legal radar over the years. It was what he did. Taylor studied the letter. No matter how obvious a case seemed, each one was unique. One could always anticipate the unexpected, but this one seemed to have merit.

Gibson Taylor called his dad, Martin, to get his opinion.

CHAPTER TWELVE

The Beauty Shop/Mid-Carolina Moe's/Gibson Files

JANIE'S SHOP HAD BEEN SET UP BEHIND her house for years, but now she rented a downtown location right next to the Laundromat. The ladies found it quite convenient.

Betty Wilson had a regular Wednesday hair appointment with Janie. When Blink was alive, he and Indie often went fishing on those days. Her usual appointment was at ten, but they moved it to the afternoon so they could leave when Janie closed the shop.

When Betty arrived, Marge Thompson was still in the chair. After she left, they'd have the shop to themselves.

As Janie finished up, she said, "Miss Margie, you're downright gorgeous, honey." She added just the right highlights. "Where's Fred gonna take you for your anniversary?"

"Why, the Epicurean. Can you believe it?"

"Lord, if my Billy was to take me there, I'd figure he's cheating on me."

"Well, maybe Fred is, but I don't want to know about it 'til morning," Marge replied.

"Naw, not Fred. He's true blue, sweetie. You're one of the lucky ones." Janie put in a touch of curl. "All done." She turned the chair around so Margie could check it out in the mirror.

"Hey, Betty. We're finished."

Marge got up from the chair. "How you doing, girl? I hate it about Blinky. I'm so sorry."

"Well, he lived hard. I knew it would happen someday. I just wish it hadn't ended the way it did."

"If I can do anything ..."

"I know, and I appreciate it, too."

Marge left, and Betty got in the chair.

"So, did you get the autopsy report from Mr. Olden?" Janie asked.

"He said they'd be glad to get the hospital lawyers to handle this for me, and not even charge me. You reckon we even need Mr. Taylor?"

"Honey child. Now you watch out. Yeah, you need him. My cousin got in a lawsuit one time when his brother tried to swindle the family car dealership from him. He said not to ever forget, you are the only one who'll look after yourself. You can't count on your mama." Janie combed out the tangles.

"Well, he does seem like he wants to help."

"I'm sure he does. There are a bunch of nurses who I see in the shop. They say Olden hates Indie. They also know pillow talk."

"Jimmy? Who's he sleeping with?"

"Now, honey, you know I can't tell. I know of at least two, though." Janie turned around to reach for the shampoo.

"Why, he told me—"

"I'm sorry, honey, what did you say?"

"Oh, never mind. How 'bout turning on the TV?"

"Sure thing." Janie clicked it on, "Look, Betty, you need your own lawyer. Trust me."

"Hm, maybe you're right. We'll at least talk to him."

Janie finished the shampoo, added a touch of auburn, and then turned on the drier. "Gotta have you look good for your boy."

"Oh, Janie. It's a legal consultation, not a date."

"You never know."

"For heavens' sake."

"You look great. Let's go."

"Where are we to meet him?"

"He said he'd meet us halfway. Mid-Carolina Moe's. He's gotta go back to Norfolk tonight."

Mid-Carolina Moe's, a popular Fuquay-Varina restaurant, was downtown right next door to the East Piedmont bank. They had the best Italian menu anywhere in the Raleigh area. The ladies walked into Moe's and there sat Gibson Taylor at the bar.

"My Lord, Betty. He's just like the picture in the Yellow Pages," Janie whispered. Thirty-ish, perfect teeth, he was a Robert Redford with dark hair. "Damn if he ain't gonna look good in a court-room." She checked herself in the mirror, and they went over to introduce themselves.

"Howdy, Mr. Taylor. I'm Janie Johnson. This here's Betty Wilson."

"Pleased to meet you." Gibson Taylor picked out a table and seated them. He motioned for the waiter. "How are you, Sam? I'll have the house linguini and whatever the ladies would like. It's on my ticket."

"Sure enough, Mr. Taylor. Anything to drink?"

"No, thanks, better not. Got to hit the road for Norfolk tonight."

"The customer knows best, Mr. Taylor. Ladies?"

Janie rested her chin on her hands and studied the menu. "Oh, the house is fine with me, too."

Betty concurred.

"I'm sorry about Mr. Wilson. Tell me what happened," Gibson said.

It took Betty a full five minutes, and Gibson Taylor let her proceed un-interrupted. She handed him a copy of the autopsy report. Taylor studied it for a moment. "Well, Ms. Wilson, it is early in the process, but I think your husband's death does warrant investigation. Have you sought out any other opinions yet?"

"No, sir. Mr. Olden did offer to handle it for me, but Janie here advised against it."

"Mr. Olden?" Taylor asked.

"He is the Administrator at Harvey Memorial."

"Yeah, he runs the place," Janie added. "I told Betty she'd better get someone else."

Betty went on. "He said he was sorry it happened in his hospital, but he'd see to it Indie was off the staff. He recommended we go ahead with the lawsuit," Betty said.

"Hmm. That is unusual. Well, Miss Janie gave you good advice. It sounds like the hospital would be supportive, but you do need your own counsel, be it me or whoever you choose."

"Oh, we choose you, Mr. Taylor," Janie said.

Betty Wilson kicked her shin under the table.

"Ms. Wilson?" Gibson asked.

"Well, Mr. Taylor. I have to tell you I've never done this before. But I'm not going to let Indie do in my Blinky and not do something about it."

"I must prepare you for the fact these things are never easy. It seems like it ought to be straightforward, but it never is. They often drag out several years. Doctors have the resources for a vigorous defense."

"Indie? He ain't got nothing," Janie countered.

"Not so much the doctor personally, but the insurance company who defends them. They do not give up easy. I've never met one allergic to money yet. Do you know who the carrier is for Dr. Jenkins?"

Betty shrugged her shoulders.

"Doesn't matter. We'll track all that down."

"How much do y'all charge?" Janie asked.

"We work on a contingency system. Most folks can't afford years of legal fees and not know how it will come out."

"What if we lose?" Betty asked.

"Then I don't get paid."

"Well, that doesn't seem very fair," Janie said.

"That's the system. Don't worry, though. After we study it in detail, if we decide to take it on, we will not lose. The question is, how much will we win?"

"How do you know?" Janie asked.

"Sutton's law." Taylor replied.

"Pardon?"

"Sutton's law. When they captured the famous bank robber, Willie Sutton, they asked him why he robbed banks and he said he went for the money. We have to study it some more. But, in a death case, with this kind of autopsy report, we don't plan to lose."

Janie turned south on 401. "So, Betty, what do you think?"

"I think he's a keeper."

"Me, too. I like how he talked at the end. You know what you said in Sunday school, Betty?"

"What's that?"

"Oh, you remember: 'There only two things in life that matter—money and sex. If you have one you can get the other.' That boy had both. What a great line; how'd you think it up?"

"Jimmy Olden told it to me."

"Oh."

Gibson Taylor filed suit within two weeks.

CHAPTER THIRTEEN

Little Orphan Annie

LUCILLE TAGGERT, OR TAG AS SHE WAS CALLED, was the first ever female attorney for Physician's Liability. It was physician-owned, and in the South most doctors were slow to adapt to women in assertive roles. Tag changed all that. In her first case, she had been assigned to a throwaway situation the company thought to be a sure loser.

It was a heart attack case. Some country doctor saw a lady in his office. She was tired and short of breath. He gave the woman a B12 shot and she went home and died. The doctor was past his prime and had just failed his boards. The company washed their hands of it, and told Tag to do the best she could. They sent her to Smithfield to fend for the old doctor herself. No one thought it could be won.

Tag had to go up against Martin Taylor. The elderly doctor Tag defended had been a deacon in the church, and had spent his whole life as a country doctor in the same town. He'd delivered babies at home, and was the team doctor for the high school. Tag was a small-town girl. She knew there would be some traction for a guy who had volunteered on the sidelines for forty years and was then still President of the Kiwanis Club, but she hadn't expected to win. Later they called it the Grandpa defense.

It was the only time Martin Taylor ever went to trial against his wishes, and he lost. Martin was a behind-the-scenes master, and was almost always able to negotiate a settlement. But the old doctor was beyond stubborn and wouldn't hear of it. "If my town won't stand behind me, then it's time for me to call it a day," he said.

The insurance company set aside $400K in reserves. Tag agreed, but in private thought she had a shot at damage control.

Martin Taylor was also concerned. He did his best for his client, but he began to fear the doc's lifetime of service and popularity would outweigh his obvious error and the doc's early senility. Martin was right. Tag won. From then on, she was the company ace. Corporate never forgot she beat Martin Taylor. He was a tough opponent, one the company had not done well against in the past.

None of that made any difference to Indie when he first showed up in his office. She introduced herself, opened her briefcase, and began to shuffle through some papers.

Indie was polite. "Ma'am, if you'll excuse me for a second, I'll be right back."

"Fine, Doctor Jenkins. We will get started in just a minute. I have a bit of preparation to do, anyway."

Indie slipped away to make a call. "Bones," he whispered. "You gotta help me, man. Here I am in all this trouble and they sent this college girl to save my professional ass. I knew they'd give up on me—I drew the damn rookie."

"Calm down, calm down. Who is it?"

"It's that Luciille Taggert you talked about. I'm telling ya, Bones, she looks like a Bobsie twin. God-a-mighty. She must have escaped from cheerleader camp."

Bones smiled slightly on the other side of the conversation; prejudice could rear its ugly head when folks were scared. "No fear. That woman's tough as a pine knot."

"You sure?"

"Positive."

"Well, she looks like a little rag doll."

"I saw her in action in Dr. Joseph's heart attack case. Once she gets in a courtroom, it's 'Beauty and the Beast.' Look, then she was pretty new in the business and she still freed him in two shakes."

"Yeah, well, he was a big-time cardiologist. And they weren't up against this Taylor crowd, either. I heard it was some divorce lawyer who decided to take a shot at the malpractice lottery."

"He didn't have a chance against Taggert. Believe me, Joseph was still just as frightened as a small child. Just do what you're told. Call me after she leaves."

"Okay."

Bones didn't tell Indie, but they had sent the Pro. Physician's Liability had to be scared.

Indie went back to his study and poured some coffee. "You care for some pound cake? That's from Ms. Watkins. It's the best."

"No, thanks, but I appreciate it." Taggert sorted through some notes.

"Tell me what we need to do," Indie asked. He sat down at the table.

"Well, Dr. Jenkins. I am sorry to inform you so early, but the company feels we should settle this out of court if at all possible."

"I hate to throw in the towel before we get started."

She turned to page six. "Here are my concerns, Doctor. We always worry about a death case, and the autopsy report is very conclusive."

"Maybe so, but it doesn't make sense."

"Perhaps not to you, but that makes no difference to a jury. The company feels it would be impossible to defend. I'm sorry."

Indie got up and paced around the room for a moment, then sat back down. "Well, ma'am, if it weren't for Betty I'd say we might be able to reason with them, but Betty Wilson..."

"Tell me about that."

"Oh, God, it's too long a story. You see, me and Blinky—"

"Blinky?" Taggert looked at her papers and scratched her head.

"Sure, Blinky, you know." Indie paused, and looked over the desk at her paperwork. "Oh yeah, uh, Randolph Wilson. That's Blinky, my patient. Same guy, but no one calls him Randolph anymore. Anyway, me and Blinky were like brothers, way back then he got her pregnant and boy was her daddy pissed off. She got thrown out of the family. They moved here. I wouldn't even have come to this little town except I swore I'd always look after Blinky and-"

Taggert raised her eyebrows.

"Oh, never mind ... That was a long time ago. I'm still glad I came. I've done a lot of good here ... I love my cabin at the river ... we've played one hell of a lot of music ..."

"I'm sorry, Dr. Jenkins."

Indie sat back down. "Well, at any rate, yeah, I guess we can talk settlement. I reckon I'm gonna get my ass—I mean, my tail kicked, no matter what."

She produced a document. "This is called a Consent to Settle, Doctor. It doesn't mean we'll settle today, but it does give us permission to do so if we can negotiate something."

"Hm. Dang, ma'am. Is it okay for me to think about it a day or two? I mean, it's my whole career on the line here."

"Sure, Doctor Jenkins. That's fine."

"And let me ask you about Bones."

"Yes, Brad Keith requested we list him as a consultant. You can go over the medical aspects with him, but don't forget, I'm in charge."

"Bones is pretty smart, and he knows a lot of medicine."

She scowled. "This is not about medicine. It is about money. Don't forget it. I know Bones. He's a good doctor, but way too soft-hearted to negotiate. I'm the boss, okay?"

"Yes, ma'am. Bones said you were a good-un. I trust him."

She closed her briefcase. "Any other problems here we need to know of?"

"Hmm. Well, Betty always hated me. And that Janie."

"Janie?"

"Betty's hairdresser. That woman yaks about everyone in town."

"I wouldn't worry too much about her, Dr. Jenkins. Hearsay is not allowed. We'd squelch her if it ever got to court."

"Yeah, but you won't in the beauty shop."

Tag laughed. "I grew up in a small town, Dr. Jenkins. I understand." She began to collect her things to leave. "I'm glad you agree, Dr. Jenkins." She turned around to pick up her briefcase. "Mock trial was a disaster."

"Mock trial? What the hell is that?"

"Oh, I'm sorry. It's just routine. We always run these through a mock trial ahead of time. In this case, the trial run was conclusive. We don't have a chance in court."

"Now wait a damn minute. Hell, you had a trial and I didn't get to defend myself? What kinda crap is that?"

"It's standard procedure, Doctor. Just to test the water; we always do it."

"Well, you might, but I don't. Damn. I know I drink a little and play some bluegrass music, but this is my reputation on the line here. To y'all it's just business, but to me it's personal."

"Oh, don't take it personal. Truly, it isn't."

"It might not be to you, but it is to me."

"Well, it isn't."

"Hell, yeah, it is. I know I ain't no thoroughbred, but I'm like a damn racehorse on a track. I run like hell to try to take care of everybody, and all you rich folks sit way up in the grandstand. Y'all watch with binoculars and bet on the ponies, then split up a bunch of money and go home." Indie began to pace again. "All I get is a bag of oats on my snout to try to get ready for another race." He jerked a Dixie cup out of the dispenser, placed it over his nose for emphasis, and neighed like a horse. "Awh, horse sh—uh, shoot, I ain't gonna sign nothing."

Tag stared for a moment, and then broke into laughter. "Look, I understand, Doctor Jenkins. I am on your team, okay? I'll bet on you the best I can, but this is a tough case."

"Okay, Okay." Indie tried to calm down. "And one more thing. Quit calling me Dr. Jenkins. Ain't no one called me that since I finished medical school. It's Indie for my friends, and if you ain't my friend, I'm in deep, uh, voodoo, as they say."

"Okay, Indie it is."

Indie studied the paper again. "Y'all don't expect me to sign today, do ya? I need some time to think about this."

"Oh, no. Of course not. These things move like sorghum molasses. No hurry."

Sorghum molasses. Indie gathered hope. Maybe they could jive okay. He figured they'd have to. For now, they were joined at the hip. "Hey, Ms. Lucille, anyone tell you look like Little Orphan Annie?"

Lucille rolled her eyes. "Yes. It has happened."

"Well, I'd call you Annie, but Bones said to call you Tag. If I gotta go through all this crap I ain't gonna be formal. Is Tag okay?"

"Sure. No problem." She broke into a smile. "Annie, Tag; either one is okay. I think Lucille is too formal, too."

"Sounds like B.B King's guitar."

"Well, now that you put it that way, maybe Lucille isn't so bad. I'll do the best I can." Tag smiled.

"Thanks."

She got up to leave and shook his hand. Her tiny hand was swallowed up by his. It again struck him just how petite she was. He looked at her one last time. She sure was young. He hoped Bones knew what he was talking about.

CHAPTER FOURTEEN

Lost Indian and Private Counsel

INDIE CALLED AFTER TAG LEFT. "Bones, can you drop by the B-&-B after work?"

"Sure. I've only got two more on my schedule, and I have to run by the hospital. Dark-thirty okay?"

"I'll be there. My turn to buy."

"Tag gone?"

"Yeah, just left. She's still in the parking lot."

"You okay?"

"I guess."

Bones made it by 8:00. "Lou, Indie here?"

"Yup, he's in the back. Been here a half-hour. Indie all right?"

"Sure."

"Well, he looks like one lost Indian. Try to take care of him." Lou led Bones to Indie's table and Bones sat down. "Whaddaya have, Doc?"

"Just coffee. Kate fried some chicken tonight. I better get on home. And make it high test, no cream, no sugar."

"The missus says for you not to drink coffee so late, Doc; it'll keep you up."

"It's okay, Lou. I must study after supper."

"How 'bout you, Indie?"

"Bacon Swiss cheeseburger basket."

"Sure thing."

Lou went to the front. Indie got up and opened the door. "Hey Lou, bring me a Pabst, too."

"Indie wanna Pabst, Pabst Blue Ribbon Beer. Aaawk!" Minnie the myna chimed in.

"Dang, Indie, you can't keep a secret in this place," Bones complained.

Indie closed the door, walked back to the table and took a seat.

"So what's the word?" Bones asked.

"I don't think I'm even gonna get off the starting block. They're already talking settlement."

"Hmm. Not unusual in a death case."

"Should I do it?"

"I would give it some thought. You've settled cases before, but this one has the potential to get out of hand."

"I know, but it doesn't feel right. I hate to pay off Betty Wilson. You know she hates me. Hell, she didn't like Blink. Besides, I really don't think it was my fault. I just can't figure out what happened."

"I know. I'm sorry."

"Hell, all she wants is the money and to be able to brag to that Janie Johnson how she kicked my ass."

"What is it with Janie?"

Indie squirmed in his seat. "Nothing."

"It is something. Better not hold out on me."

Indie got up and checked the door. "You remember the little French foreign exchange student?"

"Giselle? Every man in town remembers that girl. She had better curves than a slope shouldered guitar. How could I forget? I thought Ms. Jenkins was going to kill you."

"I shouldn't a done it. I'm still sorry."

"Well, no one could say the girl wasn't one heck of a temptation."

"I guess. Well, about Janie."

"Janie? You didn't get tangled her with her, did you?"

"Good Lord, no. Why, if Janie was the last woman on Earth ... oh, never mind. Anyway, Janie's aunt ran the foreign exchange student program at Harvey High. The woman damn near lost her job. The girl's parents were pissed over it. She told Janie and Janie told Betty all about it."

"Why does she care anyway?"

"She doesn't. It's just leverage when she needs it."

"Good Lord, Indie. I know Ms. Jenkins was able to forgive you, surely Janie could."

"Well, she ain't as kind a soul as my Immogene. She's gonna stir all that up again."

"That was twenty-five years ago. I ain't too worried about that."

"Well, I am."

"Well jeez, Indie. I know you shouldn't have done it, but any man could see how it could happen. Even as a kid, I could see Giselle was a looker. Did you tell Tag?"

"Naw, I'da been embarrassed to."

"I'll keep it in the pocket for now. If it settles, it'll never come up anyway."

"Good. Look, Bones. For Betty this ain't got nothing to do with Blink. I hate to go down in the record book as doing him in. It'll be my legacy, 'cause those two women'll talk about it for years."

"Well, by law they can't. These things are sealed up; confidential."

"Hell, fire, them women don't go by the law. They're thick as thieves."

"Hmm. You might be right. Well, one thing is for sure. I wouldn't make any decision without private counsel."

"So, who would you get? No one around here does that kinda work."

"You better get someone on the team who's all about just you. It never hurts to have someone familiar with the local landscape."

"Who would you get?"

"Roy Davidson."

"Whew. I don't know if he'd take me on or not. He got mad as hell at me when his aunt died."

"Dang, Indie, the woman was in her eighties."

"Yeah, but the family wanted me to send her to Sandhills. I tried, but they wouldn't take her. I don't think the family believed me. How 'bout you call him and break the ice for me? Y'all go to church together. He likes you."

"Okay, I'll call him first thing in the morning."

He called early.

"Bones, how are you? No trouble, I hope," Roy Davidson said.

"Nope, not me, anyway. It's Indie."

"Indie! Is he drunk again? One more D.U.I. and he's done for."

"No, no. He's in litigation. You remember when Blinky Wilson died? Betty filed suit."

"Uh, oh. I hope he wasn't drinking."

"Nope. I swear he wasn't. Hell, he was out of town. They're already talking settlement. I told Indie before he signed he should run it by you."

"Hmm. It isn't in my line."

"Please. As a favor to me?"

"I suppose. Who's the lawyer?"

"Lucille Taggert."

"Well, that's her field of expertise. Why doesn't he just ask her?"

"Come on, Roy. You know how it is. I think the world of Tag, but it is not the same as someone you go to church with. I just want Indie to cover every base before he signs off. He's got to live with it and I don't want him to worry later he forgot to do anything."

"Damn, Bones, the things I do for you. Why should I let you drag me into something outside my area of expertise?"

"Oh, come on, Roy. When the band had that intellectual property case you did great, and that wasn't your specialty at all."

"Yeah, but you didn't have Indie's baggage. I knew that song was yours; it was easy. Besides, I like the music."

"Please? You know how tight Indie and me are. I need to him if I can."

"Okay." Davidson sighed. "Send him on in after lunch. I'll be in the courtroom this morning. I'll help if I can. I'll give him twenty minutes."

"Thanks. That's great. He'll have to be back to the office at two anyway. I just want you to get a start on it."

"Okay."

Indie checked in at 1:30.

Davidson shook his hand. "So, Indie, tell me what happened."

Indie did, though his story rattled on. Roy was a quick study, and in ten minutes understood the essence of the case. "So, Indie. Have they run any numbers?"

"Nah, they ain't got that far."

"How much coverage do you have?"

"Three quarters of a mil. I had two other cases. I settled a heart attack one out of court, and then there was Sissy Hamlett's lost mammogram. I had a million, but those burned through a quarter of it."

"Why did you settle the heart attack case?"

"I didn't get a choice on that one. That was when they could settle without the doc's consent. I was pissed about that one. I thought we coulda won. I told him to go to the ER. The man died, and the family swore I never told him to go. It was a damn lie. The company was afraid to risk it."

"And Sissy?"

"Awh, hell. I hated it, Roy. It was my fault. I lost the mammogram report at the Billiard and Bowl. We found it a few months later. The science of it was the delay didn't change anything, but Sissy is slow, you know, and I felt sorry for her. Medicaid wouldn't cover all the treatment she needed, so I fell on the sword a little. The settlement warn't but a nick. We coulda won. Maybe I shoulda fought."

"Hmn. Both of those were outpatient incidents. Ever had any run-ins at the hospital?"

"Only minor ones." Indie chuckled at the memory. "I did get into it with old lady Hamlett."

"What happened?"

"That woman is so damn pious. She was still pissed about Sissy. She kept on a ragging me about drinking and quoted the Bible about how I was going to hell. Finally I told her Jesus said gluttony was a sin, too."

"Good Lord, be careful. A lawyer might say she is 'a woman of size, but even more generous of spirit.'

"Yeah, well, I got mad and called her fat."

"I don't think I'd done that." Roy couldn't help but laugh. Being disingenuous was not in Indie's make-up.

"Well, it's the truth. Anyway, she wrote me up and Olden called me into the office. Wanted me to apologize."

"Did you?"

"Hell, no. I told him if he pushed me any more I'd tell the Board what he was up to with that Columbian kid; you know, that Diosas girl. We call it the 'Sex for Citizenship' program."

"For heaven's sake, Indie." Roy leaned back in his chair and thought a moment. "I'll take on your case for the entertainment value if nothing else, but you must promise me: No public statements unless approved by Taggert. And she's the boss; I'll offer some help if I can."

"Sure, okay."

"So, you say you've got three quarters of a mill to work with?"

"Yup."

"I'll talk to Lucille. I promised Bones I would. I tell you, though; I think you had better go with her advice. I'll be glad to look it over, but she's an expert in medical litigation, and I'm not." Roy looked over the paperwork on his desk. "My caseload is awful, but I promised ... I'll do what I can. Look, these are the kind of cases lawyers dread. They are very hard to win. If Betty agrees to a settlement and Tag approves, I would sign it. Off the top of my head I would say do not offer more than a half mil, though. You need to keep some in the pocket for down the road."

"No kidding. I gotta get to sixty-five so I can get on Medicare. If I'm outta either health or malpractice insurance, I'm finished."

Roy got up, and shook Indie's hand. "I'll talk to them. Keep me posted."

"Will do, brother. Don't give up on me."

"Ah, Lord. I can't. I don't know why, but somehow I'm your lawyer, or at least one of them."

"Look at it this way. If it weren't for guys like me, you lawyers wouldn't have anything to do."

"I suppose so, but I want to retire someday, too. Try to stay out of trouble."

"I will. Thanks again."

CHAPTER FIFTEEN

Deposition and Settlement Discussions

TAG CALLED INDIE A FEW WEEKS LATER. "Gibson Taylor has called for a settlement conference. We would like to schedule it soon. Can you arrange to be off on the seventh?"

"Wednesday?"

"Yes."

"Sure. Might as well get it over with. It'll be summer before you know it. I'd rather spend it at the cabin than deal with this mess."

"I'll be there an hour ahead of time for a pre-deposition conference."

"Okay."

They met at the third floor classroom at the hospital. Tag opened her briefcase and went right to work. "Depositions are tough. I know it's hard, but you just need to be yourself. Try to give short answers. We don't think we can get you out of this. We want to settle. The less you say the better. Do not forget, they'll watch your every move. The good news is Gibson Taylor tends to be a reasonable adversary. Try not to be nervous."

"Hell, Tag, that's like telling those kamikaze pilots not to worry. You got any sake?"

"And try not to cuss."

"Yes, ma'am. Is it okay for Bones to come?"

"I suppose, Doctor. It not necessary, though. We intend to settle if at all possible."

"He won't come unless we invite him."

Tag checked her watch. "I don't have time to prep him." She looked Indie right in the eye. "I know you don't understand. Here's the thing: One of the first things they will ask is if you have talked to anyone about the case. If you say yes, they will make a note of it. When they can use the information, they will depose those people and seize on any possible discrepancy in your stories to try to discredit you. It's an ugly business." She sat back and sighed. "I know you trust Bones, and you have good reason to, but let's just hold the cards we have."

"Yes, ma'am."

Olden's conference room was on the second floor. Gibson Taylor and a couple of men Indie did not recognize were huddled in the hallway just outside the room. Tag and Indie went inside.

There was a table set up in the middle of the room with seats on either side so the adversaries could face off. A couple pitchers of water and some glasses sat on the table. There was a microphone for each participant so the event could be recorded.

Indie took a seat in the back of the room. "Let's get the back pew. I'm a half-ass Episcopalian, but today I'll be a Baptist," he whispered to Tag. She sat down beside him. "Looks like Nuremburg."

"Ssh."

A few Impressionistic paintings hung on the wall. Indie turned to Tag. "See those prints? Knock offs; not even a good Cezanne copy. Snookers got 'em at Walmart. Fine mics, though. Shure 57s. John Lennon wouldn't use anything else."

"Quiet, Indie."

"You oughta hear Olden try to sing over one of those Shures. God-a-mighty!"

"Hush!"

Gibson Taylor came in and his men sat down on either side of him. He called Indie to the table. Indie pulled out a chair for Tag, seated her to his right, and then sat opposite of Gibson Taylor. The first third of the session was to establish facts. Where did he go to school, residency training, Board Certification, that sort of thing. Indie slouched in his chair and yawned. Tag punched him in the ribs.

"Dr. Jenkins, are you current on your continuing medical education?"

"Why, yes sir, I have it right here." Indie reached in his coat pocket and pulled out several sheets of paper. A treadmill report was mixed in there, and the papers fluttered to the ground. Indie bent over to retrieve them. "Yeah, here it is. Damn, I didn't realize I had that many hours. A hundred forty-seven last year. I bet I kicked Bones' ass on that."

Tag glanced at Taylor; he nodded. "Sure, Lucille, we'll strike that line."

She grasped Indie by the elbow and whispered in his ear. "Please, Indie, no profanity. It'll make you look bad."

Indie straightened up. "Yes, ma'am, and sir. I'm sorry. I'm trying to break the habit."

"Dr. Jenkins, are you critical of anyone else's care in this case?"

"Naw, man." Indie refused to blame anyone. "But I'm not critical of me, either. I know the autopsy said Fentanyl toxicity, but it doesn't make sense."

"Are you saying the autopsy report is wrong? This is the State Coroner's office, you know," Taylor said.

"No, I'm just saying it doesn't make sense," Indie responded.

"And why do you say that?"

"Shoot fire, Mr. Taylor. Why, the dose he was on was just a tiny thing. I had my aunt on that much after hip surgery."

"Was Mr. Wilson narcotic-naive?"

"Blink? He ... uh, heck, no. Ever since Blink's back injury, he'd taken all kind of pain pills." Indie realized he might have led himself into a trap. "He had a second opinion at the Pain Center, and they didn't change a thing about my treatment plan."

"Would it have been wise to have obtained a level prior to his death?" Taylor asked.

"Well, it's not the standard of care. I've never done it."

"Do other doctors?"

"I asked Bones, and he said he didn't and he couldn't find anything in the literature to support it."

"I'm sorry. Asked who?"

"Bones. Dr. Bones Robertson. Oh, his real name is James. I have permission to talk to him. He is a consultant on the case."

"Have you talked to anyone else about it?"

"Just the team, sir." He smiled and thought of Minnie the myna bird. "I do know someone has talked to the folks in the hospital, though. They were talking about it at the nurse's station last week, but they stopped when I walked up. Oh, yeah, and I did go over it with my personal attorney, too."

"Who is that?"

"Roy Davidson."

"And what did he say?"

"He said he thought I was telling the truth, and that I'd be okay."

Taylor scribbled down a few words. "Okay, so you mentioned it to Bones Robertson. What was his take on it?"

"Like I said, he didn't see anything in the literature to say a Fentanyl level is the standard of care. Bones' smarter than he looks, too. That cat can run the table on a bubble test."

"Bubble test? I beg your pardon?"

"A bubble test. You know, those standardized computer things. Bones says all you gotta do is fill in the right bubbles."

Taylor laughed. "I see. How did you do, Doctor?"

"Pretty dang good. Me and Bones study together at the Harvey B-&-B on Thursdays after church band practice. I made the seventy-seventh percentile last year. Hell, I beat Bones the year his Marie was born—eighty-eight to eighty-five—and I ain't gonna let him forget it, either."

Taylor glanced at one of his associates and smiled. "So, Dr. Jenkins. You have stated you do not believe Mr. Wilson died of Fentanyl toxicity, in spite of what seems an obvious autopsy report. What do you think happened?"

Indie turned somber. "I don't know, Mr. Taylor. It just doesn't add up. I'll tell you what's the truth, though: I wouldn'ta done in Blink for nothing. He was my best friend, about like a brother. I'm sorry he's gone, man. I really am. I'm sorry."

Taylor reached across the table and shook hands. "I am, too, Indie."

Everyone filed out and went to separate rooms for post-deposition conferences.

"So, little Miss Orphan Annie, how'd it go?"

"Fine, Indie. I tell you one thing: I've only seen an attorney shake a doc's hand one other time. I think Gibson at least knows you're sincere."

"Did that guy win?"

"No, but we did manage damage control on a bad case. I think you handled yourself well. I liked your short answers—you didn't give him anything to hang you with."

"Hell, he already has plenty of rope."

"I believe we'll be able to avoid a trial."

"You know what? I think that Taylor knows I'm telling the truth. He seems okay to me."

"Like I said, he's a reasonable adversary."

"So you think he'll cut me loose?"

"He's not that reasonable. Besides, if he did, Betty Wilson will jump on him like a legal duck on a June-bug."

"I reckon." Indie started to cuss, then bit his lip. He got up, walked over to the window and stared out for a while, then came back and sat down. "How long you think this might drag on?"

"Oh, they can go on for years. We're going to try to wrap this one up fast, though." Tag reached over and squeezed Indie's neck and shoulders. "You need to go try to relax."

"I wish Bones coulda been here. Hey, we're gonna play at the Bomb Shelter, Wednesday. You want to come?"

"Bomb Shelter? What's that?"

"Man, that's one of the best picking place in eastern North Carolina."

"I don't understand. Is it a concert hall?"

"No, it's just a place to play bluegrass music. Sorta like the B-&-B, just no food. Plenty of beer, though."

"That's encouraging."

"You oughta come."

"I'd love to, Indie, but I'm going to to be in trial."

"I wish you hadn'ta said that." Indie gazed out the window again. "I tell ya the truth, Tag. Today brought it all back. No matter what happens, Blink is gone. We ain't gonna change that."

Indie shuffled out to the parking lot, got in the Jeep and drove home. He had promised to call Bones, and he could stand a drink. Ms Jenkins greeted him at the door.

CHAPTER SIXTEEN

Settlement Conference

WHEN TAG GOT TO THE OFFICE the next Monday morning there was a note from Gibson Taylor taped to her phone: Call Gibson Taylor how about a settlement conference 3pm Wed. week?? Hm. Only two weeks. It was a good sign. Maybe they could settle up.

She called Indie first. "Indie. Gibson Taylor called. He's talking settlement. Three p.m. Wednesday, two weeks, the 17th. We both need to go. I hope we can get this behind us."

"I dread it, but ... Is it okay for me to bring Bones?"

"Truly, Indie, he's not needed. Too many cooks, you know."

"Honest to God, Tag, he's the best friend I've got. I know he can be a pest, but the boy is smart. He can help us."

"Indie, he's but a child in an adult game."

"Well, I heard he helped you out in the Bonfield case."

There was silence for a minute. Finally Tag spoke. "Now damn it, Indie, I won that one, not Bones Robertson, and don't forget it. Other than the Smithfield case, it was one of my best. Besides, he really didn't have any exposure. If he had, he would have been doomed. All Martin Taylor had to do was ask him a question, and he'd have told the man anything he wanted to know."

"At least he's honest."

She was silent.

"Tag, please."

"He's that important to you?"

"Yes'um."

For a moment she didn't say anything. "I suppose, if he'll just sit there."

"He will, I promise."

"Okay, I'll call to brief him. But listen, Indie, it's okay for you two to review the case, it's okay for him to provide moral support, but it is not okay for him to get into the mix as far as negotiation. I do not want you to, either. I know doctors like to be in charge, but you have to let me handle this."

"Yes, ma'am."

Tag sighed. "Okay. I'll call him."

She hung up and called Bones. "Dr. Robertson, this is Lucille Taggett. We want to have a settlement conference next Wednesday. I would like for you to come. Can you get free?"

"Lord, Tag. You need me?"

"I don't, but Indie does. We hope we can strike a deal. I don't want Indie to cuss or cry."

"I'll be there."

"You just have to promise. You are there for moral support. It's my case."

"I understand. Look, Tag, I know it was an odd case, but the truth won out."

"We might not be that lucky again."

"I know. I just want to be there for Indie. "

"Okay. And I understand that. I give."

Taggert called Gibson Taylor. "Indie says he's ready. He does want to bring Dr. Robertson. We have him listed as a consultant, but he's just there for support. "

"Okay, not a problem."

"I'll listen to anything you have to say, Gib, as long as it's reasonable."

"Hell, I always am."

"Sure you are."

"I want to ask Bill Thomas from Goldsboro to mediate. Is that okay?"

"Sure."

"Lucille, let me ask you something. Has anyone from Harvey Memorial contacted you?"

"No, why do you ask?"

"Well, someone's been pushing Betty Wilson very hard. Told her to go for the max, and saw to it she understood that's all Dr. Jenkins has anyway."

"That's true."

"The woman knows down to the penny what Jenkins has left in his coverage, and I didn't tell her. What's your take on Sharma? I was all set to add him on but Ms. Wilson pitched a fit. As bad as she wants Dr. Jenkins, she seems indifferent to Sharma altogether. It is very strange."

"Sounds like a vendetta."

"I don't know if Dr. Jenkins has adequate coverage to cut a deal or not."

"Well, I think he does, Gib. For one, we are not at all certain about the autopsy. And, even if Indie will not support it, you can make the argument the hospital had time to correct his error, if there was one. We're willing to talk settlement, but not for the limits of his coverage. He has genuine regret that Mr. Wilson died. If we have a trial, there'll be more sympathy for Dr. Jenkins than you realize."

"Perhaps, but he carries a lot of baggage. Pills, booze, age. I could paint an ugly picture."

"It might backfire, Gib. You've been there."

"Yes. See you Wednesday at three."

"Where?"

"I rented a suite at the Holiday Inn, third floor, room three-oh-seven."

Tag was sitting in the lobby of the Holiday Inn at 2:50 when Indie and

Bones arrived. "Gentlemen, I believe we are close. Any last minute concerns?"

"I'm ready to be done with it," Indie said.

"Bones?"

"I'm good."

Tag studied her notes. "One last question. Why do you think Ms. Wilson didn't name Sharma?"

"Oh, that's an easy one, Tag," Bones began.

"I was asking Indie."

"Bones woulda been right. Sharma is a sacred cow," Indie responded.

"How's that?"

"Sharma came here on Senator Walton's rural health initiative. Olden and Walton have been tight for years. The hospital was a major contributor to Walton's campaign; Walton passes legislation in the hospital's interest. It's a nice relationship. The senator came through for 'em, too; he got a big rural hospital reimbursement bill passed. You can be damn sure Olden'll not touch Sharma."

"Besides, we can't see Sharma had any more to do with it any more than Indie," Bones added.

"He would be another well to tap, though."

"So would the hospital, but Olden won't let her." Indie frowned. "Don't matter, he didn't do nothing. I ain't pointing fingers."

"Okay, Indie. They don't seem to be inclined to add Sharma on anyway."

"You can be sure Olden wants to keep the focus on me." Indie looked around the lobby. "As close as Olden and Betty are, I promise you she knows it, too."

Tag pushed the elevator button. Indie took a deep breath.

It was small group, just Tag, Indie, and Bones, then Betty Wilson came in with Gibson Taylor. There also was Mr. Bill Thomas, who Taylor introduced.

Mr. Thomas laid out the process. First Mr. Taylor would have the floor, followed by Tag. Then the two sides would separate into groups in the adjoining rooms and Taylor would communicate between both until an agreement was reached. With that, he gave the floor to Gibson Taylor.

"Our experts have reviewed this case at length, and they concur with the State Coroner's autopsy report: The cause of Mr. Wilson's death was Fentanyl toxicity. However, we don't believe that Dr. Jenkins made this error with any malice."

Betty winced.

Taylor went on. "We have discussed it with Ms. Wilson, and she is amenable to reasonable settlement considerations. She asked to speak for a moment. "

"Fair enough." Tag looked up from her notes, waved her hand, and agreed to proceed.

Betty Wilson went on about how she loved her Blinky so, and he had been worth a million dollars to her. Then she turned and pointed right at Indie. "And you, Dr. Jenkins, you of all people. My Blinky trusted you with his life and you killed him, and—" She began to sob. She was out of control, and had to stop.

Indie started to stand up, but Tag held his shoulder and kept him in his seat. "It's okay, Indie," she whispered. "You'll get your turn in a minute."

Bones kneaded Indie's neck muscles like Ms. Jenkins did when he worried.

Tag fidgeted, and then spoke. "We understand Ms. Wilson's feelings; her husband is gone. But, we have some concerns about the autopsy report and our experts wish to review this issue further. However, we will consider reasonable settlement offers." She looked at Indie, "Dr. Jenkins?"

Tag grasped his elbow, and whispered in his ear. "No cussing, Indie."

"Yes, ma'am." He cleared his throat. "Now, Betty, first of all, you know as good as anyone in town I loved Blinky Wilson like a brother. Ain't no way I killed him, and Mr. Taylor knows that." Taylor fixed his eyes on his legal pad and jotted down a few notes. Indie scratched the bald spot on his head. "I was good to him, and you know everyone wasn't. I was his doctor and he told me everything, and I mean everything."

He paused to let it sink in. If they wanted to get in the mud and wrestle, he'd bring everybody to the courthouse. "I really don't think I did anything wrong, but I'd be okay with some kinda settlement, maybe something for the grandchildren's college fund or something, I don't know. But, I sure am sorry he's gone, and I want all y'all to know that." His voice took on a higher pitch. "I, uh ... well ... uh ... I guess, uh ... I ain't got nothing else to say."

Tag patted him on the arm.

The mediator had them break to adjoining rooms for further discussion.

Someone had placed a pitcher of water and glasses on the round table in the hotel room. The bed had been removed and two couches and a glass coffee table sat in the middle of the room. The three of them all sat at the table.

Indie poured some water and spoke first. "God, how 'bout that bull of Betty's?"

"What was that all about?" Tag asked.

"She's just being Betty."

"Damn right, Indie," Bones replied.

Thomas the mediator came in and sat at the table. "Any numbers, Tag?"

Tag said, "They called the meeting. We're here to listen."

"Taylor said they want a million."

"That's just to impress Betty," said Indie.

"I know," replied Thomas.

"My top dollar is four hundred grand. Our experts believe the autopsy may have technical limitations," Tag said.

Thomas raised his eyebrows. "I assure you they don't see it that way."

"We'll offer three-fifty because of what we know about the report. My guess is Taylor expects around three-hundred."

"I think he expects a little more than that," said Thomas.

"Our offer is three-fifty," Tag said.

"That's all you want to open with?"

"Three-fifty. We've already invested too much for experts."

"Okay."

Thomas was gone for fifteen minutes. When he came back, he sat down, looked everyone in the eye and said, "They are holding a hard line, but Gibson led me to believe that he might be able to sell six hundred thousand."

For a moment, Tag did not say a thing, and did not look at Thomas. She tapped on the table and then looked him in the eye. "Hm. Maybe four-fifty, and we'd have to think on that."

Thomas didn't say anything. Bones' right foot shook. Indie took a deep breath but Tag just stared into Thomas's eyes without blinking.

Thomas stood up. "Four-fifty. It's going to be hard, but I'll be back."

Thomas went to Taylor's room and made his case. "Four-fifty, guys. I can read Taggert. That's all she's going to do."

Gibson Taylor turned to Betty. "Now, Ms. Wilson, I think we ought to do this. At the outset, I didn't think they would go more than three hundred. There are problems with the autopsy, and I'm not certain they realize the extent of it."

"I don't know. Blinky gone ... and for less than a half million ..."

Taylor held her hand, "If we go to trial we'll eat up two-hundred grand in expenses. I recommend we strike a deal."

Betty paced around the room. "My Blinky's dead. This is so hard ... I don't know. Is it okay if I walk outside and get some fresh air? I need to think for a minute."

"Sure, Ms. Wilson. Take as long as you need; we'll wait on you."

Betty went down the hall, then outside and around the building, mumbling to herself. When she went back in the lobby she walked to a pay phone.

"Jimmy? They're only talking four-fifty. You told me I could get three-quarters, minimum. What the hell's going on here?"

"I'm sorry, sweetie. I would say turn it down. If Indie had any decent insurance you could get a mil. Damn, Betty. The man died."

She froze.

"Betty ... Betty ... Tell them to go to hell."

Her lips were dry and began to crack. "Okay, I'm will go back in there and tell them to go to hell."

"That's right, sweetie. That's right."

She walked back into Gibson Taylor's room, sat stiff on the couch, and brushed her hair back. "I feel much better. I'm ready to talk." She sighed and asked for water. "My feet are killing me." She took off her high heels and put them on the coffee table. Mr. Taylor brought her a glass and set it on the table.

Taylor called Thomas in, who took a seat. "My client has had some time to think, Bill. I think we can finish up today."

"Good. I think you're doing the right thing, Ms. Wilson. Then four-fifty is acceptable?"

Betty interrupted. "Four-fifty, hell! I want everything he has. You tell that damn Henry Jenkins if he doesn't give me three-quarters I'll take everything he has right down to that motorcycle." Gibson Taylor's jaw dropped as Betty took one of her high heels and cracked the glass top of the coffee table. "I have my rights!!" she shouted. She stood up and her knees hit the table and tilted it. Her glass slid off, shattered, and the water spilled across the floor.

Snookers said later the hospital got a bill for a new table. The Holiday Inn sent it to Gibson Taylor first, and he scrawled "No Way, Personal/Confidential," and forwarded it to Jim Olden. Olden paid for it and had Snook deliver the check.

Bill Thomas waited for a sign from Taylor, then left to break the news.

"Sorry, guys. The woman is just not going to negotiate. She claims this is worth a million. She won't settle."

"I'm afraid this has to do with bad blood," Indie replied.

"We want to send back a message," Tag said.

"Yeah, tell Betty I said go to hell," Indie said.

"Indie!" Tag admonished.

"Okay, then. Quote General McAuliffe. 'Nuts.'"

Tag laughed. "That won't do either, Indie. Can I meet with my client in private for a moment?"

"Sure, Lucille, take your time." He stepped back into the center room and closed the door.

"Okay, Indie, where are you coming from?"

"Damn it, Tag. I don't mind being reasonable, but I'm telling ya, I think the autopsy is wrong. Betty Wilson is under Jim Olden's influence."

"How do you know that?"

"Snookers."

"Who?"

"Snookers Molesby. Snook is in maintenance at the hospital," Indie said.

"He's an old golf pal of mine," Bones added.

Tag threw Bones an icy look. "So, Indie, what does this guy say?"

"If they max out my malpractice insurance, I'm off the staff, and Olden knows it. Sumbitch," Indie explained.

"Ssh, Indie. You're getting too loud. Why does Olden hate you so bad?"

"I know too much. You see, Betty hated Blinky 'cause he got her pregnant and her daddy disowned her. She hated me 'cause I supported Blink. And there's that little Colombian intern who works in Olden's office? We call it the 'Sex for Citizenship program,' and—"

Tag threw up her palm like a policewoman at a crosswalk. "Okay, Indie. Stop. I've heard enough. Let them back in. No use to run the table on you this early."

Tag opened the door and Thomas came back in and started to sit down.

"You don't need to sit," she said.

"So what's the verdict?"

"We do not believe any settlement in excess of four-hundred-fifty thousand is reasonable at this time. We will take further developments under consideration as the case matures."

"That's it?" he asked.

"Yes." Tag was firm.

"Amen," Indie said.

"Understood," Thomas said. "Anything else?"

"Yes," Tag said. "Tell Ms. Wilson I agree with Indie: Nuts!" She smiled.

Thomas grinned. "I'll believe I'll leave it with your first statement, Lucille." He turned around at the door. "Tell you what, though, this thing could be over-tried."

"Let's wait and see if they come back," Tag said into the quiet.

"Hell, Tag, I appreciate you standing up for me."

"No use to settle for the max ... yet."

"So this act's over?" Bones asked.

"Maybe, but I need to talk about this Snookers guy."

Thomas opened the door a few minutes later. "The queen has left the building. I'm sorry I wasn't able to make it work."

Tag turned to Indie. "God, what have you gotten me into? You know this means we've got to go to trial?"

"Don't worry, Tag. It'll be all right. Don't worry 'til Bones says worry."

She didn't comment.

CHAPTER SEVENTEEN

Mason Marley

MASON MARLEY LIVED IN A SMALL, white, frame house on the river, about two miles upstream from Indie's cabin. Both Indie and Bones liked to visit her. They all loved the river. Indie loved spring, but Bones was more partial to the summer than any other time of year. When they would go out for a ride in Indie's fishing boat, they often stopped at Mason's. Sometimes they'd stop in Lawson's Cove and Indie'd jump in for a swim.

Mason was confined to home, but she loved to hear Indie talk about his days on the river. "I'm old as dirt but the river makes me feel clean as a baby after a bath," he'd say.

By June, the case seemed dormant, but they knew it wasn't dead. It was too hot for golf that day. Bones went out to visit and take Mason her blood pressure medicine.

Mason was blind and in a wheelchair from post-polio syndrome, but she remained fiercely independent. Wheatie Willis kept up her yard, and an Indian woman, Atsa Paaki, helped in the house.

Wheatie had just finished mowing the grass and waved as he backed out of the driveway when Bones pulled up.

Atsa was elderly, but quite active and the best cook around. She had lived at Mason's as long as Bones could remember. She came to work for Mason after her husband was killed in WWII. She spoke broken English and often pointed to her eyes and then to Mason's mouth.

When asked what it meant, Mason said, "She says she has eyes like an eagle, but I am her voice. She doesn't speak English well."

Most people couldn't understand Atsa, but she and Mason communicated just fine. Every once in a while Indie would be there, too, talking to

Atsa, and Bones felt like an outsider. He would ask Indie what they were laughing about and he would say, "Ah, hell, just old stories, Bones. You have to be ancient and dip snuff to understand Atsa."

Bones went to the porch and opened the screen door. "Mason? You home?"

"Come on in, Bones."

Mason was listening to a book for the blind in her wheelchair.

"How are you, girl?"

"Oh, just fine, Bones, and you?"

"Good."

"Y'all been out in the boat much?"

"No, ma'am, not enough."

"Well, you need to get Indie out there. You know how much he loves the river."

"Yes, ma'am."

"I hope you'll stay for supper. Atsa has cooked up some catfish."

"Salt and peppers?"

"Yep."

"Believe I will."

Mason rolled into the kitchen. She and Atsa talked in some words Bones didn't understand and Mason tapped on the table a few times. "She says she'll set an extra place."

Bones had three servings and then pushed the empty plate away. "Lord have mercy, Mason. That was some kinda good." Atsa held out a catfish on a spatula and raised her eyebrows. "Oh, can't eat another bite." He rubbed his stomach, and said, "Full." She waved her hand and put it back in the skillet. "Mason, those were as fine a salt-and-pepper cats as I've ever had."

Atsa put on a pot of coffee.

After supper, Mason motioned to move into the parlor. "Atsa is a fine cook, huh, Bones?"

"You want me to help her get the dishes?"

"It's okay. She'll finish up. She likes to watch old Lawrence Welk shows in the back before she turns in."

Bones started toward the parlor.

"No kidding? Lawrence Welk? Who'd thought that?" Bones chuckled. Atsa could barely speak English, and she was digging Lawrence Welk. "I guess Mr. Welk's German-Ukrainian-North Dakota accent doesn't bother her a bit."

"Music is an international language, Bones. You know that as well as anybody."

Bones sat in the parlor's stuffed armed chair, sipped his coffee and watched Mason roll over and pull out a cassette tape, feel the Braille words on it, then put it in the player to her right. "Here's something new for you, Bones."

"What's that?"

"A Czech bluegrass band. Your kind of music has started to get around."

"You know, Mason, I've often wondered. How did you come up with the name Mason? It seems unusual for a little girl, though I have to admit it fits you nowadays."

Mason opened a small wooden box on the coffee table, and retrieved one of her favorite Cohiba Cuban cigars. She lit it, took a few puffs, and then flicked an ash to the side. "Oh, now, Bones. My, my. If I get into all that, I might need one of those 'Zan-Xan' pills you talk about to get to sleep tonight."

"Jeez, Mason, I'm sorry. I didn't mean to upset you, or your reflux, either, for that matter."

Mason laughed out loud. "I'm just teasing. Your mama is right; you are far too sensitive."

"I reckon so."

Mason pointed her cane to her left and toward the cabinet. "How 'bout getting me one of those feel-goods?"

"Scotch? I can go the Kelvinator and get you a Pabst if you want."

"I believe I'll have a scotch. There's some Oban in there. Care for one?"

"I appreciate it, but I must get home in a little bit."

"What time do you need to leave?"

"Kate has Bible study tonight. I'm good for an hour or so."

Mason rolled over toward the wall. "There's a picture over here somewhere." She tapped the paneling with her cane. "Here it is. See it?"

"Yes, ma'am." The photograph was an old black and white in a little golden frame, somewhere around WWII. Bones studied the picture. It was of a pretty girl, no doubt. Delicate little curls, dimples, all decked out in an Easter dress and sunhat. Charming. "Is that you?"

"Me? Heavens no. That's Priscilla Marley. She's gone now."

"I'm sorry. Your sister?"

Mason laughed again. "You are so gullible; you'd never made it as a lawyer." Mason took a long puff on her Cohiba. "I knew her well, and she was a lovely child. I was once Priscilla, but they renamed me after I came down with polio."

Bones walked over and took a better look. Sure enough, it was Mason. One could see the resemblance around the eyes and the bridge of the nose. "Son of a gun, it is you, or was, anyway. How come they changed your name?"

Mason turned quiet, took two long draws on her cigar, and then picked a bit of tobacco from her tongue.

"Hey, Mason, we don't have to talk about it."

"It's okay. If not my doctor, who needs to know?"

Muffled Lawrence Welk music came from Atsa's bedroom behind the kitchen.

"When I got polio it was a different world. Daddy had TB, and he had to go to Asheville. They thought the mountain air might help some, and they sent him to the sanatorium for what little treatment they had. If you came down with the consumption, it was a death sentence. I understand why they did it, but I knew I'd never see him again."

"Must have been terrible."

"It was; it surely was. Well, Daddy knew he was dying, so he had my name changed to Mason."

"I don't get it."

"You can be sure as a little girl I didn't, either. I cried for days. Mason?! 'Daddy,' I asked, what kind of name is that for a girl?!'" Over time, though, I began to realize the merits of Father's wisdom. He knew as a young lady in a man's world, and a handicapped girl at that, I would have to be extra tough to survive."

"I think he accomplished that."

"You remember when Johnny Cash came out with a *'Boy Named Sue'?* Daddy had the same idea years ago, just in reverse. *'A Girl Named Mason.'*"

Bones and Mason talked for a while longer. Bones got up to leave, then stopped and turned around. "Hey, could I come back tomorrow? I have a buddy in trouble. I'd like your advice. Confidential, of course."

"Of course. I've been worried about Indie, too. Such a vulnerable man he is."

"Dang it, how'd you know?"

She smiled. "Now Bones, you know I can not betray my confidants." She turned serious, and spoke in a low voice. "Did you look at my hedges when you came in?"

"I can't say I did. I noticed those salt and pepper cats right off, though."

"You must learn to be more observant. I think the hedges look wonderful."

"Come on, you're killing me. What's up? You are not talking 'bout hedges."

Mason leaned out over her wheelchair. "Wheatie was in the hospital the Saturday night Blinky died."

"Really? Did Sharma admit him?"

"No, Jerry Cecil."

"Our internist?"

"Yep. Wheatie didn't get his Demerol that night and checked out against advice. My question, Bones, is if he didn't get it, who did?"

"Well, I don't know. Did Dr. Cecil order it?"

"I don't know, check the record." Mason sipped the last of her scotch.

"Hmn. He probably thought Wheatie was just upping the ante on his dope. Wheatie's hard to take care of. I'll bet Cecil was just glad to get him out of there."

"So is there any connection?"

"Hmm. Could be. Would Wheat talk to me?"

"A cheeseburger at Harvey Billiard and Bowl will buy you all the time you want."

"You are a sweetheart!" He planted a kiss on her forehead. Mason blushed. "A regular Sherlock Holmes sweetheart, you are!"

"You forgot something."

"What?"

"My medicine."

"Oh, sorry, I did forget. I left my bag out in the car. I'll get it."

"And tell Indie I'm in, but we have a long way to go."

"Yes, ma'am."

CHAPTER EIGHTEEN

Pickin' at Indie's Cabin

IN THE SUMMER, THE DAYS WERE LONGER, and there was always a lot of music. Snookers called on Friday. "Hey, Bones, you up for a jam session?"

"Sure, when?"

"Tonight."

"They not going to play cards at the B-&-B?"

"Indie said he needs a break. He misses Blink so bad. He says poker ain't the same without Blinky."

"Six months. Poor Indie. It's hard to forget." Bones knew Indie wasn't going to be able to get over Blinky until the case was resolved. "I saw him at the hospital today. Y'all going to the Bomb Shelter?"

"Nope. Gonna be at the cabin."

"What time?

"Dark-thirty. Darrell is off the road, so he'll be there. Moose is gonna pick the banjo."

"Good, I'm in."

"How's Indie holding up?" Snookers asked.

"Okay, I guess. He needs a break, though."

"I was gonna bring him some Galax strawberries."

"Good Lord, Snookers. Those are nothing but fermented fruit in a Mason jar of moonshine. Be careful. Indie needs to keep his wits about him."

"Olden told the trustees today Indie wouldn't settle with Betty and it was gonna have to go to court."

"Ms. Wilson is a fool to take his advice." Bones shook his head.

"You ain't kidding."

"I need to talk to Indie."

"Some strawberries will make him feel better."

"The last thing he needs is a D.U.I. right now, Snook."

"He'll be okay. Ms. Jenkins is gonna drop him off, and I promised you'd drive him home."

"Lord, Snook. Dark-thirty?"

"Yep."

It was a good session. Moose Dooley was the best five-string man in the county. Darrell Brookes was in off the road, and everyone wanted to hear him play the mandolin, so Bones switched off and played guitar. Snookers held down the bass, and Indie played as fine a fiddle as he always had.

About midnight, Bones said, "Let's pick one more and take a break, boys. How 'bout *Going Down That Road Feeling Bad*?"

"That one makes me cry," Indie said. "Especially now."

"Might make you feel better."

Everyone went to the ice box for a beer, then Indie went outside and Bones followed. Snook walked over to his pick-up.

"I got some new info, Indie," Bones said.

"Hell, Bones, it ain't gonna save me."

"I don't know, man, listen—"

Snook called out from his truck. "I got some of them Galax strawberries in the back. Want some?"

The two walked to Snooker's pick-up. Snookers opened the hatch to the camper and retrieved a cardboard box with a dozen or so Mason jars. He unscrewed the top off one and put it under Bones' nose.

"That stuff's like lighter fluid. Strawberries soaked in moonshine. How do y'all drink it?" Bones asked. It was too strong to smell, much less swallow.

Indie caressed the jar in his left hand, and fanned the fumes across his nostrils with his right palm in a gentle motion. "Your problem, Bones, is you ain't got no culture."

"So, how's it going?" Snookers asked. He looked at Indie and then at Bones.

"Terrible." Indie took a swig.

Bones looked around and lowered his voice. "Let me tell you what Mason said."

"Whatcha got, Columbo?" Indie munched on a strawberry from the jar.

"Wheatie Willis told Mason he was in the hospital the night Blink died. Wheat swears he didn't get his Demerol that night."

Indie put down his jar. "He was on a drunk for two weeks after Blinky died. I do remember he fussed at me for being out of town."

"What'd you tell him?"

"I told him to go to hell; I had to check on my mom."

Snook reached in the bed for a second jar. "He raised hell about Dr. Cecil. Said he was a prick, and if you guys were gone he'd see Sanjay from now on."

"Are you sure?" Bones asked.

"Sure I'm sure. Wheatie said Jerry Cecil was as dumb as Blake and if Cecil wouldn't give him his medicine he was gonna fire him. Heard him say it myself."

Indie looked at Bones and finally said, "Are you positive, Snook?"

"Hell, yeah. Everybody knows Cecil's a jerk. Y'all ready to go pick?"

Bones said, "I think Wheatie is right, Indie. It jives with what Mason said, too."

"When it comes to Demerol he might be. He's unreliable, but Wheatie knows hedges and narcotics." Indie paused. "Damn, Bones. I hadn't thought about it." He scratched his head. "I guess I shoulda asked him a few more questions when he got on me." He raised his eyebrows and looked Bones right in the eye. "You think Blinky got that Demerol by mistake, don't you?"

"Could have."

Indie put his Mason jar back in the cardboard box in the bed of Snook's truck. "That's a great theory, Bones, but I don't recall anything about Demerol. Blinky had Haldol, but no Demerol... at least I think... no I'm sure. Demerol. Damn. We better check Wheatie's chart."

"I did, today. Cecil ordered up the Demerol, but I think Wheatie never got it. It fits. What if somehow Blinky got Wheatie's Demerol by mistake?"

All of a sudden, Indie was stone cold sober. "Damn, Bones. How you gonna prove that?"

"I don't know, yet. Snook, can you do some surveillance work at the hospital? You got to be discreet."

"Huh?"

"You know: Not talk."

"Sure, Doc. I ain't told no one but Donna."

"Snook! I told you. No one, man, and I mean no one. What did you tell her?"

"Hell, only that Indie's in hot water with Olden. That ain't news. She won't talk. She don't kiss and tell, and she sure ain't gonna talk about such as this."

"If you and Donna were to split, she'll hold you hostage."

"We ain't gonna split."

"That's what you said about the last three."

Indie set down his jar. "Come on, boys. Settle down. Snook's all we got over there, Bones. He'll be quiet." Indie grabbed Snookers by the suspenders. "Now look here, pal. I got you that job over there. You have to leave this with us. Olden would kick your ass from here to Ocracoke if he thought you helped me." He smiled and eased the suspenders back to Snooker's chest.

"You better listen to Indie, Snook. If this isn't handled right, Indie's in a world of trouble, and you could be, too. This could get out of hand. Betty Wilson is determined to hit the jackpot; Olden is going to do what he can to help her, and you could get fired."

"God-a-mighty. You boys worry too much. Let's go back in and pick a few," Snook said.

Indie had some spring in his step after the talk outside, and decided to do his John Hartford imitation. He put a plywood board down, tapped on it to 'tune it up' a little, and then sawed down the *'Lee Highway Blues.'* It was a favorite for Bones, and Indie rendered it to perfection, all the while clogging away on that board. It would have made Hartford proud.

"Indie, the missus said no later than two a.m. We better go to the house."

"Yes, sir, boss Bones."

Ms. Jenkins came out to meet them. "How is he, Bones?"

"Fine, Ms. Jenkins. Snookers only let him have one Mason jar."

"Appreciate you looking after him."

"Yes, ma'am. We all need somebody."

"Anything new?"

Indie woke up. "Tell you what, Mama. Bones' gonna save this chief's ass, you wait and see. I didn't pick no dummy for a doctor, I tell ya."

Bones laughed. "Shoot, you only picked me 'cause I can play the mandolin."

"Naw, Bones, I picked you 'cause you're a damn Boy Scout."

CHAPTER NINETEEN

Martin Taylor Summit Meeting

"SO SNOOK, WHAT DID YOU FIND?"

"Not much, Doc, but I did get a couple things."

"Let's see."

Snook handed Bones a piece of paper. "Here's Wheatie's copy of his complaint."

"Where did you get it?"

"Wheatie found it. It took a while. He'd left it in an old stack of bills by the TV. His trailer is a wreck."

"Good work." Bones studied the yellow copy. It was legit, no doubt about it. Wheatie had filled it out. "Man, is his writing bad."

"His? C'mon, Doc."

"What else you got?"

"Me and Donna went through the files down in PR. She works in Public Relations, you know."

"I'm sure she's good at that."

"Dang right." Snookers smiled. "Yeah, here's the kicker. The hospital copy ain't anywhere in the department. Wheatie's sure he turned it in. He only has his copy, so I figure that's true. Me and Donna turned the place upside down, Saturday. I told you she'd come in handy."

"Whatever. Anything else?"

"Yeah. I got the pharmacist to pull the medicine record from that night."

"Dang, Snook, he might talk."

"Not a chance. He hates Olden. He got passed up for head pharmacist by that little pissant cousin of Jimmy's after all those years of working nights. He won't tell."

"I hope not. Would he testify?"

"Nope. Job scared. He did give me a copy, though. Made me swear I wouldn't tell where I got it. He won't let us keep it; said I had to bring it back."

"Let me see." Bones looked over the requisition. "Damn. Six fifty-milligram doses checked out to the floor. But no record Wheat ever got it. And by the chart, neither did Blinky. It just frigging vanished."

"So did I help?"

"I don't know. It just doesn't make sense. I wish there was some way for me to get this information in the right hands."

"What about that lawyer lady?"

"I don't know. She thinks I'm meddling now. She says Indie can't win. I know she's right, but I'd like to sow some doubt. Maybe he can settle without breaking the bank."

"I'll tell Donna to keep her eyes open at the hospital. We've got a date tonight."

"Don't talk about it."

"You're too uptight. You want me to help or not?"

"Snook, somehow I need to talk to Betty's attorney and explain this to him."

"Ain't that against the law?"

"It's not exactly against the law."

"Then why don't you just let the lawyer lady talk to him?"

"Oh, well, even though it's not against the law, they don't want me messing in this thing, Snook. I can't do that."

"Why don't you just mail it?"

"I might have to." Bones fished around his pocket for his DayTimer to check his schedule. "Oh, well, somehow we'll get something done. Me and you need to play golf sometime, pal. I've about let my game get away from me."

"Anytime, Doc. Give me a call."

"Okay. Hey, Snook, let me ask you something. You played in the Magnolia Seniors golf tournament last year, didn't you?"

"Yeah, how come?"

"Do you ever run into a guy named Martin Taylor?"

"The lawyer?"

"Yeah, he's a hell of a golfer."

"No kidding. He made the quarter-finals."

"Where is he now?"

"Somewhere in the Virgin Islands. Retired."

"Does he ever get back this way?"

"Yeah. He plays some tournaments on the coast every so often."

"I've been fighting a hook. Is he any good with that kind of thing?"

"They say he knows the game."

"How would you find him?"

"Hm. I know a guy who caddies for him whenever he plays down there. Taylor has a place near Morehead. He let my buddy stay there; he said it was some kinda crib."

"Really? I'm going to be down that way. I want to take a week to tune up before the County Tournament in August. I sure would like to get up with him."

"I'll see what I can do."

Three days went by. Bones walked in his office to start the day, and threw his coat across the chair. The phone lines were lit up. It was going to be a busy one. His private line rang.

"Hello? This is Martin Taylor."

Bones was near speechless. "Yes, sir, what can I do for you?"

"I understand you've got a hitch in your swing. I might be able to help out a fellow golfer."

"Is this really Martin Taylor?"

"Yes. Good to speak to you, Bones. I hear your game has gone south."

"Well, it's not too bad, but I've been fighting a hook. Getting a little quick, I think."

"Hm. You're probably over the top. I'll be in Morehead City the week of the Fourth of July. We have a condo on Bogue Banks. Why don't you come down and we'll get in a round?"

"Gee, well, I don't know, I gotta work and—"

"It won't hurt to take Wednesday off. Hell, all doctors take Wednesdays off."

"I could get there Tuesday night. I'll try to get off work early. Eight p.m. is the best I can do. Maybe we could get in a round the next morning."

"Tuesday night would be good. Captain Bill's has an all-you-can-eat flounder special. It'll be packed. The traffic will be lighter at Tony's Fish Market. Meet me there. I'll get us a private room."

Bones didn't feel too guilty. Taylor was now retired, and this was in Indie's best interest. A meal and a round of golf couldn't be too far out of bounds.

Bones arrived at Tony's at eight o'clock, approached the desk, and lay his card on the counter. He carried a mandolin in a Calton coffin case, and set it down at his feet. "Hello, there, ma'am. I'm here to meet Martin Taylor. We are to have a private room overlooking the Sound. I like to watch the wild ponies over on the banks."

"Hey, aren't you Bones Robertson? Is Neuse River going to be at Kinston this year?"

"Yes, ma'am. Has Taylor arrived? He might hire us for a big gig."

"Yes, sir. I assume the smoking section is acceptable?"

"Sure. I'm bluegrass, ain't I?"

Bones picked up his mandolin case. A customer recognized Bones. "Y'all got a gig down here, Doc?"

"Uh, yes, ma'am. Private party."

"Oh. I wish I could come. Tell Moose I love that banjo."

"Yes, ma'am. Look for us at Kinston next winter."

The two made their way to the back of the restaurant. Their footsteps on the hard wood floor ricocheted like the clip-clop of the ponies out on Bougue Banks. Bones loved the ponies; he saw them as survivors. Legend had it their ancestors swam to shore off Spanish ships that ran aground in the sound years ago.

They two reached the back room, and the young lady swung the door open. There sat none other than Martin Taylor.

Taylor was reading the paper. He looked like a Southern Gentleman. A diamond stud held his tie in place. There was a small American flag on his lapel. He had a slight wisp of a beard, and favored a cross between Rhett Butler and Confederate General Joe Johnston. He looked up and flipped his newspaper onto the table.

"Mr. Taylor, this is Bones Robertson. He plays the mandolin for Neuse River."

Martin slipped the young lady ten bills. "Another Oban, Miss."

"Yes, sir, Mr. Taylor." The young lady left to get Martin a scotch.

Taylor closed the door.

Bones shook his hand. "You know, Mr. Taylor, everyone knows me, and no one knows you. I guess in our lines of work it is the only way we can get anything accomplished."

"Good to see you again, Bones."

"Good to see you, too, sir, I guess. I must say, though, I'm glad you aren't chasing me."

Martin laughed out loud. "I'm retired, son. No one's going to chase you again, anyway. I put the word out on the street."

"How's that?"

"You're too damn honest. Everyone's scared of the nice guys."

Bones scratched his head. "Scared? Dang. Well, I assure you, Mr. Taylor, the feeling is mutual."

"Say your game is off?"

"Yeah. I need some advice."

"I'll help if I can."

The waitress opened the door. "I meant to ask. A scotch for Mr. Robertson, too, sir?"

"Sure, that's fine."

"Oh, okay. Let's see. Hm." Bones' eyes wandered around the room. "Uh, one thing I wanted to tell you is I've got a buddy with the same problem. Is it okay for me to talk to him?"

"Hmn. Well as long as it's generic, I suppose so. But just because I might give you good advice doesn't mean it will apply in every case. He might have a different game."

"I understand. I'm not binding you. Just generic advice, that's all."

"Fine, no problem. So, what's the trouble?"

"Like I said, I'm hooking it pretty wild. It gets me in trouble sometimes. My pal's got the same problem."

Martin stood up. "Stand opposite of me there, Bones. Show me your set-up."

Bones stood as if he were ready to hit the ball. Martin rolled up his newspaper, and handed it to Bones. "Use this." Bones gripped it like a club as Taylor watched. "Hmn. Your set-up's okay. Grip's a bit strong, though. Turn your left hand to where only one knuckle shows. You need a weaker grip to fade the ball."

Bones adjusted his grip. "Like that?"

"Yeah, that's it. Sam Snead used to say hold it as gentle as if you wanted to take a small bird back to the nest. You're too tight. You'll strangle the little sumbitch like that."

Bones flopped his wrists in a lazy way. "Like that?"

"Better."

"You think that'll straighten it up?"

"It might. You don't hit a double cross, do you?"

"Hell, no. I ain't that bad."

Martin laughed. "Let me see your backswing."

Bones took it back just short of parallel.

"Ah, there's part of the problem."

"What?"

"You need to finish your backswing. If you're too quick, you'll be over the top. From there you're going to hit a wild slice unless you trap it; then she'll go left."

"I never slice. Trap hook, that's it." Bones took a few imaginary swings. "I've got my clubs out in the car. Want me to go get 'em?"

"Hell, boy, use your imagination." Taylor watched a couple more passes. "Hm. I'm betting you're just impatient. You have to give it some time." Taylor lit a cigar and took a few puffs. "Golf is like sex. You have to have the right rhythm and wait on it. There's nothing to it."

"I don't know whether I can trust a man who says ain't nothing to golf and sex. Those are the most complicated subjects in the world."

"No, that would be litigation."

The waitress brought their drinks. Martin left a ten. "Thanks, kid. Keep the change. If you don't mind we will need some privacy. We're in high-level negotiations."

"Really? Wow."

"We'll ring you if we need anything."

"Yes, sir."

Martin raised his glass and took a sip of his Oban.

"Yeah, I guess litigation is pretty complicated," Bones said. "You got time for a good story?"

"Sure. You're always good for that. Cohiba?" Martin took another puff, and offered Bones a cigar.

"Uh, gee, I better not. Heart trouble runs in my family."

"Suit yourself."

"Years ago I had this patient. Everyone thought he'd died from a medicine called Fentanyl, but he didn't. It was a tox screen error, and—"

Martin cut him off. "For God's sake, I'm retired from all that now. I play golf, damn it, and I don't want to hear about that kind of crap. You know I can't talk about these things if I'm not involved in 'em."

"Yes, sir, well, okay." Bones paused. "You guys sure are secretive. Can I just tell you one thing?"

"Maybe."

"Hm. Let me put it another way. The key to my pal's trouble is in the music."

"Music? How's that?"

Bones pulled his mandolin out of the case. "Ever seen one like this?"

"Looks like a little guitar. Most unusual. What's it made of?"

"Carbon fiber. Sort of like modern golf clubs. Carbon fiber is near indestructible. It don't matter how long that baby sits in that case, or what kind of elements it's exposed to, it lasts forever. And you see the case it's in? We call them coffin cases. To play your tune all you do is take the mandolin out of the coffin case."

"I know everyone in golf, and no one in music."

"If you ever need to know a player, I know 'em all. Matter of fact, you take on my game and I'll play the mandolin for you myself. Professional courtesy."

Martin chuckled. "Whatever, Bones. Why do I need to know about mandolins? I've made it all these years and haven't been a player yet."

"Never know what'll help you in life, Martin. The mandolin has taken me a lot of places. Ever heard of a music Green Card?"

"Can't say as I have."

"A lot of lawyers dig traditional music. You remember George Anthony, the mediator in the Bo Bonfield case?"

"Of course. It was the most unusual one I was ever involved in."

"Shucks, Martin. It was the only one I was ever in."

"I guess I ought to apologize. You were in it too long. I knew you didn't have exposure from the start."

"It's okay. You did what you had to do. Anyway, George plays traditional Russian folk music these days."

"I never knew that about him."

"I'm telling ya, the music gig is another world. And George holds the card; the Green Card, that is."

Martin tapped his pencil on the desk, and then jotted a few notes for further reference, a sure sign of interest for a lawyer. "Are you leading me on some kind of wild goose chase?"

"I promise I'm not. These synthetic mandolins are prototypes right now. But they will be the ticket; you can count on it."

Taylor rang the call bell. "Another Oban, and we're ready to order, please." The story seemed worthy of his time. Martin settled in to hear more.

CHAPTER TWENTY

Green Cards

THE WAITRESS SET THEIR DRINKS on the table. "What'll you gentleman have this evening?"

Martin studied the menu. "What's the special today?"

"Bluefish, sir. Fresh catch. They're excellent."

"Sounds good. And I'll have a baked potato," Martin said.

"And you sir?" the waitress asked.

"Steamed shrimp in butter, ma'am."

"Yes, sir. They are good, aren't they?"

"Yes, ma'am. Oh, and sweet tea, too," Bones added.

"Sure enough."

The young lady left to place their order.

Martin was quiet for a moment and then asked, "So, Bones, what is this Green Card you refer to?"

"It's a long story, but I promise you it's the truth."

"Good. All I ever wanted was the truth. Back when I was a lawyer, I had enough lies told to me to last a lifetime. More lies than Hollywood told about Daniel Boone. I'm retired now, so the truth is all I want to hear. Go on."

"So, you remember George Anthony, right? The mediator guy?"

"Certainly. A good man."

"I run into him every once in a while. He's a guitar player. A good one, too. Man, the guy can pick."

Martin rolled his hands in the air. "Keep moving, Bones."

"Well, one day we were in Winston-Salem for a show at Ziggy's. The Seldom Scene was the main act. A doctor friend of mine, John Starling, is the lead singer. What a hot band. The opening act was George, of all people; he's a guitar sideman for a guy who plays Russian folk fiddle tunes. After the show we hung out and told old war stories for a while."

"Bones, I'm afraid I'm lost. Any judge in the country would object by now for lack of relevance."

"I'm getting there. So, George tells me about a young Colombian nurse who's an illegal alien, right? Turns out some administrator had tried to finagle a bogus green card for her. She had some people in Russia, and the guy leaned on this Russian fiddler to help him out. He figured he'd get George in a compromised spot, double-cross him, and then put the heat on in a case they had going on at the time."

"George is straight up; I can imagine how that went over."

"Exactly. George and his Russian fiddle man were quite offended. They wanted to press the issue, but the administrator realized he had tried to tap the wrong well. He covered his tracks, never got in any trouble, and it all died down."

"I've got a feeling a man shouldn't mess with that music crowd. I understand they're thick as thieves."

"Yeah, and so are lawyers."

"No comment." Martin smiled. "So, what's this got to do with anything?"

"The Green Card kid those guys told me about at Ziggy's? She turned out to be none other than Maria Diosas."

"And who is that?"

"She's an L.P.N. Used to work in our hospital."

"So?"

Bones looked around. "She and our administrator made beautiful music, you know."

"He's a musician?"

"Hell, no."

"You said she used to work in the hospital?"

"Yeah, well, she's gone now. She went to Russia. Her grandparents live there."

"And how do you know that?"

"Indie's wife heard it at the Beauty shop. She told my wife."

"Who's Indie?"

"Oh. Indie's a doc in town. A lot of people think Indie is kind of rough, but he's smart and he cares about his people."

"I see. Do you know why the woman left town?"

"I don't know for certain. I think this administrator guy sent her."

"What happened? Did his wife find out about them?"

"I don't think so."

"The relationship just went bad?"

"I'm not sure."

"What was it, then?"

"Mr. Taylor, come to think of it, I don't know. I do know Snook said Mr. Olde— Uh, this guy was just as happy since the green card didn't pan out."

"Who is Olde?"

"Oh, uh, well, uh ... that's Mr. Olden."

"Why was he happy?"

"Dang, Mr. Taylor. You sure ask a lot of questions. I never thought about it. Snook said Jimmy was tired of her leaning on him so bad."

"You mentioned this Snook. That has to be the one from Harvey County who's a golfer."

"Yeah, that's the guy. He's one hell of a player. We played together at Harvey High. Snook won State two years in a row. Hey, try one of these shrimpies. They're good."

Martin fished one out of the bowl. "Did this girl know a lot of people in town?"

"I got a feeling she knew more than one. Man, was she a looker. Hmm. Hey, she did know this Demerol junkie."

"Bones, you're going in circles. If I were still a lawyer, I wouldn't want to talk to any of these kind of people; too unreliable."

"Yeah, you're right about that. I didn't mean to get off the subject."

"Hmn. Okay. Let me ask you something. Your buddy who's hooking the ball? What does he do?"

"He's a doc."

"Really? What kind?"

"Country doc, like me."

"Is he any good?"

"At golf or doctoring?"

"Either."

"He's got his troubles, but he's a good doc; not much of a golfer. Plays a mean fiddle, though. Hey, at least he isn't tangled up in narcotics. He doesn't even keep Demerol in his office. Said Jim Beam is better than that crap."

"My guess is his charts are a jumble."

"I'm sure they are. But, he is quite likeable. Heck, one time he got audited. The tax man was there in a suit and tie, you know, and he asked to see this doc's records. Doc said, 'Sure, man, no problem,' and led him to a closet where there were stacks of old shoe boxes filled with receipts and ledgers that all spilled out on the floor. The IRS guy sifted through that mess for about an hour, and couldn't make head nor tails of it."

"Did your friend get a fine?"

"Heck, no. After an hour, Indi....uh, he thought the timing was right and asked the man if he liked fishing. Turned out the agent did. Doc knew the best spot on the Neuse, and suggested they take a break. Once they were out in the boat, he asked the man if he liked Jim Beam, and you know the rest of the story."

"I'm afraid I might."

"Yeah, they put some steaks on the grill, and after supper they went back to that big pile of paper at the office. The agent took one look and said, 'Awh, hell, Doc. I think we're about even. Let's call it a day.' Shoot, they are still friends! Just don't underestimate these old docs; they've been written off before."

"Trust me, Bones. I won't. So, this hospital administrator, does he have a thing for women?"

"Sometimes. He likes the young ones. I could tell you more ..."

"Never mind, I'm out of the business. I don't need to know anyway."

"So you think you can help me?"

"I don't see much way to straighten out your game without a round of golf. You said you were staying until tomorrow, didn't you?"

"Sure."

"Give me a night to think about it. I want to call my pro in St. Croix. Meet me at the Club Car Diner for breakfast—seven-thirty a.m., sharp. We'll hit Bogue Banks Club after that."

"Will do."

Bones reached to pick up the check, but Martin snatched it away. "My turn to buy."

Bones guessed he had made it in the world. Who'd ever heard of a lawyer to pick up the tab for a doctor? Martin slow-tapped his pencil eraser on the table, and then turned it around and jotted down a few more lines.

Bones pulled the mandolin out of the case. "Whadda you wanta hear, Martin?"

"Whatever, Bones." Martin was amused. No doctor had ever played the mandolin for him after dinner. "Maybe '*Lost Indian*'?"

"Uh, lost... uh no. How 'bout 'Cherokee'? It's one of my pals' favorites— mine, too. I wish you could hear Mike Marshall's chord solo version. It's a thing of beauty, and even better on that Gibson of his."

Martin laughed. "'*Cherokee*' it is, Bones. If a doctor plays the mandolin for me after dinner, he gets to choose the song."

Martin lit a Cohiba, and leaned back in his chair. His smoke rings broke up in the ceiling fan that wobbled overhead.

Bones rendered *"Cherokee,"* a complex chord melody number, to the best of his ability. It was a good rendering for a doctor.

The two men relaxed. Life was too short to fight all the time.

"Let me at least get the tip, Martin."

"Okay."

Bones tossed ten on the table. "Ten bones tip from Bones, Martin."

Martin laughed. "Good enough. I'll pay the bill." They walked out to the parking lot, and Martin climbed into his silver Mercedes. "'Night, Bones. You're right. That 'Cherokee' is a fine tune."

"Sure enough."

"You'll like the Club Car. Best breakfast on Bogue Banks. See you in the morning." Martin waved and drove out of the parking lot.

Bones checked into the Sea Eagle Motel to crash for the night, and set the alarm. There was no way he was to be late. He called Indie to update him. The line was busy. Bones figured to catch him the next morning.

CHAPTER TWENTY ONE

Dealing Cards with the Old Men in the Club Car

BONES CALLED INDIE FIRST THING in the morning. No answer. He worried for a moment and then called Snookers.

Donna answered the phone.

"Hey, Donna, Dr. Bones here. Is Snook there?"

"Sure, Doc, hold on." She put the phone down. "Snookie? Snookie baby! Get out of the shower honey, Dr. Bones's on the phone."

Snookers came to the phone.

"Snookie?" Bones asked.

"Uh, yeah, whatcha need?"

"You seen Indie? I can't find him. Is he okay?"

"He went down to the cabin with Ms. Jenkins. Said Sharma is on call and not to bother him."

"Oh, okay. Good."

"Whatcha up to?"

"Got a game with Martin Taylor today."

"God-a-mighty, Bones. I thought you were just gonna ask him a question on the telephone. Good Lord. Hey, Donna, Bones's playing golf with Martin Taylor today!"

"Hush, Snook. Any advice?"

"Where you playing?"

"Bogue Banks Club."

"When the wind comes in off the Sound, don't hit a draw."

"That's the only shot I got, Snook."

"Better learn the fade, Bones. Good luck. Martin Taylor. Damn. You're a player."

Bones hung up and called Kate. "Hey, sweetie. Everything okay there?"

"All good. Marie called. She got an 'A' on her trig final."

"Great. I'll give her a call tonight."

"Well, you get on home. There's a lot of sharks down there. You aren't used to swimming in the ocean. That undertow can take you right out to sea."

"For heavens's sake, honey. I'm just playing golf."

"I know. But be careful."

"I will. Don't worry. I'll call when I get in."

Seven-thirty AM. Martin Taylor pulled his Silver Bullet Mercedes along-side Bones' Scout. "Top of the day to you, Mr. Taylor."

"Son, it is too early to be that cheerful. Let's get some coffee."

"Yes, sir."

The Club Car was an aluminum-skinned '50s-style diner. The atmosphere was somewhere between an Air Stream trailer and a small airplane hanger. But they made up for the lack of sophistication with the best short-order grill on the North Carolina coast.

The men took a booth in the back.

"Y'all want some coffee?"

"Yes, ma'am. High test. No cream, no sugar. We aren't woke up good yet," Bones replied.

Martin waved a hand in agreement. "Okay, Bones, you intrigued me with that story you told me last night, but I've worked this as far as I can. I talked it over with my pro. I do have a return message."

"What's the word?"

"He's not sure how he can help from a distance."

"Dang it, Martin. My buddy's game is a shambles. All you lawyers ever want to do is talk about sending messages back and forth. Shoot the dadburned messenger."

Martin laughed. "Now, Doctor. Surely you don't mean it. Why, as far as I know the messenger could be sympathetic to your cause."

The waitress brought the coffee. "What'll you boys have?"

"Bacon and egg omelet for me, hold the cheese."

"And you, sir?"

"Waffles and sausage."

"Dang, Martin, you don't eat any better than I do."

She left. Bones inched out over the table. "So who is this messenger person?"

"Messenger? Oh, I meant pro. Besides, you know that loyalty list thing you talked about back in the Bonfield case?"

"Yeah. I can't believe you remember that."

"A mind like a steel trap, son. Here's the thing. A pro is always loyal. He's sympathetic even though he's never seen you play."

"For my game?"

"Sure. He'll keep you on his list if you need a lesson."

"So, he'd work with either of us?"

"Of course, he's a pro."

"Well, then who is it?"

"Bones! For God's sake, we don't need you in espionage." Martin waved to the waitress and asked for more coffee. "Don't worry. He's very loyal. Neither of us has to worry about him ever being a traitor. As they say in the CIA, friends can be enemies, and enemies can be friends. You don't even know this, but he helped you back then. We've done business for years. Pro can be trusted."

"Hmn. Okay, Martin. Don't shoot him, then. What does he need?"

"First of all, I've been asked to break confidence enough to facilitate communications with you going forward. The code name is Navajo," Martin said.

"Got it."

"The Navajo says to disturb the ancestors is contrary to tradition. And the women of the tribe consider it sacrilege."

"What the heck kinda talk is that?"

Martin added some cream to his coffee and stirred a moment. "Look, kid. I've been around golf all my life. Wives often carry a grudge about all the time a man can invest in the game."

"Well, maybe some wife was the trouble in this case. The woman never gave the fellow any space. Wouldn't listen to him, either,"

"And when that is the case, I advise the people involved not to try to change what is. Stick with the game he has. You start swinging at snakes, son, and they'll bite you every time."

"How big a bite, you reckon?"

"You don't need to get sucked into this kind of game. A thousand-dollar Nassau with automatic presses can get out of control. Besides, if a man goes out of town for lessons, it takes time and money. And the hometown guys resent a player who looks to an out-of-town hot shot for advice. Pro says unless the man has an awful lot of game to work with to settle for what's he's got. An angry spouse can be a wild card."

"Did he not offer any words of wisdom? You know, some kind of take home message?'"

"There was one."

"And?"

"I told him you were a musician. As it turns out, Navajo plays a little. Big band stuff mostly. Benny Goodman, Glenn Miller, *Chattanooga Choo-Choo,*' that kind of thing. The message is when you swing, use your music. You know how good Snead's rhythm was? Navajo said set the swing to waltz time. Think Lawrence Welk. A one and a two ...'"

"Lawrence Welk? That's for old people. We do some waltzes in blue-grass. *'Kentucky Waltz,' 'Tennessee Waltz.'* I know all about waltzes. They are in three-quarter time. Bluegrassers love a good waltz, but they are better known for cut-time numbers; fast pieces."

"As in breakdowns?"

"Yeah, like breakdowns. *Foggy Mountain Breakdown* was the 'Bonnie and Clyde' theme. Hell, Martin. You know more music than you let on."

He laughed. "My contacts say if you set your game to cut time you'll be too quick and get over the top. Thus your hook. See, it all fits together. You're just impatient, Bones. You have to wait on it."

"God-a-mighty, Martin. All you guys do is sit and wait. I see those lawyers down at the courthouse all the time. All they do is drink coffee and let their meter run like a dang cabbie."

"And all you doctors do is run like those wild ponies out there on Bogue Banks. Just stop and listen to the wind talk rather than try to outrun it. Only God can do that."

"And the wife? Would she ever listen to the wind?"

"Of course not. But Pro has seen it all. He says hold what you got."

"Yeah, well, we tried that."

"Pardon?"

"Oh, uh, nothing." Bones thought back to settlement conference. "I'm sorry, my mind was just wandering there." Bones polished off the last piece of toast. "Well, dang it, Martin. Somehow this needs to be revisited. I wish Pro would talk to the wife. See if he can convince her. I think the man's game is not as simple as you think."

"Most of these guys know better than to go against a spouse. It never works out."

"Pro would help out my man if he knew him."

"Your buddy needs to get his own people. Someone close he can call on at a moment's notice. If he's serious about his game, that's what he has to do."

"Maybe. I just worry they're not as tough as your guys."

Martin laughed out loud. "Never underestimate local talent."

"I guess."

"Don't feel too bad, Bones, for a doctor you're all right." They ordered up one last cup of coffee and finished their breakfast.

"Hey, you know you used to talk about the CIA and that friends and enemies thing? At least we aren't like that," Bones said.

"How's that?"

"Did you ever see that documentary on the Bay of Pigs? It was a CIA saga."

"Hm. I'm not sure."

"It was all about loyalty. The way I see it, as much impact as we can have on other folk's lives, we have a responsibility to choose our loyalties very carefully."

"I agree."

"So, I figure we're better off than those CIA guys."

"Why?" Martin asked.

"They threw that woman out of an airplane there at the end. If we fail to line up our loyalties with precision, at least we don't have to go that far to resolve our differences with people."

"Don't be so sure."

"Oh, hush."

Martin laughed again. "Okay. Tell you what. I'll give it some thought."

"Good, good. That's all I ask."

"We better go. I've got us a nine-thirty tee-off over at Bogue Banks." Taylor reached for the check, but Bones picked it up. Breakfast was cheaper, and would leave it Martin's turn at dinner. Martin made more than he did and could afford it.

They dropped by the Sea Eagle to get Bones' clubs, threw his sticks in Martin Taylor's Silver Bullet Mercedes, and headed out to the golf course. "So, Martin, how long you going to be in town?"

"Leaving on the seven a.m. commuter out of Kinston Friday, then I'll go sit in Atlanta a while before going back to St. Croix."

"Well, you be careful. You know about those small airplanes. Don't open any doors."

CHAPTER TWENTY TWO

A Gentleman's Game

NEGOTIATIONS BEGAN ON THE FIRST TEE. "My standard match is a twenty dollar Nassau, with automatic presses," Bones opened.

"Fine by me."

"What's your handicap nowadays?"

"Six. And you?"

"Seven."

"One a side? The underdog should get the benefit of the doubt."

Bones countered. "Better make it one on the front and then adjust. The handicap sheet is lagging behind a bit."

"Sounds like you; always compelled to play fair." Taylor had not forgotten the Bonfield case.

"I'll win my share." Bones reached in his bag. "Titleist. Blue and green dot."

Martin held his out for inspection. "Pro V, black dot."

"Got it. Let me ask you something. How did you craft that agreement in the Bonfield case?" Bones asked.

"My Lord, son. Please. If you're going to be in this business, you must learn discretion. Besides, it's a trade secret. We have to keep some of our work in the pocket, you know."

"I guess. You lawyers sure are a secretive bunch. Everything's some kind of code."

"Of course. We're like the Code-Talkers in WWII. You remember the Navajo?"

Bones hesitated. "Uh, yeah. The Navajo."

"Yes. Do you know how dangerous it was to be a Navajo code-talker?"

'Uh, not exactly."

"You better go read your history books before you decide if you're going to be in this thing. Lawyers always have some Navajo-type as a broker; you can count on that."

"Yes, sir." Bones flipped a tee into the air. It landed on the turf, bounced once, and then pointed toward Martin. "Your honor, your honor. Tee it up, Taylor. May the best man win."

Martin pulled out his Callaway, and smacked his opening drive 240 yards right down the sprinkler line. Bones came over the top a bit, and hooked into the first cut of rough. The game was on.

"I've always liked golf. It is the last gentleman's game, one that respects the old traditions," Martin said.

"Yeah, well, I see you aren't exactly hitting a MacGregor persimmon driver, brother Taylor. I believe that is one of those synthetics, isn't it?"

"Shut up, kid."

Both played well on the front nine. Bones carded a 38, Martin was in at 37. With the stroke, they were net even at the turn. "No one's behind us," Martin said. "Let's stop and get a burger at the turn."

They took a seat at the bar. "Two burger baskets," Martin ordered. "So, about this buddy of yours. Does he bet on his golf game?" Martin asked.

"Anything else, gentlemen?" the waitress asked.

Martin ordered a couple Buds.

"He's better at cards."

"Does he overplay his hand?"

"Never."

"How much does he play for?"

"More than penny poker, but he's not a high-roller. Usually, they won't play for more than a few hundred dollars."

The waitress brought their burgers. "Oh. Not worth a man's time." Martin opened his hamburger bun and poured on some more ketchup.

"I'll grant you my buddy isn't flush, but I think this game has another angle."

"High stakes or just penny poker, Bones?"

"High stakes."

"How much?"

"I don't know yet. Maybe millions."

Martin put his hamburger down.

There was silence.

"I don't know man, millions as in plural. Five, maybe ten. I don't know. Hell, Martin, you're the dang expert." Bones blurted out the words.

"Millions? How sure are you of that?"

"Confident."

Martin counted the seconds. They blinked. Finally Martin spoke. "You already said you man isn't a high-roller. Just where is that money going to come from?"

"It's in the case, Martin. We'll have to get it out of the case."

"I don't know, Bones. I like the old ways. Tradition, honor, purity of the process."

"Okay, I've got an old wooden driver in my Scout. You play the back nine with that. It ain't warped too bad." Martin smiled. Bones went on. "Martin, you've got one problem here. You said you like the truth. And for you that is the ace card in the poker game. I know you. You said you can't stand a lie."

"Damn it, boy. Don't tell anyone. I was a lawyer, you know."

"Yeah, well, I'm a doctor. I can't afford to be misunderstood."

"No kidding. You ever heard about the Dr. Cohen case?" Martin asked.

"No, sir."

"A doc in Missouri almost wound up in jail for trying to influence a judge."

"I just want some advice. I'm not trying to influence anyone. Just advice."

"I understand."

"So how do you think a wife would react in a situation like this?" Bones asked.

"Hmn. If you are right with your dollar figures, I'm sure she'd listen. She's the queen in the chess game. If she doesn't co-operate, you might as well go home." Martin ordered a second Budweiser. "Another beer?"

"Oh, no thanks. I don't have any strokes on the back nine. I better have my wits about me. Look, Martin. With this woman, money talks. Hell, several mil is real money, even for a lawyer."

"Well, I'm not involved. There's nothing I can do," Martin said.

"Good Lord, man. You really mean it about the purity of the process, don't you? Use one of those intermediaries. Maybe they'll translate. Code talk, you know. Messenger model."

"Hmn. I don't mind floating the concept, but I'm confident my contacts would not run the logistics."

"That's okay, I wouldn't expect them to. I've got a plan. I just want 'em to know this is legit so no one will throw up a roadblock when the time comes."

"Damn it, Bones, you better not try to finagle me. Don't forget; never try to subterfuge a lawyer."

"Heck, Martin, you already said you weren't a lawyer anymore."

"Yeah, but I'm an ex-lawyer. You can count on that."

"Yes sir. I understand, and I respect that, and won't forget. I promise; I'm just looking for the truth. And thirty percent of those kind of numbers would be a lot of jack. A man could retire off that."

"Are you after the truth or retribution?"

"Come on, Martin. I can't stand a hypocrite. I just want to find out what happened. My man has some game. I don't want him to lose it all."

Martin turned up the last of his beer. "Let me think on it. Let's finish up."

They got in the cart, and headed for the tenth tee.

A couple of Buds didn't impair Martin's golf game in the least, but Bones struck it well, too. After some give and take on the inward nine, they were both plus two for the side, and all even at the eighteenth tee. The seagulls rode the wind that came in off Bogue Sound. The flagstick bent in the distance and their pant legs flapped in the breeze.

Martin struck a solid power fade, and held it in the wind before the ball settled in the right rough just shy of the water. Bones hit his standard trap hook, and watched the ball bound down a gentle slope and on toward the left rough. It trickled over a hill, and out of sight.

"Dang it, Martin, I'm going to have to learn to hit a fade into the wind. You know what Trevino said, 'You can talk to a fade, but a hook won't listen.' That's near out of bounds, I'm afraid."

"Naw, you're in. I saw it come to rest."

"Really? Man, you can see everything."

The match was going to boil down to a few final swings. Martin surveyed his circumstances, and pulled an eight iron. He hit a terrific shot. It checked up on two bounces, and stopped just four feet from the cup.

Bones crested the hill. When he got to his ball, he was out by a foot. Match over. He raked the ball from the rough and took an inconsequential swing. The ball flew on a dead-on beeline, rattled the flagstick and dropped just an inch from the hole.

Martin reacted. "Damn good shot, Bones!" Then he shouted, "By God, I'll sink mine, I'm not dead yet."

"Martin!" Bones tried to get his attention, but Martin was on a run for the green, so Bones let him putt out.

Martin sank his putt, the moved in Bones' direction. "All slick. Fine match." Martin extended his hand to shake.

Bones handed him two twenties. "The match was over in the fairway, Martin. I was out by a foot. I just wanted to see how you'd do under pressure. Who knows, I might need to know sometime." Martin smiled, folded the bills, and put them in his money clip without comment.

They mulled the match over at the nineteenth hole. "Fine play, Bones. I've got to go. Got a bit of business to tend to. Might even take a nap. Getting some age on me, you know. I've had some time to think about it. I'll make a few calls. The process has to stay pure, but it's not too far out of bounds." Martin said.

"That's great. Wait a minute. How'd I convince you?"

"Hell, Bones. I have to trust you. I knew you were out of bounds; I saw the ball come to rest. I just wanted to see how you would do under pressure. I might need to know sometime."

"I can't get nothing on you."

Martin laughed and lit a Cohiba. "One more point."

"Yeah, what's that?"

"It was a foot and a half."

Bones laughed. "Maybe so."

Martin took Bones back to his car. "Enjoyed the game. Here. Take this." He pulled out a dollar bill, ripped it in half and handed him one half of it.

"What's that?"

"You'll know soon. Don't lose it."

"Has this got something to do with the Navajo?"

"Hell, boy. Don't you mention that Navajo again, you understand? No one knows the Navajo. Go do your homework, I tell you."

"Okay, man. Okay. Whatever." Bones put the torn bill in his wallet. "See you around, Martin."

"Play hard."

"Yes, sir."

CHAPTER TWENTY THREE

The Navajo Has Spoken

BONES DIALED INDIE AT THE OFFICE before he left. No answer. He called Kate.

"Kate? How's the old home place?"

"Good. So, how did it go?"

"I held my own, but Mr. Taylor sqwuanked me out of forty bones. I hit one out of bounds on eighteen. He won, one-up."

"Then you did okay. Did he help you?"

"Hm. I think so. He referred to the Navajo and kept talking in some kind of code. I think he knew I was telling the truth."

"Hon, you don't know how to do anything but. I promise that lawyer could see it. They have people tell them so many lies they can spot the truth in a minute."

"Well, I hope so. Hey, is Indie still at the cabin?"

"I saw Immogene at the grocery store yesterday. She said they were going to stay two days and come in tonight. You need to come home, too. I got Jimmy Martin playing." She turned up the stereo. *"Hold whatcha got, I'm a-coming home, baby ..."*

"Yes, ma'am, I'll be right on. Getting ready to leave right now."

As Bones walked through the door to his house, the phone rang. It was Snookers.

"Hey, Doc, there gonna be a jam soon?"

"I don't know, why do you ask?"

"Some boys from out of town were down at Johnny's Jewelry and Pawn today. Said they wanted to play and they're looking for Indie."

"Who was it?"

"I dunno, but I ain't sure they was pickers."

"Why do you say that?"

"The one that said he played the banjo had a Porsche. Ain't no banjo man got a Porsche."

"Where were they from?"

"Virginia plates, that's all I know."

"Damn."

"What's the matter?"

"Awh, nothing." *Virginia. Had to be Martin Taylor's people.*

"You okay?"

"Uh, yeah, Snook. Yeah, I'm fine. Hey, none of 'em looked Native American, did they?"

"No. How come?"

"Just curious. Hey, when you going to teach me how to fade the ball?"

"Anytime, Doc. You gotta learn all the shots to play that game."

"Yeah, I know. I hope I've got enough game. You run with a fast crowd at times. I'll give Indie a call."

Bones dialed up Indie's house that night.

Indie answered. "So, how'd it go?"

"I couldn't tell for sure, but I think he'll at least run our theory by Gibson. There's more to this than Fentanyl."

"That's all you can do, brother. I appreciate it."

"What do you know about Navajo code-talkers, Indie?"

"They were some of the most important folks in the World War Two. Under-appreciated, to say the least. Very dangerous position."

"You think this thing is like dealing with the Mafia or something?"

"Naw, the stakes aren't that high. It's more like a high-dollar poker game. Don't worry 'til Indie says worry."

"I guess. So, when are we jamming?"

"Tomorrow."

"Okay, I'll be there. I'm glad it isn't tonight. I need to stay home."

"Yeah, boy, you do."

"Why do you say that?"

"That's what my Immogene said, that's why. When she talks, I listen."

Bones laughed. "Been at the cabin two days, have you, Indie?"

"Hush up, boy. You just stay home tonight and I don't care if that Columbian Green Card girl was to show us naked in your front yard."

"Yes, sir, Dr. Indie."

Bones went back to the den to find Kate.

"So what'd Indie have to say?" she asked.

"He wanted to play some music, but he said I needed to wait 'til tomorrow."

"Honestly, James Robertson. You've been gone; and for a doctor you can be so dumb."

"Who, me?"

"Yes, you."

CHAPTER TWENTY FOUR

Ancient Tones

INDIE CALLED THE OFFICE ON FRIDAY. "Hey, Bones, I might be late on the the jam."

"How come?"

"Tag's in town. She and Gibson Taylor have been talking for a couple days. She wants to meet right after supper. It might take up to an hour. I hate to hold everybody up. We don't have enough time to get down to the cabin."

"Why don't we just play at the Holiday Inn? Richard'll most likely let us."

"That'd be good."

"What time you want to play?"

"Eight okay?"

"Sure. If you get hung up with Tag and can't make it, let me know, but we'll shoot for eight."

"How's Tag?"

"As far I can tell, okay. Why?"

"Uh ... I tell you, Indie, I was just trying to help."

"She didn't say anything, Bones. I don't think she knows."

"Okay. I'll see you at the jam. I'll call Richard to be sure he's all right with eight p.m."

"Richard, Bones Robertson here. Anybody playing the lounge tonight?"

"I wish I could tell you J.D. Crowe, but no, nothing going on."

"You want some free entertainment?"

"Y'all just stay downstairs. Last winter when III Tyme Out was here and you jammed with them in the hall, some of the customers griped."

"Where else can you get free bluegrass 'til three in the morning?"

"If it was up to me ... but the customer knows best."

"I understand. We'll be there around eight."

"Good. We've got the Southeast CB Convention in town. As soon as I get them fed, I'll come down. Might sit in on one myself."

Bones called the boys.

Indie was out of his meeting by a quarter of eight. Bones met him in the lobby. "All good?"

"All bad, I guess, but she's still confident this is gonna settle. She talked to Gibson on the phone while I was there." Indie sat down in one of the lobby's wing-back chairs and turned up the TV. "Hell," he whispered. "They're gonna do whatever they're gonna do. This ain't my game."

"Well, let's go pick. All the boys are coming."

They made their way to the lounge. Bones looked around. "I guess we're a little early; no one's here yet."

"Let's get 'em outta the case and tune up."

They broke into 'Salt Creek'.

A stranger at the bar took notice. "You boys play 'Sally Good'un'?"

"Sure, man."

When the man stood up he was almost as tall as Bones, nearly six-two. He had high cheek bones and a deep, reddish-brown complexion. His face was etched with a road map of wrinkles.

Indie noticed a turquoise bracelet. He had on a string tie. "I dig those boots, man. Are they snakeskin?" Indie asked.

"Rattlers. Kimble Bee Gilchrist is the name. Everyone just calls me B.G. It's for bluegrass."

"Pleased to meet you." Indie shook hands. "You a picker?"

"Yeah. Okay for me to join you?"

"Sure."

"Let me get my guitar out of the car."

"Great. We've got several guys who should be here soon. There are some fine players around here," Bones said.

The man returned in a moment. He carried a Calton guitar case. He opened it as they watched.

"Damn, man. I haven't seen one of those in years. A 'thirty-six Herring-bone. Where'd you get it?" Indie asked.

"I bought it from Chris Hillman in California right before he joined the Byrds. I deal in 'em. Banjos, guitars, fiddles. Mandolins are my specialty. I even make a few." The man opened his wallet and produced a card: *K.B. Gilchrist—EXPERT.*

Indie turned the card over, and then put it in his pocket. "I'll hold onto it."

"Keep this, too." It was half a dollar bill.

Bones grabbed Indie's elbow. "Indie, we need to go outside."

"What's the matter?"

Bones tugged harder on his arm. "C'mon." He turned to the man. "Sir, could you excuse us a minute?"

"Sure."

Bones hustled Indie out into the hall. "Indie, Lord have mercy. Look, man, don't tell Tag. Oh, my Lord."

"What the hell are you talking about?"

Moose and the boys were filing in. Snook set his bass fiddle on the floor. "Hey, y'all ain't leaving, are you?"

"Nah, we'll be right back. Y'all go on in and get started. Some cat has a thirty-six Herringbone. You need to check it out. We'll be back in a minute."

The boys went to the lounge to set up.

"What the hell's eating you?" Indie asked.

"I wasn't trying to cause trouble, but, well, you know how I played golf with Martin Taylor? He, uh ... he said not to say anything but ... well, look at this." Bones reached in his wallet and produced the other half of the dollar bill. "He gave me this."

Indie turned the bill over in his hands a few times. "And what does it mean?"

"Honest to God, I don't know."

"You ever heard Bill Monroe talk about the Ancient Tones?" Indie asked.

"Yeah, I think that was how he got Peter Rowan to change a flat on his bus."

"No, Bones. Ancient Tones. Monroe said they were carried by the wind. Not everyone can hear them. We need to go listen to this man."

Bones went back to the lounge with Indie ambling in behind him. The session was already in progress. Moose hammered the *"Bluegrass Breakdown"* on the banjo. B.G. flat-picked some fine guitar. This was not the kind of player who shows up in town every day.

They played for two hours before anyone suggested a break. "Gonna have to give an old man a rest," Indie said. "Prostate ain't what it used to be. You smoke, B.G.? I'm gonna go have a cigarette. Care to join me?"

"Sure."

Bones followed them outside.

"So, what's your business in town?" Indie asked.

"I'm always on the look-out for an instrument bargain. Buy, sell, trade. Just got back from Oklahoma. A man from Tupelo, Mississippi named Crow put me on a flathead in a shop out there." He got the banjo out of the trunk.

"Very nice. I don't have anything like that."

"Know anyone who does?"

"Might. I'll check around." Indie took a drag off his cigarette.

"Of course, I deal in smaller ticket items, too. Stewart Nye jewelry, wood carvings; about whatever you need in the arts line. Like I told your buddy there, I build mandolins, too."

"You have one here? I'm a mandolin nut," Bones said.

"Not with me, but I can bring 'em."

"Great." Bones handed him a card. "I'd love to see them."

"Y'all want to play a few more?" B.G. asked.

"Sure, let's go back in." Indie stamped out his cigarette, and they went back inside.

CHAPTER TWENTY FIVE

Slow Waltz

THE SESSION WORE ON, A CROWD BEGAN to gather. Richard Bailey, the manager, dropped by and picked a few on the banjo. Donna came to check on Snook and sang a fine version of "Steel Rails." B.G. was the best flat-pick man to come through town in a long while.

Bones took a rest. He watched the crowd. Everyone knew everyone in Harvey County. Maybe no one was supposed to know about the case, but he wondered. Everyone loved Indie, but it seemed they were closer to him than ever. Folks came up and patted him on the shoulder or asked for his favorite tunes. A couple well-wishers high-fived him. In the low light of the bar, he looked a bit like Anthony Quinn as he prepared for a last fight, but Bones sensed Indie wasn't out yet. He was more popular than outsiders knew.

Bones got back in the mix. As the session wore on, the room grew hotter. It was a packed house. Indie got warmed up on the fiddle and began to sweat. He stood with a wide stance to keep his balance, and weaved and bobbed with the music like an old punch-drunk fighter. Everyone brown-bagged, and the bartender mixed rum and Coke one after another. "Love it when y'all pick, Bones. Thirty percent increase in tips every time." He smiled and poured another mixed drink. The room grew thick with smoke, but it didn't bother Indie. He played stronger by the hour.

B.G. had to ask. "Dr. Indie, do you know everyone in the county?"

Bones stepped in. "Yes, sir, he does. Everyone loves Indie—"

Indie put an arm around Bones' shoulder. "Now, B.G., you can't take Bones too serious. He's a nice boy, but he's my doctor, so he's a bit prejudiced."

"But it's true, it's tru—" Bones protested.

Indie put his fingers over Bones' lips and sealed them in a gentle way. "Patience, my boy. It'll be all right."

Bones got back in the session, and B.G. turned to Indie. "Are all your people so loyal?"

"There's one woman in town who ain't." Both men laughed.

Elisa Reyes from housekeeping spotted Indie. "Dr. Indie! I work late. You good man, Dr. Indie." She turned to B.G. to explain. "Dr. Indie, he save my little Nina. I have no money, and the other doctors want fifty dollar. Indie see her. He even speak Spanish. She have 'Smilin' Mighty Jesus.' Very sick with fever in her head." She broke into tears, and buried her head into Indie's chest. He patted her on the back. "She finish school this year. We very proud of her. I never forget you, Dr. Indie."

"Lord, Miss Elisa, that spinal meningitis is scary." Indie had a sheepish smile. "It warn't me, it was Jesus and Rocephin."

Elisa was unconvinced. "Jesus sent you to me. Why you here?"

"Oh, some of the boys are gonna hang out and and jam a while."

"Last time they leave their underwear in sink. Tell them I ain't their mama."

"Yes, ma'am."

"You play 'El Commanchero' for me?"

"Sure, Elisa."

"Very good, Indie. I off work, have to go home, but I come back. You play late?"

"Yes, ma'am."

"I be back."

"Another satisfied customer, Indie?" B.G. asked.

"She's a sweetheart. Still my patient to this day."

"Where did you learn Spanish?"

"Oh, I picked it up from one of the migrant workers. He had a bad back. We bartered Spanish for doctoring."

"I see."

"They call it marketing. Hell, I'm a man of vision."

Someone called for the *'Lee Highway Blues,'* and Indie sawed away on it.

"Indie, how 'bout kicking off *'Sweet Blue-eyed Darling*?" Moose asked.

"Sure." Indie rosined up his bow.

"Hey, can you sing it in French, Indie?"

"Shut the hell up, Moose." Indie smiled. "You boys are just jealous you weren't the ones Giselle wanted to get tangled up with."

Moose laughed. "If I had, my wife woulda killed me."

Elisa came back after supper. Indie saw her, and kicked off *'El Commanchero'.*

"Oh, that so good. You play waltz, Mr. Indie?"

"Sure. How 'bout the *'Kentucky Waltz'*?"

"Yes, very good." She spotted B.G. "You new in town, my friend? I not know you."

"Yes, ma'am."

"You here to help Mr. Indie?"

Indie intervened. "It's okay. He's one of us. No worry."

She extended her hand. "My name Elisa. You friend of Mr. Indie, you friend of mine. If you need extra towels, you call. I'm head housekeeper."

"So, B.G., what'll it be?" Moose asked.

"Hmn. Gotta keep the ladies happy. How 'bout a waltz tune? Seems like all the women I know like those three-quarter-time numbers. Which one did Elisa call for, was it the 'Kentucky'?"

"Don't you want to play one last cut-time number?" Bones asked.

"I like cut time, but you gotta satisfy the women folks, you know," Indie said.

"Mr. Indie is right, Señor Bones. Ladies love a waltz," Elisa chimed in.

"A waltz it is, then," BG said. "After that I gotta turn in. I must say, Indie, I've enjoyed the session. Yeah, a waltz sounds about right. If we play a breakdown this late I might not be able to sleep."

"I'm okay with a slow waltz, about eighty-percent pace," Indie said.

"That's good. Let's play it a little slow. Eighty-percent sounds about right," B.G. replied. "We ought both to be able to sleep on that. It's like golf; if you try too hard you can strangle the deal to death."

"You play golf?" Bones asked.

"Hush," Indie whispered.

Indie kicked off the *"Kentucky Waltz."* Elisa swayed to the music.

BG got ready to turn in.

"It's early, B.G. Play one more good 'un," Indie suggested.

"Well, okay, just one more ..."

Seven AM, Saturday. Gibson Taylor called B.G. "So, what's the word?"

"Man, it was a great jam. I've only been in bed three hours. Indie and Bones were singing harmony with that housekeeper on *'Glory Hallelujah'* when I turned in."

"No, no, B.G. What did you find out? I got to get home. It's against my religion to work weekends."

"Oh, yeah, well, let's see. I tell you boss, that Indie is quite popular. Significant social capital. I would be very wary of court."

"I agree. Any feel for a dollar figure?"

"I think six hundred will cut the gig."

"The woman wants three quarters. Hell, if we go to court we'd eat up way more than the difference. I tell you, though, Ms. Wilson is a stubborn woman. I feel like telling her she isn't the one who died. What do you think Dad would say?"

"I believe he'd say if she doesn't loosen her grip, she's will strangle the negotiations to death."

Gibson laughed. "I think you're right. She wants to choke the old doc, but if she can't get a hold of herself she'll derail the whole thing. I'll talk to her before conference Monday."

"Good luck."

"Thanks."

CHAPTER TWENTY SIX

Settlement Conference: Take Two

BONES CALLED TO CHECK ON INDIE Sunday after church. "Good jam Friday, huh?"

"Excellent. B.G. was a player, huh?"

"Yeah, boy. What time is your settlement conference in the morning?"

"Eleven-thirty. Can you make it?"

"I'll be late. The office is wild on Mondays, but I'll be there as soon as I can finish up. What did Tag say?"

"She said to come on but be careful. She senses an opening."

"How come she worries so bad? I know not to talk."

"She said it was okay. But I would let her handle it. The deal is close. Everyone feels good about it. I'll be glad to get it over."

"I'll be happy for you, man. Sure will."

Eleven o'clock. Indie met with Tag.

"Indie, you look great. All spiffed up." Tag dusted off his sleeve.

"Never know I fiddled away half of Friday night, huh, kid?"

"I don't want to know about it."

"How does it look?"

"I've been over it with Gibson. He's willing to come off seven-fifty a little. If we can get out for six, I think we should."

"Bones said he'd be here after a while."

"Okay."

Bones made it by the first break.

"Hey, bud," Indie said. "Have some of these chicken strips. Elisa had the kitchen send 'em up."

"Thanks."

Indie pulled one out of the box. "Tag?"

She shook her head. "How do you guys eat so much and stay so slim?"

"I work out," Bones replied.

"For me it's cigarettes," Indie quipped.

"So, how's it going?" Bones asked.

"Good. We're close." Tag tended to her legal pad.

"Geez. I still think something is wrong with this case," Bones said.

She took a deep breath and visibly counted to three. "Bones, there is something wrong with all of them. It has enormous inflammatory potential. Death cases are always hard to predict in court. We need to avoid going to trial, if at all possible."

"Heck, you whupped Gibson's daddy in Smithfield. They've got a long memory."

Tag stood up. "No, no. Look, Bones. You stay out of this. You love stories. Let me tell you one. That doctor reminded me a lot of Indie. I really liked the man. He was hell bent on going to trial. I did my best to talk him out of it. I really didn't think he could win. Anyway, it was a long, drawn-out ordeal." She paced around the room. "We eeked out a win and then he died of a heart attack a month later. He won, but he lost." Tag was silent for a minute. "You know how you guys talk about when you lose a patient? That's how I felt."

Bones scratched his head and didn't speak for a moment. "I'm sorry, Tag. I didn't know it ended up that way. Hey, it ain't your fault. Everybody thinks a doc can predict this medical stuff, but we can't any better than anyone else."

"Maybe so. We can't with the legal business either. Still, it's my job to get this behind Indie as soon as possible." She turned away for a moment.

"I'm sorry, Tag," Bones apologized.

"It's okay, Lucille," Indie said. "He didn't know. He's just trying to look out for me. Go ahead and do what you have to do. I'm ready."

She sat back down. "Okay, they'll be back in a minute."

"No problem. I've made my peace."

"Bones?"

"Yes, ma'am."

Gibson Taylor knocked, and then came in the room. Betty sat down. She crossed her arms and legs and did not speak.

Gibson opened. "Lucille, if we can be reasonable today, my client desires to settle."

"And?"

"We believe if this went to trial, it has the potential to be a million-dollar case. However, we do find Dr. Jenkins relationship with the patient to be a mitigating factor. And we both know trials are time-consuming and expensive."

"Go on."

"Yes, well, we feel seven hundred is beyond fair."

"Four-fifty has been our max for some time, Gibson."

"I realize that, Lucille, but the times they are a changing. Here are the figures for similar cases across the country. You can see they are all in excess of a million dollars. We think seven- hundred-fifty-thousand is most reasonable."

"Yes, but these are all metropolitan areas. This is Harvey County. It is rural. Our mock trial indicated it could go as low as three hundred."

Betty frowned.

Tag went on. "Twice that seems more than generous. Six hundred. That is a final offer."

"May I meet with my client in private?"

"Sure, take your time."

They went back to Gibson Taylor's headquarters on the next floor.

"Betty, now I know you think this is a million-dollar deal, but we do this all the time. We've done an excellent background check on this Dr. Jenkins. We believe he has more support than what you might realize. If we went to court, after expenses you'd be lucky if you clear four-fifty. I don't think it's likely, but it's possible he could walk."

"He better not."

"Tell you what. My usual fee is thirty percent. We need to wrap this up. I'll knock it down to twenty-five. You need to take the six-hundred, and I need to get out of this thing. Tag beat us one time in the past. I have a bad feeling about it."

"A bad feeling? What kind of man talk is that? Are you going by woman's intuition? She's just a little bitty girl. Why are you scared of her? You aren't in her pocket, are you?"

"Absolutely not! Not under any circumstances, Ms. Wilson. No. Look here, you're making this far more difficult than is has to be. Why are you trying to strangle the old goat?"

"I just want my fair share. I say no."

Gibson walked around the room for a moment, and then sat down. "Suit yourself. You'll need to sign these papers, then."

"What are they?"

"Informed consent. It releases me of any responsibility if this goes wrong. And it might."

"It better not. And I ain't signing shit." She flung the papers across the room, then retrieved several of them, tore the documents in small pieces and proceeded to jump up and down on the tattered remnants.

Gibson gathered up the shredded documents, placed them in an envelope, and put it in his briefcase. He smoothed back his hair. "Well, let's go back in."

They went to Tag's headquarters and sat down again.

Gibson sighed. "My client and I have discussed this again. We are not prepared to accept any offer of less than seven hundred-fifty thousand dollars."

Everyone sat in stunned silence.

Betty got up to leave.

Indie had to comment. "Hey, Betty, you didn't wear your high heels today. They show your ass better, you know."

She stomped out. Tag elbowed Indie, but suppressed a smile, and Taylor did his best not to laugh.

Gibson turned to Indie. "Indie, I wanted this to settle, I give you my word on that. I think it was the right thing to do."

"It's okay, Mr. Taylor. Not a problem. I believe you."

Gibson opened the door to leave and then turned around. "I think this thing can be over-tried. It's a mistake for us, too. Damn. I guess I'd better go find my client." He left.

Tag finally spoke. "What is it with her, Indie?"

"I don't know. I've known Betty a long time. She's always had it in for me, and in more ways than one."

"How do you mean?"

Indie thought back to when Blinky got Betty pregnant, and then to that night at the Harvey Country Club when Betty made a pass at him. He shifted in his chair. "Awh, you know Tag, just mad, that's all."

Tag was certain there was more to it, but Indie wasn't ready to talk. She jotted down a memo. "Ms. Wilson's got a mean streak, all right. I hate to see her at trial."

"Don't worry, Tag. Bones predicts a winner," Indie said.

She laughed. "It's a long shot, but I'll concede you can't count Bones out. He's forecast a couple of strong closers in the past."

Indie gave a silent thumbs-up.

Bones smiled.

CHAPTER TWENTY SEVEN

The River

THE NEXT SATURDAY MORNING A RAP CAME on the Robertsons' door.

"What's that, honey?"

Kate rolled over. "I don't hear anything."

Bang, bang, bang. "There it is again. Someone's at the door."

Bones pulled on a shirt and went downstairs.

It was Indie. "Bones, old boy. I'm worried about you. Part of your medical education is severely lacking. Summer's a-wasting away. We need to go while we can."

"What are you talking about?"

"Oh, hell, Bones. I ain't talking bubble tests. I'm talking fishing. You ain't been fishing in a year. We're going down the river."

"Let me check in with Kate. I don't know what's on the calendar for today."

"To hell with your damn calendars and schedules. Atsa made some streaky meat sandwiches, and I've got a six pack on ice. Let's go."

"Well, I don't know, I—"

"I even packed your Co-Colas. Let's go to the river. I want to test the boat."

Bones looked out. Indie's battered john boat was on the trailer behind his Jeep. "Damn, Indie. You're crazy. Come on in." Bones turned on the coffee pot. "Wait here a minute. Let me go speak to her real quick." He went upstairs.

"Hey, sweetie. It's Indie. Says he needs to talk. Okay for me to go with him?"

"How long?"

"I don't know. Maybe we can go out tonight. I won't be gone too long."

"We'll talk about it when you get back."

"Anything special on tap?"

"Not a thing, dear. You go on."

Indie turned the Jeep south on Lee Highway and headed for City Landing.

"The boat running okay?"

"It sprung a leak. Buddy patched it up."

"Sure it's fixed?"

"Yeah, he checked it out yesterday."

"So, what's up?"

"Nothing. You just need to go fishing, that's all."

"It's seven o'clock in the morning. Why did we have to start so early?"

"'Cause that's when they bite."

"Everything okay with the case?"

"Hush. We ain't talking about nothing but beauty today."

The paint on Indie's old wooden boat was a cracked and peeled. It had once been a deep, sea green, but after years of sun exposure, was now more the hue of a faded lime. The outboard motor was a 3½ horsepower Evinrude, but they'd paddle when they were around a fishing hole.

Indie pulled the cord. It didn't want to turn over. He took off the cowling and banged around with a screwdriver, then pulled again. "Damn. I told Buddy to check the plugs on this sumbitch."

"You sure he fixed the leak?"

"Yeah, yeah."

Indie opened up a beer. He scraped the spark plug with steel wool, and pulled the cord again. This time it sputtered to life. A few empty cans and milk cartons floated nearby. "Damn. Someone dumped their trash." He eased over that way, and scooped them up with his net. They went back to the dock for a minute. "Throw that crap away, Bones. I can't stand for folks to mess up my river."

They headed out. The water was quieter upstream. A formation of water-bugs left behind a wake off the boat's starboard side. Every so often Bones would get his line tangled in the bushes, but Indie freed it up when he did. They meandered up the river past the farms and fields.

"When is old man Turner going to get that junked car out of the water?"

"I told him not to. The fish hang out there," Indie replied.

They went over and put in a line, but had no luck, and after an hour turned north and moved on.

"Don't ever swim in this part of the river, Bones. It ain't safe. How 'bout manning the ship? I'm gonna take a smoke break. I'll sit up front."

The two slowly started to switch seats.

"Seeing as the gas can is back here with me, you sit as far up there as you can," Bones grumbled.

"You worry too much."

Indie sat on the bow and lit a cigarette. At least for the moment, he was captain of his ship. "I love this part of the river. Look at those turtles. You hear the birds? It was a good day's work when I got my cabin." He put his hand over his eyes to shield the sun. "We're only a mile and a half north of town, but it might as well be a thousand. This stretch right here is the prettiest part of the county."

"I agree. There ain't a finer spot on the river than between here and Mason's."

Neither man spoke for a while. They rode along as free as two boys on a raft. The only sounds were the whir of the outboard motor and the wake as it washed up behind them.

"Reckon we ought to try the far bank?" Bones asked.

"Naw, we ain't had a nibble all day. Let's get some lunch. Pull over there in Lawson's Cove."

They tied the boat to a log in a quiet spot in the cove and took a break. Indie had a couple beers and Bones got out a Coke. They unwrapped the sandwiches, and Indie opened a bag of chips.

"You ain't worried?" Bones asked.

Indie got down off the stump that served as a seat and lay back on the leaves. He watched the clouds drift by. "Hell, no. I'm worried about you, though."

"Me?"

"Yeah. Look man, this is just a thing. It'll pass. Betty's always been this way, and she ain't gonna change. Time has a way of smoothing things out; just like with those rocks."

"I guess."

They got back in the boat and trolled toward the cabin. Bones threw out a line. All of a sudden the bobber sank and the pole bent almost double. "Lord have mercy, Indie!"

"Hold onto that sumbitch. You got a pike there!"

The old flat-bottom boat pitched back and forth. Indie got up and inched over to Bones to help.

"Watch out, Indie, you're gonna fall in."

Indie held the side of the boat with one hand and Bones' fishing pole with the other. Water splashed everywhere. They kept tugging. Bones looked at Indie. He was old and half drunk with a cigarette dangling out of the corner of his mouth, and yet his hands were as steady as the best neurosurgeon in the Tobacco Triangle.

"Reel that sumbitch in, Bones. You got him."

Indie was right. It was an old black fish. She wiggled all around the bottom of the boat. Bones wrestled it into the cooler while Indie laughed. "Look at that damn pike. I ain't seen one that size in years!"

They slammed the lid. The box jumped around as the fish flopped inside.

"You done good. It was all assholes and elbows for a minute there, but you done good." Indie put up the gear. "We ain't gonna do better than that. Let's go to the cabin and dry off." He manned the stern and revved up the throttle. The old engine strained and the boat lurched forward. "I'd like to fiddle a couple before we go."

"Sounds good. Whatcha gonna play?"

"How bout 'Mama Don't Allow'?"

"Yeah, that's a good one. 'Mama Don't Allow' ... Oh, Lordy, Indie."

"What's wrong?"

"Dang. I forgot. Turn this thing around!"

"What's the matter?"

"I gotta get home."

"How come?"

"God-a-mighty, Indie. It's Kate's birthday. You know how she loves a celebration."

"You better get your ass outta here."

They turned back. "Lord, this thing's slow, Indie. I told ya, you needed a bigger motor."

"Hell, I never get in a hurry out here unless you come along."

"Won't it go any faster?"

"Sorry, Bones."

"Damn."

Bones called home from the pay phone at the landing. "Hey, hon, I'm headed for the house."

"I thought you were just going to be out 'til lunch. It's three o'clock."

"I'm sorry. I just lost track of time. Hey, you wouldn't believe the fish I caught today."

"Fish?! You went to the river?"

"Oh, well ... uh, yeah ... But you know how it is, honey. Indie can't think anywhere else. I'll be right home."

"Okay."

"Kate? Kate!?" Bones walked through the house. There was a small sliver of birthday cake on the kitchen table, along with a note: *Went to mom's for my birthday. I won't be gone too long, Kate.*

Bones took the slice of birthday cake into the den, and flipped on the T.V. Some mindless show blared away. He began to talk to himself. "Here you're trying to help Indie and you go and do something this stupid." Indie was right. "Boy, for someone with all your book learning, you sure can be a dumbass."

CHAPTER TWENTY EIGHT

The Eye of the Storm/Jury Selection

THERE IS ALWAYS A LULL IN THE DOCTOR BUSINESS in the summer, and it was in the lawsuit business, too. Bones didn't talk to Indie about it unless Indie brought it up, and that wasn't often. Both doctors settled into a routine of seeing patients and played music on the weekends. Indie spent a lot of time on the river. Bones went fishing with him a couple times and played some golf with Snookers. It was almost as if life were back to normal.

Indie knew it was temporary, though. Every so often Tag would call with an update, and he'd keep Bones in the loop.

"She's doing her best to get it settled, pal, but it ain't gonna happen."

"I'm sorry, Indie."

"Yeah. It ain't Gibson Taylor's fault. I'm telling ya, Betty's not gonna be happy unless she kicks my ass, and she wants it to be public."

"At least you got some of the summer off."

"Yeah, well, it's just the eye of the storm. You know how those big hurricanes kick up come fall. We ain't seen trouble yet."

"We'll get through it, " Bones reassured him, but he knew Indie was right.

Indie called one Friday. "Hey, Bones. I'm gonna be at the cabin this weekend. Can you drop by tomorrow?"

"Sure, Indie. What's up?"

"Heard from Tag today."

"What's the word?"

"Trial."

"Hm. Not surprised. I'll be there. Maybe we can go fishing."

"Sounds good. Come as early as you can."

"Yes, sir."

Indie would get a sense of dread every fall. It didn't last long, but when the leaves began to fall, he'd drink a bit more for a few weeks. "Just don't care for this time of year," he'd say. "Everything goes dormant, the cycle goes in the garage, the days get shorter, and now it reminds me of the beginning of the end for Blinky. Add a trial to it and I don't guess me and fall are ever gonna get along."

"I'm sorry, Indie."

"Oh, well, it's just a thing."

"So, when is it on?"

"Third week of September, the twenty-first. Damn. Gonna mess up Fair week."

"Hm. At least you won't miss as much work. Folks don't go to the doctor the week of the Fair if they can get out of it."

"Yeah, but I'm afraid it's gonna wreck our gig."

"Not a problem, Indie. I heard from the manager last week. He changed our Wednesday afternoon show. We're gonna be on the grandstand Friday night. Court will long be out of session by then."

"Good."

"So what all did Tag say?"

"At least we drew Judge Hamrick."

"Lord, Indie how'd you luck out on that? You take care of him some, don't you?"

"Yeah, but he's officially Jerry Cecil's patient. He ain't gonna say anything, 'cause he don't want his wife to know he has a chart at my place."

Bones laughed. "Not being a member at the Country Club has it's advantages."

"Yep. You know, I gotta give Tag her due. She's done her best. I told her when we got started Betty wasn't gonna be reasonable. I think she's decided we know the landscape around here."

"So what's the agenda?"

"She said it'd be jury selection first. It'll be the Wednesday before the trial starts."

"Hm. At least I can get by for the afternoon."

"Tag'll love that." Indie laughed. "She said to go ahead and call Roy Davidson. Even Tag agreed we stand a better chance with the juror mix if we have a local there."

"Sure Indie. Will do. Roy knows the street, that's a fact."

"Yeah, he knows every scoundrel in town."

"Both the legal and illegal ones."

"Man, I love his Christmas party. That gumbo is the best."

Indie laughed. "What a mix; the judge singing with some guy he sentenced to jail the year before. The police, the criminals, the bank president, and the janitor; Roy's an equal opportunity attorney."

"I'm glad we got him."

"It can't hurt, and it might help."

"Yep. I agree."

The morning of jury selection was a slow process. There was a large jury pool sequestered away. Behind the scene, the felons and anyone who worked in the medical field were eliminated. By 10:00 AM, Judge Hamrick had the first cattle call, and filled up the seats for potential jury members.

Each stated his or her name and profession, and then asked if they knew any reason they could not be objective. One stated he wanted to be on the panel. He began to cry and said he was in AA now, but when he was a drunk, Indie was the only doctor in town who would take care of him. He was axed immediately.

At least a half dozen were eliminated because Indie took care of some of member of the family, and two were let go because they knew Bones and Indie were close.

Indie turned to Tag. "Hey, kid, maybe they won't be able to seat a jury."

Tag told him to hush and punched him in the ribs, but she chuckled.

Roy Davidson went to work. He canned the paving contractor who'd worked for the hospital and put down the driveway at Olden's farm. One woman was a widow whose husband had died under Indie's care, and he axed her, too. Another was a man who had been a client of his in a D.U.I. case, and then stiffed him on his bill. He pared the list away.

Gibson Taylor objected to Rossie Douglas when he found out he was the guy who re-haired Indie's fiddle bows. And Buddy, Indie's boat mechanic, wasn't in his seat more than thirty seconds.

Both teams got input from their clients, too. When Gibson Taylor took his list to Betty Wilson, she knew Mrs. Sylvia Evans played bridge with Indie's wife, and tossed her. By lunch the two sides had a rough list. They agreed to come back after lunch to finish up.

Hospital attorney Jackson Leggett had been sent by Olden in the event his interests needed to be represented. Gibson Taylor made sure Leggett reviewed the list. "Any objections, Jackson? Speak now or forever hold your peace."

"We don't have a dog in the fight," Leggett said about the hospital. "Looks okay to me."

Indie and Bones met at the B-&-B for lunch.

"Man. I'm already tired of this, Bones. I don't see how we can predict what they're going to do anyway."

"I don't know. I've read about this business of jury selection. They say it's getting to be a science. The big ones try to stack the deck before the trial ever starts."

"I don't think it's that exact an art, pal."

"Think of it like golf. A good hustler cuts his bets at the first tee, and knows how to shave the margin before he ever hits the first shot. What kind of game he plays is immaterial, as long as he knows the opponent well enough. If he's gathered the right information, then what follows is predictable."

"Hm. Maybe so, but I think you're reading too many spy novels. You still gonna come over this afternoon?"

"Wouldn't miss it. I know Tag wants to hear my theories as to emerging science of jury selection."

Indie smiled. "I'm glad I get to watch that."

The teams met again in the afternoon. They vetted the prospects for the final cut at the attorney's table. Tag and Roy poured over what small details they had. For the most part, Indie and Bones just sat back and watched from the row just behind them.

Tag shuffled thorough the final choices. "Everyone okay with Joseph E. Watson?"

"Okay with me," Davidson said. "He's quiet. He retired after thirty years with the State Credit Union in Raleigh, and moved to the county last year to take care of his mother."

The team was pleased Taylor approved. People who stayed in one job a long time were often conservative, and tended to opt for lower settlements. Watson was old, a slight man with horn-rimmed glasses. They hoped he wasn't demented.

Several were ditched because they hated doctors in general, and two were omitted because they thought all lawyers were crooks. Three more passed. They were close to full.

Tag was nervous about Sally Goodwin, who owned the other beauty shop in town, and afraid she'd talk. She leaned back to ask Indie.

"They've got Janie Johnson working the street for them," Indie said. "We need a beauty operator, too, if we can slide one in there. Besides, Sally's a good'un." Indie laughed. It went by Tag, and she didn't object.

Bones got bored and began to snooze. Indie outright snored.

"What about this Wanda Meyer?" Tag asked.

"Wanda? Don't trade her for any two!" Bones startled and woke up.

Tag turned to Gibson Taylor. "Can you excuse me a minute?"

"Sure."

Tag turned around. "Okay, Sherlock, How do you know this one? Is she an old girlfriend?"

"No, no. She ran the pig races at the county fair for years."

Tag looked over her glasses. "What in this world is a pig race?"

"Shoot fire, that's the biggest attraction at the fair. The little porkers run at the top of every hour. There's a chicken-wire pigpen track where they race. The pig that wins gets an ear of corn for a prize. They announce it by a bugle call that sounds like the start of the Kentucky Derby. Heck, when we played our fair gig they sounded the bugle and everyone left our show, right down to my own mama. I've known Wanda for ages. She'll not dig Gibson Taylor at all; too fancy. Leave her in."

Tag rolled her eyes. "Lord have mercy."

By now Indie was wide awake. He laughed so loud Judge Hamrick had to call him down. Later Indie said Tag might not frequent the pig races or eat vinegar fries at the Harvey County Fair, but she was smart enough to take any help she could get. Wanda passed.

Tag collected herself and resumed the business at hand. "Bonita LaTrice. I think—" Tag started.

"Bonita!" Indie interrupted. "Damn!"

Tag slammed her papers to the desk. "Is this another pig-racing crony?"

"Hardly. I need to talk to you outside."

Tag turned to Taylor. "I'll need to meet with my client in private."

"Sure, Lucille. I might suggest you need to wrest control of your team."

Hamrick buried his face in his robe.

Tag and Indie went out in the hall.

Indie looked around. "Man, she's Blinky's old flame!"

"Are you sure?" Tag asked. "That's prejudicial. She'll have to be ditched.

Gibson should know better."

"Gibson don't know, 'cause Betty don't, either," Indie countered. "She never found out. You know what? Bonita was good to Blink. Shoot, he and Betty didn't have ... uh, well, never mind, but I tell you the only reason Blink didn't leave was 'cause he was too good a guy and hated to hurt Betty. Too damn good for his own good he was."

"Wouldn't she favor a settlement for Blinky?"

"If Blink was alive she would, but not for Betty. I guarantee it. She hated that woman with a purple passion," Indie said.

Bonita made it to the jury.

Tag brushed her hair back, pursed her lips, and exhaled slowly. "God, what have I gotten into?" she wondered aloud.

When he found out, Bones he was estatic. "See, Indie. I told you, I told you. I knew that jury science stuff would come in handy, and ain't no one from the city got a clue about it, either. No way Bonita's gonna go against you."

"I hope not. Where does she get her hair done?"

"I don't know."

"Hm. I guess we shoulda done some more homework, but I still think we struck a lick."

"Me, too, Indie."

CHAPTER TWENTY NINE

Indie on Trial

TRIAL BEGAN THE THIRD WEEK OF SEPTEMBER just as Judge Hamrick promised. It was nine months after Blinky died. Indie seldom talked about the trial being a burden, but he spoke of Blinky often. "None of us got as bad a deal as Blinky," he'd say.

Indie and Bones sat in the back of the courtroom and waited for the proceedings to begin.

Indie turned to Bones. "This place makes me claustrophobic. There ain't a window in the joint."

Bones patted him on the knee. "At least you got on your fish tie."

"If I had to wear one, at least it'll remind me of a better place."

Tag was up front at the bench in discussion with Gibson. "Tag looks the part, huh?" Indie commented.

"Looks older now, doesn't she?"

"Maybe it's the pinstripe suit."

"Yeah, quite professional."

"Hate I called her Little Orphan Annie."

"She's used to it." Bones checked his watch. "About time to get started." He looked off to the side. Betty Wilson came into the courtroom. "Good Lord, look at her."

"My God, she looks like a hooker. Are those fish nets? Shield my eyes, son. That gives legs a bad name."

Bones laughed out-loud. Tag turned around and stared. She walked back to their seats, separated them, and sat down between them. "Behave, boys."

"Yes, ma'am."

"Gotta take away your playmate, Bones."

"Good luck, pal." Bones saluted Indie.

"Thanks."

The judge arrived. Bones passed Indie one last note. *"Let me know if Judge Hamrick needs any medicine."*

"You're crazy, boy." Indie stuck it in his pocket.

Proceedings opened.

Testimony began with pathologists on parade. They were all the same mold: dark suits with a bunch of charts and graphs. At one point Indie fell asleep and snored right there in the courtroom. Tag poked him in the ribs and woke him up.

Tag got on him afterwards. "For God's sake, Indie. Couldn't you at least pretend to be interested?"

"Hell, Tag. I've known those guys since med school. They're all alike. They hang out with dead people 'cause they can't talk to the live ones."

They were all just alike and so was their testimony. Fentanyl is an excellent medicine, they said, but has to be used with care. They cautioned one has to be aware of patient differences in metabolism, like that was news to anyone. The eyes of the jury glazed over. One of them noodled on a sketch pad. Every so often, old man Watson would nod off.

One expert said Fentanyl should not be used except by certified pain specialists. Bones and Indie thought it was a ridiculous assertion, and Tag took note of it.

Betty Wilson took the stand. Gibson Taylor's team had done their best to exclude anyone from the jury with prior knowledge of the Wilsons. Still, though, it was small town.

"Everyone knows everyone for miles and miles around," Indie whispered to Tag.

When Betty went on about how much she loved Blinky, two of the jurors smirked. Indie turned a laugh into a cough. He passed a note to Tag. *Hell, they haven't had sex in a decade.* Tag kicked his shin under the table, and passed a note back. *DON'T GO THERE.*

Indie scribbled a response and passed it back. *Yes, ma'am,* it read. *But only out of respect for Blinky.*

Indie took the stand. He wore his best outfit, a tweed coat with patches on the elbows. There was a hole just over the left breast pocket from a cigarette burn, but it was a small one. He hadn't wanted to wear a tie, but wore his dark blue one with the fish on it. It matched his navy slacks. Ms. Jenkins had pressed them that morning. He could have passed for a rumpled college biology professor. Bones suspected Indie bordered on uncomfortable.

Indie turned his chair to face the jury. It wasn't orchestrated, it was just Indie. Later, he said, "Well, Good Lord, Bones. How else would you talk to the folks?" He did not know any other way.

He crossed his legs and slouched in the chair. If he'd had a cigarette and a drink, he would have been right at home. At times it was like he wanted to reach out to the jury and invite them to his campsite for a chiliburger and a beer. There wasn't a formal bone in the man, even in court. The jury watched his every move.

Gibson Taylor began his questions. When Indie wanted some time to think about his answer he'd cough with the timing of a standup comic, and pause to gather his thoughts. He only cussed once.

Taylor asked him why he didn't order a Fentanyl level before restarting the patch Saturday morning.

"I've been in practice a long time, Mr. Taylor. And I've seen a lot of Fentanyl prescribed. I have never seen anyone order a Fentanyl level."

"After Mr. Wilson's death, don't you think it would be a good time to revise your standard of care?"

"No."

"It seems obvious you should."

"It might to you, Mr. Taylor, but even in retrospect Fentanyl levels aren't that reliable."

Taylor stopped for a moment.

"Hot as hell in here, ain't it, Mr. Taylor?" Indie tugged at his tie.

The jury laughed out loud.

The judge made them strike it, and Tag wagged her index finger as a warning to behave, but Indie had the jury in his hand as sure as if he were sawing the "Orange Blossom Special" on his fiddle.

Gibson came back to the subject and hammered away on the Fentanyl. "Dr. Jenkins, on admission, you stopped Mr. Wilson's Fentanyl. You documented in the record you suspected it caused his problem. After that, why would you reinstate this medication? After all, it was the medicine that killed Mr. Wilson, was it not?"

Indie sipped on his water. He took his time and didn't get flustered even once. He answered point by point. "Well, Mr. Taylor, first of all, Blink was never intolerant of Fentanyl. If it hadn't been for his patch, he'da done some powerful suffering his last few years. On admission we were still sorting it out, but even in retrospect, I don't believe it caused the change in his status."

Betty Wilson checked her makeup on her compact mirror, and picked at a hole in her fish-nets.

Indie went on. "Blink was my best friend, and I couldn't allow that him to suffer. Matter of fact, he asked me to start the patch again."

"But should you give a medicine just because the patient asks for it?"

"If it has always worked you should."

"Even if you are aware it may harm him?" Gibson asked.

"He ... Heck, Mr. Taylor. There was no indication he'd ever had any harm from it. Matter of fact, there is considerable doubt as to that now." Indie sipped on his water again. "Ain't nothing worse than a doc who won't listen to his patient." He rubbed his thumb across the face of his watch in an aimless way. "I'll bet most of the folks on the jury have seen it more than once." Indie scratched the back of his neck. His eyes wandered around the room. "I've seen it so many times. A patient knows exactly what works for them and some stubborn doc won't listen. I listened to Blink, and tried to help him."

Several jury members nodded. Tag hoped at least one had a family member had dealt with an arrogant doctor somewhere.

Gibson sensed a loss of momentum, and tried to reverse field. "Dr. Jenkins, I am certain you have to agree that Mr. Wilson's cause of death is straightforward. His Fentanyl level was ten times normal."

"Well not necessarily, Mr. Taylor. Dr. McBride will explain it better than what I can. I'm just a country doctor like Bones there, but it has to do with the Fentanyl intravascular shift at the time of cardiac arrest." Indie went into an in-depth review of the scientific literature. The jury began to take notes. Indie got into it like a med school professor. The judge let him go the easel to draw out some diagrams. Then he walked right up to the jury box, and said, "Now, if y'all want to ask anything, you just go right ahead."

Gibson jumped up and objected. Judge Hamrick sustained.

Indie apologized. "I'm sorry, Your Honor, but that's what I'd do at the office. I like for folks to have a chance to ask questions."

Hamrick struck that, too, but he smiled as he did so.

Bones wasn't surprised by Indie's grasp of the material. Indie liked to read, and could take a bubble test with the best. He was far smarter than what all the stuffed-shirt guys knew, and he could smoke all of them on the Boards, especially Dr. Blake, who'd never even passed. Bones sat back and listened with the pride of a professor watching his star pupil ace his oral exams.

Gibson Taylor decided to turn the witness over to Tag.

"Indie, just to be sure everyone knows, just where in the world did you learn all that?"

"Shoot fire, Ms. Tag. Me and Bones read the New England Journal, the American Family Physician, and take the Home Study program every month. Bones won't let me listen to one bit of bluegrass music until I've memorized the monthly CD the Academy sends. On the years we are up for Boards we take Core Content. Bones says, 'Be Prepared.' I always did say he was a dang Boy Scout." The jury laughed.

Gibson jotted down a note. *Call Dad re: Bones.*

Indie was on a roll. She decided to let him run. "Dr. Jenkins, one of the pathologists made the statement Fentanyl should only be prescribed by Board certified Pain Specialists. Your opinion, sir?"

"Mercy, Ms. Tag. If we did that there sure would be a lot of suffering going on. We don't even have a pain specialist in town. All those folks would have to get in the car and go to Raleigh. Well, they could go to Dr. Grey, but he's in trouble with the Board. Why, the drive alone'll kill your back. It does mine. It'd take 'em three months to get an appointment, and them doctors charge about two hundred dollars. I just went up to twenty–five last year, and that's too dang high, but the insurance is getting up there pretty good."

"One more question, Dr. Jenkins. Would you tell the jury what kind of patient is a candidate for Fentanyl?"

"Sure. You can use it on anyone with severe pain. You shouldn't use it on narcotic-naive patients, though."

"I'm sorry, Indie. Tell me what that means."

"Oh, just that if they've never been on narcotics before they might react to it the patch, so you don't use it first. That sure warn't the case with Blink. The poor boy had been on most everything there was and none of it controlled his pain. You can use Fentanyl on frail little old ladies. My mama is dying of cancer, and it's the only thing that's helped her. I wouldn't let Blinky suffer any more than I would let my mama."

"Mr. Taylor? Any further questions?"

Taylor waved his hand to indicate he was through. Judge Hamrick called for a break.

Everyone went out in the hall, but Indie had managed to line up a conference room for his team.

"How'd you come up with this?" Tag asked.

"It's the old black waiting room. They been using it for storage but the custodian cleaned it out just for me. He said it was for people of color and Choctaw was good by him."

The room was small but comfortable. "I believe we could play some music in here on the bad days," Bones said.

Tag didn't notice the remark. She was near giddy. "Honest to goodness, Indie, that might have been the all-time best testimony by a country doctor I have ever heard."

"Just told the truth. Warn't nothing to it."

"And you hardly cussed at all," Tag said. "I'm as proud of you as if you were my dad."

"Thanks."

Tag said, "You know, I have all respect for the Taylors, but I think Gib lost some of his enthusiasm for the case. If you were that type of guy, you could have almost made him look bad."

"Well, I'm not one to take advantage of my opponent just because he's young and inexperienced." Indie laughed, and then turned serious. "No, I figure I don't need to burn any bridges with the man. I respect him, and this thing is a long way from over. If it was blackjack, I'da had a hand of nineteen today. I didn't need to draw another card."

Tag agreed. "Better to cash in while you are ahead, Indie. You timed it right. Now if I only get as good a testimony out of Dr. McBride, we might have a chance."

In the Taylor camp, Betty Wilson was oblivious to the day's testimony. "Well, that Indie Jenkins is a fool. Thinks he's smarter than all those experts. Janie done me proud when she picked you out of the phone book, Mr. Taylor. I think you showed Indie up good."

"Thank you, Ms. Wilson." Gibson Taylor decided to leave it at that. Today was a disappointment, but if the case went bad, it'd be someone else's fault than his. He took some notes to document Betty Wilson's assessment of his performance. He had a feeling he might need them later.

CHAPTER THIRTY

In the Case

TAG CALLED FOR A MEETING that night at the Holiday Inn. They all shook hands, and Indie and Bones sat down.

Tag began. "I've read the analysis from this expert and I like what he has to say. Tell me more about him."

"It was Bones. He heard about him years ago. That boy remembers everyone he runs into."

"I hope we can work with him, and his theory. Our regular experts were unanimous. They said settle. Not defendable."

"This guy's good, Tag," Bones said.

"He better be. The coroner's office is going to testify this Fentanyl level is iron-clad."

"Awh, what do they know?" Indie asked.

She rolled her eyes, then opened her briefcase and got out a legal pad. "Okay, Bones. Tell me about this expert."

"Well, first off, he's from Texas. He's a straight-shooter."

"Wonderful." She scratched some notes.

"I went to a Board Prep Course. Some guy there was giving a Toxicology lecture."

"And it was on this subject?"

"No, but he was extra-sharp. I remembered him from back then. When I called about this Fentanyl thing, he knew all the answers right off the top of his head."

"See, Tag, I told you Bones would help," Indie said.

"Are you guys related or what?"

"Naw, but he's on to something. This ain't no hare-brained idea."

"So, tell me."

Indie continued. "A Fentanyl level drawn at sudden death ain't worth a damn."

"You'd better find a different way to say it, Indie."

"Really, Tag. It's a lousy test. Wait 'til you hear McBride explain it," Bones added.

"Shouldn't he be here?"

"He's on the way. He flew in his own plane, and he called from the airport. Trust me, he's sharp."

"I hope so. He's our only expert right now. Pathologists are reluctant to go up against the State office; too much pull with the Board of Medical Examiners."

"We haven't been able to get anyone in the state to testify. I tried to contact Dr. Turner at Tobacco Triangle Institute, but he hasn't returned my calls."

"Dang, I hate that," Indie said.

"At least he's not on Gibson's witness list. Hopefully we'll get to him first." Tag pushed her hair out of her eyes and took a deep breath.

Someone knocked. "I bet it's Larry," Bones said. He got up to open the door.

It was McBride. Larry was an ex-fighter pilot. He had on an Italian suit, but his shoes were some kind of boxy military style. He extended his hand. "Bones. Always a pleasure." He walked over and gave Tag's hand a vigorous shake. "Nice to meet, you, Ms. Taggert. These boys speak highly of you." He turned to speak to Bones again. "Good to see you. How's the family?"

"Good, good."

"And I take it this is Dr. Jenkins?"

Indie shook hands. "Yes, sir."

"I must say, I feel like I'm meeting a legend. Bones sure has talked a lot about you."

"Not all bad, I hope."

"Oh, no. All good."

McBride opened up his briefcase and produced volumes of charts and graphs and launched into a detailed explanation. This was a take-charge man. Bones hoped Tag wouldn't be put off by him.

When he finished, Tag took a deep breath. "Sir, that is impressive, but if you explain it that way to the jury they aren't going to understand a word you say." She slouched back in her chair and blew her bangs out of her eyes.

McBride went through his presentation again. This time he talked slower and paused to make eye contact with Tag. She shook her head. "Dr. McBride, I am confident you know your business, but you have to connect with these jurors."

"These are the facts. Precisely what do you propose I tell them? I am one of the world's authorities on the metabolism of Fentanyl. The paper I presented at the International Society of Toxicology is now considered the definitive word on the subject. My team did a multivariate analysis which clearly demonstrated the limitations of free Fentanyl levels in the setting of acute cardiac arrest."

"Slow down. Tell me again why the jury is going to understand this?"

"They should have no difficulty. This was a well-designed, double-blind study, irrefutably conclusive at the P-point-oh-five statistical level, and—"

"All right, Doctor. Let me think ..." Tag said.

"Do not misconstrue my objectives. I will not misrepresent my statistical analysis for any purpose; however, a careful review of the literature ..."

Tag help up her hand. "I'm sure, I'm sure, but—"

Indie stood up. "Hell, Larry. Just tell 'em when someone dies all of a sudden, a bloodstream Fentanyl level ain't worth a fart in a whirlwind."

McBride laughed. "I better not say it quite that way either, Indie, but I get the idea."

"Well, do your best. You're all we have," Tag said.

McBride smiled. "I flew fighter jets in my other life, Ms. Taggert. I'm used to being the ace in the hole. I am accustomed to situations that involve high pressure. In comparison to my other life this is, let's see ... how would you civilians say it? This is a walk in the park."

"In other words, no sweat," Indie said.

The next morning they got to the courthouse, and everyone paced around in the hall. Elisa Reyes was there from the Holiday Inn. She spotted Gibson Taylor and Betty Wilson as they walked in.

Elisa pointed at Ms. Wilson. "Mr. Indie, he save my Nina. He nice man." She turned to Gibson. "*Señora* Betty just want money; no good."

The court deputy tugged her arm and motioned for her to follow, but she slipped his grasp. She waved her arms wildly, sputtered Spanish, and then broke back into English. "*Señora* Betty just mad Mr. Indie no would sleep with her at country club; she jealous!"

The deputy placed his hand over her mouth. She struggled to free herself, but the deputy began to drag her from the courthouse.

Indie spoke up. "Y'all don't get on Elisa too bad, she can't help it."

Gibson did his best not to laugh. "It's okay, Dr. Jenkins. We didn't get inside the courtroom. No contempt charges are necessary. I would ask that your people see she refrain from future outbursts. Tell her I need some more towels at the Holiday Inn, and I'll let it go at that."

"Yes, sir," Indie replied.

Betty Wilson was furious, and had to excuse herself.

Tag had to ask. "Indie, why didn't you tell us? It does speak to Ms. Wilson's character, although I doubt we would have tried to use it against her."

Indie was silent for a moment. "Well, hell. I hated for anyone to know Blinky's wife made a pass at his best friend. When he was alive, I figured it would hurt his feelings. Now that he's gone he can't defend himself." Indie took off his bifocals to clean them. "It ain't no more complicated than that."

Dr. Larry McBride took the witness stand. He favored Tom Cruise, and the jurors followed his every movement. He toned down his scientific explanations, and they were almost bearable. No matter how hard Gibson Taylor pushed, he stuck to the same theme: Fentanyl levels were unreliable if obtained at the time of sudden death. Near the end, Gibson had to ask. "Sir, are you saying the State Coroner's office is wrong?"

"Yes." McBride paused. "I am certain they are not malicious, but yes, they are wrong. It is a very common error."

Gibson paced for a moment. "Dr. McBride, the cause of death seems quite obvious here. Sir, do you have any other theory as to this patient's cause of death other than Fentanyl toxicity?"

McBride hesitated. "Mr. Taylor. I am confident Mr. Wilson did not die from an overdose of Fentanyl. I have been asked by the defendants to explore other possibilities, but I am not ready to speculate at this time."

There was a short break, then McBride was back to the stand. Gibson asked him to explain again, and this time McBride went on a wild tear. He put up charts and graphs, used some kind of fancy light pointer, and went over all the stats in detail. He went on almost an hour. Bones thought it was great, but Indie passed a note to Tag. He's losing 'em. Get him off.

There was nothing she could do.

Gibson folded his arms.

The State Medical Examiner's Office waited in the wings.

McBride wound down.

"I open the floor for any discussion or questions."

Two jurors were asleep, and juror Watson snored again. The judge banged the gavel. Watson startled and dropped his glasses.

"You must stay awake, or risk contempt, sir."

"Yes, sir."

The State Chief Medical Examiner took the stand. He had on a white lab coat. His name, DR. BOYLES, was stenciled on his jacket in Carolina blue. He had a stethoscope in his right pocket. His gray hair was neatly combed. The man looked the part.

Indie penciled a note. *Hell, he hasn't used that stethoscope in ten years.*

Boyles took the stand.

"What did you think of Dr. McBride's presentation, sir?" Gibson asked.

"We have used serum Fentanyl levels for many years, and find them quite reliable. We run into this sort of thing all the time."

"What do you mean?"

"Defense teams will go to any length to discredit the office. You have to realize this man is paid quite handsomely to try to confuse the jury. If Dr. McBride's theory were common practice, any pathologist in the state would attest to that fact. I find it of note the defense had to go all the way to Texas to find a doctor willing to testify. This is nothing but statistical mumbo-jumbo. I'm certain the jury understands."

Tag took her turn at him, and couldn't shake the man. At every turn he stuck to his guns. "Nothing but a theory," he said, "only an attempt to obscure the truth. Mr. Wilson," he concluded, "died of Fentanyl overdose. There is no other logical explanation."

At the end of the day, Tag suggested they return to their headquarters at the Holiday Inn. "I appreciate your testimony, Dr. McBride. All I could ask is for you to cast doubt. I guess you did that."

"I was very disappointed in Dr. Boyle's testimony. He is not abreast of current literature," McBride said.

"Yeah, me, too. Paternalistic S.O.B., huh?" Tag commented.

"Yes."

"If you'll excuse me, I'm going back to my room. I'd like to prepare a counter-attack. I do not appreciate his assault on my character."

"Okay, Larry. You done good. We know you were telling the truth," Indie said.

"Thanks, Indie." McBride closed the door behind him.

Indie rubbed his chin. "That McBride is sharp."

"He is, but the guy from the State connected with the jury. It's an uphill climb," Tag replied.

"You know, I'll still got one more theory," Bones said.

Tag sighed. "Yes, Bones. What now?"

"I think Blinky got some Demerol."

"And what does Dr. McBride think of this?"

"I haven't run it by him yet, but….."

"Don't you think that might be a good idea?"

"Well, I will if you give me the green light, but I am sure it's possible."

"And what makes you so certain?"

"'Cause Wheatie Willis is positive he didn't get his Demerol injections the night Blinky died; we just can't prove where it went. Wheatie is sure, though."

"Who?"

"Wheatie. He's a Demerol junkie."

"Does the record show this?"

"No, ma'am. Not exactly, anyway. But there is a discrepancy in the pharmacy records."

"But there is nothing to suggest this in Mr. Wilson's chart?"

"No ma'am, but it fits."

"You have to have more. It doesn't seem so neat to me. Why are you so certain?" Tag asked.

"No really, Tag. It is more than just speculative. It fits. Really," Indie said.

"Who is this Wheatie?"

"Well, he's not exactly a model witness. I'm looking for another one," Bones said.

"Any hope?"

"I don't know."

Tag sighed. "I wish you could prove that one, Bones. It would mean the hospital was involved."

"She's right," Indie said.

Tag scrunched her forehead. She started slowly. "So, Bones, hmn ... just what do you think McBride would say?" Tag asked.

"I think he'd say it was theoretically possible."

"You love that word, don't you?"

"What?"

"Theoretically."

"Well, it is."

"Yeah and they'd shoot me down faster than your Tom Cruise if I even mentioned it. You need more than that. Okay, though. Run it by McBride and get back to me."

"Yes, ma'am."

Indie stood up and took off his coat. "Damn, if this thing ain't hot. Hey, Tag, you ought to come to the jam session tonight."

"Yeah. Come on by," Bones added.

"Good grief, boys. How do you do this all day and play half the night?"

"Endorphins, I reckon," Indie said.

"You're going to wear me out. I'm going to do some paperwork and turn in," Tag said.

"Never know what you'll learn. Bluegrass music has many lessons," Indie said.

"Whatever. I'm done for this day."

Tag stayed to catch up on her work, but Indie and Bones left to get their instruments and head to the the lounge. Indie had long since ditched the coat and tie. "We can be normal at least for awhile."

The jam session started out with Indie in a playful mood, He called for *"I'm in the Jailhouse Now,"* and then *"I'll Break Out Tonight."*

Moose said he wanted to hear a love song. "Hey, Indie, call Betty Wilson to come up here and we'll play *'Love Come Home.'* Tell her I copied it so she could sing it tonight. It was filed under *'Love: Requited and Unrequited.'*"

Indie laughed harder than anyone. "She might think it's unrequited, but I don't want no part of that woman."

The session broke up, and everyone promised to return the next night.

Bones flung the coffin case over his shoulder, and headed down the stairs. At the lobby floor, he opened the stairwell door, and ran smack into B.G.

"Dang, B.G., I'm sorry. I almost ran over you."

"Not a problem."

"Man, you need to break out that old herringbone again and play a few tunes with us. We're off the clock up there. I promise we won't talk about the case. Come join us tomorrow."

"What're you carrying there—your old Gibson?"

"No, brother. This is my modern mandolin. Carbon fiber. Indestructible, timeless, synthetic, but still real. It's one you would want to see."

"Sure, let me take a look at it. I love these old coffin cases." B.G. opened the case, pulled out the mando, and strummed a few lines of *"Lonesome Old Graveyard."*

"Didn't you say you like mandolins?"

"I can appreciate them like fine wine. Has anyone at the hospital ever seen it?"

Bones shook his head. "Nope. If they knew what it was worth, I figure they'd do their best to steal it."

"Maybe if they thought they could profit somehow ..."

Bones smiled. "Before it's over the rumor mill will say we're desperate to keep the secret hidden in the old coffin. They'll have to dig deep to get it out of the case and show it to them, don't you think?"

B.G. placed the mandolin back in the case, and secured the latches. "I've enjoyed playing with you. I gotta split. Headed out west."

"Hate to see you go. What's your trip for?"

"Partly business, partly family. My grandparents live out there."

"Have a good trip."

"Thanks. The Navajo always respect their ancestors, don't forget that."

"Sir?"

"Look, Bones, you seem like an honest boy. Just remember you can always trust folks who respect their ancestors."

"Sir, are your ancestors Navajo?"

"My mother is. My father was Hopi."

"I see. Did you know Indie is part Choctaw?"

"Hm. Interesting." B.G headed for the door, then turned around. "Do you know anything about what the Navajo did in World War Two?"

"A little. I know they were the code-talkers."

"That's right; code-talkers, wind-talkers. It is a very intricate language."

"I've always heard we wouldn'ta won the war without them."

"You can be sure the enemy knew it, too. It was very dangerous work."

"It sounds like it."

"No doubt. Each code-talker had a bodyguard. If the enemy was about to capture them, the bodyguard's job was to kill the Navajo, rather than risk them being tortured and give up the code."

"Wow."

"Now you know why no one can give up the Navajo. Do you understand?"

"Yes, sir."

"Then listen to to wind, young man. Listen for the ancient tones."

"I promise. No one knows the Navajo."

"Good. I'll be on my way."

CHAPTER THIRTY ONE

Snookered

SATURDAY SEEMED LIKE A GOOD DAY to get away from everything. Bones called Snookers. "I'm freed up for the day. Kate went to visit her mom. Can you play?"

"Hell, it's Saturday, ain't it? I was getting ready to go hit a few balls and pick up a game. Meet me in an hour."

"Okay."

"You come right by the B-&-B don't you?"

"Yeah."

"How 'bout bringing me a liver mush and egg?"

"Okay."

Snook was set up hitting balls on the practice range at River Run when Bones arrived. The sun was up, but the dew was still thick. Bones traipsed across the Bermuda, and the wet grass clung to his shoes. He watched Snookers. His shots were all the same: a high fade at the apex and then a gentle descent. One could have covered the shot dispersion with a blanket, or at least a bedspread. "Dang, Snook. I don't think you need much practice. You gonna turn pro?"

"No reason to change lifestyles at this age." Snook hit a few more. "You better learn that fade, Bones. It comes in handy sometimes."

"Tell me about it. Here's your sandwich. I brought you a cup of coffee, too."

"High test?"

"Of course."

"Good man."

"So, what's the hospital gossip?"

"Olden's bragging. As far as he's concerned, Indie is done buried."

"Somehow we need to use that."

"Olden needs to get the crap scared out of him."

"Yeah, but how?"

"I dunno." Snookers handed Bones an envelope. It was sealed and taped. "Here. Indie said to give this to you. Said it was important."

Bones opened it. *DIG DEEPER. CHECK MANDOLIN HISTORY BE-FORE PURCHASE. NAVAJO.*

Bones looked around and stuffed the note in his pocket.

"What did it say?" Snookers asked.

"Jibberish. Some kinda doctor writing. I couldn't read it all."

"You can't read it? God, it must be bad."

Bones didn't comment. "I'll call him. How come Indie didn't bring this to me?"

"Said it was like golf; he had to go by the rules. He said you'd under-stand."

"I'm not sure I do, but okay."

"Maybe I better go check on him."

"You're gonna stay and play, aren't you? The Member/Member is coming up. Indie said your game needed help."

Bones stared off in the distance.

"Bones?"

"Oh, yeah ... yeah, Snook. I'm sorry. I was just distracted. Did you say Indie said I needed help?"

"Yeah. He said he had some money on me and you in the Member/Mem-ber."

"Indie does like to bet a little, huh?"

Snook took another swing. "He said he liked his odds better if you'd learn to fade it." He handed Bones a club. "Look here, Doc. All you gotta do is take your normal grip, but just show one knuckle instead of two on your left hand. Got it?"

"Yeah."

"Then open your stance just a hair."

"Okay."

"Now, swing across the line of your shoes."

Bones hit a low rope hook.

"Hell, Bones. You double-crossed it. Try again. Think of pitching a bucket of water out to your right and not back over your shoulder the way you always do."

Bones swung again. Perfect high fade. "Hey, thanks, that's it."

"Any time. Let's go tee it up."

They stopped at the turn. "I better split, Snook. Got some doctor stuff to tend to."

"Hell, you always got doctor stuff, Bones."

"What'd you shoot?"

Snook tallied up the card. "Two under."

"Thirty-five. Good nine."

"I've got you down at thirty-eight, that right?"

Bones looked over the card. "Nah, I had a bogey on eight. It should be a thirty-nine."

"Hmm. You still a seven handicap?"

"Correct."

"You owe me a burger."

"I'm like food stamps for you, Snook."

"Sorry, Doc."

"Can you meet me in the doctor's lounge Monday morning? I need to talk to you about some hospital stuff."

"Sure. And work on that fade. Indie's got money on us. You can't let him down."

"Okay, Snook. I'll call Monday morning and remind you."

Bones called McBride at home that night. "McBride? Bones here. I appreciate your testimony. I think you helped Indie some. Sure didn't hurt."

"Thanks."

"Would you testify again if we need you?"

"Sure, you know us pilots; any excuse to fly. Just get Tag to approve the expert witness fee and I'm there."

"Okay. Might call you."

"Hope to hear from you. The fishing on the coast is good this time of year."

"Yeah, the spots run best in the fall. Uh, Larry, one other thing. I've been thinking about our man's case. Don't you think it acts like serotonin syndrome?"

"Yeah, it does, but I've been over the chart. Except for the Haldol, nothing would have interacted, and there wasn't enough of it to matter."

"What if he'd gotten some Demerol?"

"He didn't."

"But what if he did?"

"Sure, Demerol could very well do it."

"Can I ask you a theoretical question?"

"Sure."

"Is there any way to find out if a patient had had Demerol injected some nine months ago?"

"Yeah, well, most patients wouldn't sign up just for the fun of it, but you could do a bone marrow normeperidine residual level."

"What about Blinky Wilson?"

"Given he's dead, I don't guess he can consent. It's a fine idea, but I don't think his wife would agree to anything you suggest."

"Yeah, I guess you're right."

"Why do you ask?"

"Awh, just a theory. Might have to call you back in, though. Tell the wife and kids hello."

"Will do."

CHAPTER THIRTY TWO

Monday, Monday

SIX AM, MONDAY. BONES' ALARM went off to "Jimmy Brown the Newsboy."

"I sell the morning paper, sir, my name is Jimmy Brown—" He hit the snooze button and grimaced; he'd almost overslept. He called Snook.

Ten rings went by. He began to get nervous. Twelve. "Dang it, Snook. Answer the phone."

"Hello?" Donna answered.

"Hey, Donna. This is Dr. Bones. Is Snook there?"

"Snookie! Dr. Bones' on the phone."

"Tell him I'll be right there," Snook shouted.

"Hold on a minute, I'll get him." She put the phone down.

"You aren't going to play golf today, are you, shug? I thought you were gonna take the day off with Miss Donna."

"Uh, yeah, Donna. I ain't gonna be long, baby. I forgot. I promised to meet Bones early today. How 'bout I bring you some coffee and donuts from the Coffee Club?"

"Well, I won't make up the bed. Don't let the coffee get cold, Snookie."

Snook came to the phone. "Hello."

"Snookie?" Bones asked. "Dang it, Snookie. Indie's life is on the line, brother."

"Yes, Bones. Of course. Donna said she'd turn me loose for a minute, but not to be late. We're gonna go down the beach today, but I can run by, no problem."

"I guess it ain't a problem, Snook. Get over there now."

"Sure, Bones, I'll be right there."

Snook made it on on time.

"Dadgum it, Snook, don't scare me like that. How could you forget?"

"I'm sorry, Doc. You gotta understand. A girl like Donna will make a man lose his head. I made it, didn't I?"

Bones looked up at the clock in the doctor's lounge; seven AM sharp. He motioned Snook over to the patient print-out station. "Hey, Snook. You got time to follow me over to the shop and then the office this morning? The Scout has been acting up and is due for an oil change."

"Sure. I'll wait on you to make rounds."

Bones opened the refrigerator, and got out a Coke. "Anyone watching that TV?"

"Hmm. I'll check." Snook looked around the corner in the TV room. "Somebody must have left it on." He walked over and flipped it off. Snook waved his hands wildly, and then scribbled a note. He pointed to the adjacent room and handed the note to Bones. *Blake's eating breakfast in the conference room.* The door was ajar.

"What's wrong with you, Doc? You look like you feel bad," Snook asked.

"Awh, nothing. Kind of worried about the Scout. Hate to have to replace her. Hey, Snook, I must tell you we had a great jam this weekend. Indie sure can saw on a fiddle when he's had a few."

"Did y'all play at the cabin?"

"Yep. Great session, but I worry about Indie. He's drinking too much. I'm afraid he's going to talk," Bones said.

A chair squeaked in the next room.

Bones went on. "But Indie has an out. Our tox man from Texas says the Fentanyl test done at autopsy is not that great a test. Tag just knows she can get out for a reasonable settlement. You know, young attractive female lawyer argues for old half worn-out doc. The grandpa defense. Hey, he might even get off. All it takes is one juror."

"Damnation, Bones, Indie's a regular Houdini."

Bones pulled up his list of patients. The printer whirred away as it printed out his patient list. "Unfortunately, they could still nail him, though." He paused. "We not supposed to talk about it, but if anyone did a lipid-bound Fentanyl level—"

"What the hell is that?"

"It don't matter, 'cause no one's gonna do it. As long as Blinky stays buried a few more weeks, Indie might have an out. McBride thinks he can at least get him out light. Hell, he might walk."

"Damn. You think anyone will figure it out?"

"Are you kidding? Betty won't know they need to exhume Blinky. You can count on that."

Snook raised his voice. "Man, if Olden knew, he'd have Blinky dug up in a skinny minute. He'd have a fit if he found out."

"Ssh. Quiet, Snook."

The back door of the adjoining room squeaked open. "Hey, Snook, hush up. Someone's coming in." The door slammed shut.

"I believe someone's left." Snook laughed.

"Quick, see where he goes."

Snook cracked the door and peeked out. Blake was on his way down the corridor that led to Jim Olden's office.

Bones looked at his watch. "Give it a minute." He let sixty seconds tick off. "Tell you what, Snook. Anything you need to be doing for Mr. Olden?"

"Hmm. Yeah. I was supposed to change his fluorescents today."

"Go down there and ask if this would be a good time."

"You want me to change 'em out?"

"Sure, and check and see if Blake is there. Call me back."

Bones waited. Five, then ten minutes went by. The phone rang. "Sorry, Doc, I had to change out three bulbs."

"Was Blake there?"

"Yep."

"You aren't calling from Olden's office are you?"

"No, I had to go down to the nurse's station."

"Is that Dr. Bones?" a female voice asked.

"Yeah," Snook replied.

"I need to talk to him." Snookers handed her the phone. "Mrs. Thompson's blood sugar is three hundred. I just left you a message at the office."

"Give her five units of regular. Be careful. She'll bottom out on you in a heartbeat."

'Thanks."

"Put Snook back on."

"Yes, sir."

"Snook, be careful what you say over there."

"I will, Doc. Tiffany says hello. You talk and I'll tell Donna."

CHAPTER THIRTY THREE

Bee Bridges BBQ

A MAN APPROACHED THE COUNTER at Bee Bridges Barbecue. He was just shy of middle-aged, with sandy hair, a sparse beard, and wire-rimmed glasses. He looked artistic. Reg, the proprietor, did not recognize him. The gentleman sat two tweed mandolin cases down by his feet. The waitress brought him some tea.

"I must say, young lady, your iced tea is especially good. Could you direct me to the local music store? I wonder if you have any mandolin enthusiasts in these parts? If so, I would like to inquire as to their interest in my work." The accent had country flavor with a western tinge; sort of a southern-fried Montana twang, but also had a hint of British.

Reg walked over. "You ain't from around here, are you?"

"No. Montana. We have a new mandolin company. Weber's the name. Carlson Weber."

"You looking for mandolin players?"

"Yeah."

"Well, hell, we got one of the best, Dr. Bones Robertson. Ever hear of him?"

"Yes."

"Well, good. Around here if you don't know Bones, you don't know nothing about mandolins. He plays the first Saturday of the month at the B-&-B, and over at Harvey Methodist, too. He just called in an order for some 'cue. Should be here in a minute."

"Good. I'll wait."

Reg spotted Bones as he walked in. "Hey, Bones. This man has some mandolins he wants to show off."

"Great. What you carrying?"

"New company. Weber."

"I've heard of them. Good reputation."

"Care for a booth in the back?"

"Okay." They sat down. "So, is your design new?"

"It is a new company, but we believe in the old ways. Tradition, you know. We believe these are the most Loar-like mandolins on the market, except for the neck design. We found the mortise and tenon to have superior stability to the dovetail without any degradation of tonal quality."

"Say they sound like the Loars?"

"Yes. We're from out west. Like the Navajo we respect our ancestors."

"Respect your ancestors?" Bones asked.

"Yes. Like you, I am of Scots-Irish descent, but the West is well versed in the Native American ways."

The waitress came up. "Bones, I think your take-out is ready."

"Oh, go ahead and bring it. I think I'll eat here. Let me take the slaw home to Kate, though, she loves it."

"What about you, sir?" the waitress asked.

"What do you recommend?" he asked Bones.

"What did you say your name was again?"

"Carlson Weber."

"Get Mr. Weber a chopped tray."

"Yes, sir."

"And some extra sauce and hushpuppies. We could use a pitcher of tea, too."

"Coming right up."

"Have you ever seen a carbon-fiber mandolin, Mr. Weber?"

"No, but I've heard of them. Prototypes right now, aren't they?"

"Yes."

"You ought to come out west sometime."

"I'd love to. Too busy doctoring."

"You're gonna waste your whole life away."

"I guess. Look, I know this guy who's a dealer. Goes by 'B.G.' He might have interest in a Weber. Maybe we could broker a deal."

"We believe the mandolin we already own is of greater value," Weber said.

"I understand. I realize it might not be an even swap. We can talk some bones to close a deal, and we're willing to negotiate."

Weber looked around. No one was near by. "This B.G. would have to have a legitimate response."

"I understand. And how will I know of your interest?"

"You will hear from the Navajo," Weber replied.

"My guess is the market for carbon-fiber mandolins will be strong some day. Would you like to see it?" Bones asked.

"Very much so," Weber said.

"We believe we will have it ready for your appraisal soon," Bones offered. "I would not make any final decisions until you see what it has to offer. It will be in a Calton coffin mandolin case. I haven't told Ta... er... her yet, but, uh ... well, no one knows ..."

"The waitress brought the 'cue. "Dr. Bones, you ain't selling your Gibson, are you? My boyfriend has always liked that mandolin."

"No, ma'am, the Gibson is not for sale. Might let my little carbon one go, though. Need to thin the herd, you know."

She looked disappointed. "Let me know if you ever consider selling the Gibson."

"I'm still loyal to old Gib. Not for sale. This man has brought some new players to the mix, though. Look at these babies."

Weber opened one of the tweed cases. It was a beautiful mandolin; curly maple, tobacco sunburst varnish finish.

The girl let out a low whistle. "Boy, wouldn't Richard love one of those. How much?"

"Not on the market yet. These are only prototypes. We hope to go public soon, though," Weber replied.

She pooched out her lower lip, and left to retrieve their bill.

"Bones, I'm certain you recognize our limitations in this transaction. Is it your belief the owner will be able to convince a third party to consider the value of a synthetic in Harvey County? It is rural, you know. These parts of the country tend toward the traditional."

"I understand. A carbon-fiber mandolin can not equal the value of a Loar. We respect our ancestors."

"Excellent. We will await further intelligence before pricing our proto-types."

"Agreed."

Bones finally pushed his plate away. "Man, I don't think I can eat another bite."

"Same here. You folks have, as you say, excellent 'cue."

The waitress brought the tab. They left enough change for a tip, and head-ed out the door.

Weber had one last thought when out in the parking lot. "Bones, you realize the synthetic is still in the case? Until we see it, my client is honor-bound to approach the retail price for the mandolin he has. He will insist your client respond appropriately. He has no choice."

"I understand. With patience, you may be able to surpass the market. If the instrument is really prized, the bidding can get carried away."

Weber looked around the parking lot. "Like five mil?"

"Possible. We realize no one has ever approached that kind of figure around here. Depends on what's in the case. We believe the circumstances might be extraordinary." Bones checked one last time to be sure no customers were in the parking lot. "Mr. Weber, I am being as straight with you as I can. We aren't sure yet. We just want some time. Look, we both know as good as a Loar is, even it won't bring five mil. But if we had a Strad violin equivalent, then who knows; maybe more. Yes, we are not certain yet, but we have reason to believe it may be one of those one-in-a-lifetime mandolins."

"But by your own admission, this is not even a Loar; it is a carbon-fiber prototype. Untested."

"I agree. And in general, I'm not that big on carbon synthetics. But when you need a mandolin that can withstand the elements, and this one can, they can't be beat. Look at it this way: You guys have a modern streak when you see a way to improve your market share. Otherwise, you'd still use a dovetail on your neck joints."

"And I take it you believe we need to consider a nod to modern in this situation?"

Bones smiled and nodded.

"However it goes, I thank you for your expertise. I am confident my client also respects your position." Weber extended his hand and they shook.

"Tell your man I said hello, and to fully consider all reasonable offers," Bones said.

"Agreed."

The plan was in motion. But, if they couldn't see inside the coffin, there would be no business to conduct. Bones got in the Scout to drive home. Betty Wilson would never agree to exhume Blinky if she had any notion it was going to help Indie. Bones didn't even know for sure Tag would go along. All he could do was hope they would give it consideration.

CHAPTER THIRTY FOUR

Bluegrass Encryption

SNOOK CALLED. "DOC, THE RAT SNATCHED the cheese right off the trap. Olden is meeting with Betty Wilson as we speak."

"Way to go, Snook. Would you speak to Indie for me?"

"What do you want me to tell him?"

"Tell him you taught me the fade real good."

"Okay."

"See you, Snook."

"Call me."

"Will do."

Room 438 Harvey Holiday Inn. B.G. knocked, and Gibson Taylor opened the door. "Come in and tell me. What's the word?"

"My western tour is booked."

"Wonderful. Montana is beautiful this time of year."

"Mr. Weber awaits your arrival. The Navajo has spoken."

"Definitive or smoke signal?"

"Definitive."

"Excellent. Give my regards to the travel agent. When should we dig our foundation? I'm working on a building."

"Break ground at six bells on seventh morning. Sunrise, graveyard shift."

"I hope we get rain."

"Yes, sir. It would soften things up. I'll be on my way."

"Good to see you, B.G. Take care. Give your mother my best."

"In my father's memory." B.G bowed slightly, then turned and left.

Gibson lit a Cohiba.

Everyone waited.

CHAPTER THIRTY FIVE

Anger Management

OLDEN CALLED JACKSON LEGGETT, the hospital's attorney. "Jackson. We have a problem."

"What's wrong?"

"Dr. Blake dropped by. He had some bad news."

"Ole Blowhard?" Leggett asked. "What's up with him?"

"He overheard Bones in the doctor's lounge. Bones told Snookers Molesby they have an out for Jenkins."

"Impossible. The case is airtight."

"Don't be so sure. Better come by."

"I'll be there."

Storm clouds were gathering. Leggett arrived and parked in the executive lot. He fished around in the back seat and found an umbrella. Once at Olden's office he left it at the door. "Looks like rain is on the way. We need it."

Olden said, "Yes, we do."

"So what's the problem?"

"I don't know exactly. "This McBride is willing to testify that Blinky Wilson should have had a different test at autopsy. There is a better test available, and the State didn't use it. They can cast reasonable doubt as to whether Fentanyl was the problem or not. Look, Blake wrote it down for me- 'lipid-bound Fentanyl level.'" He handed the paper to Leggett.

Leggett looked it over. "Jim, this is a civil case. They don't have to worry about reasonable doubt. They only have to demonstrate there might be a chance Jenkins did wrong. For these malpractice cases, it isn't innocent until proven guilty; it's guilty until proven innocent."

"Well, damn it, I've heard that legal crap from you before and you let him slip by. By God, you better not take any chances this time."

"I still think you should let it settle and go away, Jim. They are floating around a half mil."

"No! Hell, no! Are you in or not?" Olden stood up and paced around the room as he spoke. "Well, are you?"

"Calm down, Jim. I'm in."

"I can fire you, you know."

"Yes, sir. Look, Jimmy. You better get some kind of confirmation on this."

"Dr. Blake knows what he's talking about."

"Hell, Jim. He didn't pass his Boards. He sure isn't an expert in toxicology. Why don't you call Roger Turner at Tobacco Triangle? I've used him several times. He's first rate."

"Good Lord, Jackson. That is one arrogant S.O.B. Surely someone else….."

"Jimmy, he's the best in the state."

"I am a C.E.O., and he treats me like a child. I don't have to tolerate such behavior."

"Call him. You can't afford to miss on this."

Olden rubbed his chin. He paged his secretary. "How about getting me a Dr. Roger Turner on the phone? He's up at Tobacco Triangle Institute."

"Yes, sir."

Olden held for a minute, and then Turner came to the phone. "Dr. Turner?"

"Yes?"

"This is Jim Olden in Harvey County. I need to ask a question."

"Go ahead."

"I have to meet with Dr. Blake today. I hate not to be prepared. He says we need to be doing lipid-bound Fentanyl levels. Are they the gold standard now?"

"Oh, yes. At least in cases of sudden death, we do not use a standard Fentanyl level. Not enough predictive power." Turner paused. "Jim, why do you want to know? And why does Blake care? He shouldn't have any particular interest in this subject."

"Uh, oh, well, we have a case going on, and ..."

"A case?! Damn it, Jimmy, last time you drug me into one down there, I was in and out of Harvey Country for three months."

"Oh, I'm not going to involve you, Doctor."

"Hell, you better not. Leave me out of it. That damn Leggett never did pay my expert witness fee."

"Now, Dr. Turner, this is just between me and you. But, are you sure?" Olden said it again. "Lipid-bound Fentanyl level."

"That's the best test today."

"What about the free Fentanyl level?"

"Great test if the patient is alive. Lousy if they died."

"Are you sure?"

"Of course I'm sure. In death cases, we use the lipid-bound. It's a better test. We've used it here at T.T.I. for a couple years now."

"I see. Well, I guess Blake was right."

"Well, good. I have a busy schedule. I'll come if subpoenaed, but I don't have time for it right now."

"As it turns out, it doesn't matter. The case is about to wrap up, and we already have one of these, let's see ..." Olden looked over at Leggett and snapped his fingers. Leggett handed the paper back to him. "uh... one of these lipid-bound Fentanyl levels. We won't need you to testify anyway; it's already a done deal. I thank you for your time."

"Good day, Jim. Don't call me back unless you have a court order." He hung up.

Olden turned to Leggett. "There you have it, Jackson. Bones was right.

They got the wrong test at autopsy."

"Hell, it's not that strong an argument, Jim. I'm telling you, let it settle. I don't feel good about this."

"Are you on board or not?"

"You're paying the bills." Leggett sighed, and got up to walk around the room. "We're on board."

"Betty should be here shortly. You need to convince her he should be exhumed."

"I need to? This was your idea."

"You're the lawyer. You'll think of something."

Betty Wilson was puzzled to see Jackson Leggett pacing around Olden's office. Mr. Olden had seemed so confident. "What's wrong, Jimmy?"

"Betty, Betty. Appreciate you coming by. Uh, we have run into a little snag on the case."

"What kind of snag? You said it was a sure thing."

"Oh, it is, Betty. It is. We just want to cover every base, that's all. About Mr. Wilson—"

"Blinky?" No one, not even Olden, ever called him Mr. Wilson.

Olden cleared his throat. "Betty, we feel the case is coming along quite nicely, and want to reassure you that we are not concerned. However, we do suspect that a wrinkle has developed we should discuss with you."

"A wrinkle? You said this was as good as a mutual fund. I want my damn retirement."

"Oh, it is, Betty. I don't want you to leave any stone unturned; that's all. It is a bit of a legal concept, so I thought it best to get Mr. Leggett to review this literature with you."

Leggett began to stammer. "Well, uh, Ms. Wilson, you see ... at the time of Blinky's death a 'serum Fentanyl level' was the gold standard of, uh ..." He coughed, and got up to get some water.

Betty looked over her glasses and clutched her purse. Her eyes flit back and forth between Leggett and Olden.

Leggett resumed. "However, the test did have some limitations. Since then, there is a new one that may well be more conclusive." He sat back down.

Betty sat and tapped her foot. She muttered something.

"Ma'am?"

"Oh, nothing."

Leggett went on. "Should Dr. Jenkins' counsel realize this, they could take the position that not having this piece of data leaves some doubt as to the certainty as to the cause of death. This would not be true, of course, but they could portray this as a weakness in the case, and make it a possible defense strategy for their team."

Suddenly Betty blurted out her words. "What is this about?"

Olden took her hand. "Betty, unfortunately, some of these lawyers can be quite clever and hide the truth."

Jackson Leggett scratched the back of his neck. "From what I know, I would think this test could get you close to your million dollars. Without it, they might be able to reduce their exposure." He paused. "Look, Ms. Wilson. I'm not your lawyer. I represent the hospital. I would suggest you take this information to your attorney. I cannot be in the position of representing both your interests and the hospital's."

"What is he saying, Jimmy? You said we were in this together. Matter of fact, you told me we had this thing sealed up. What is this?"

Olden took over. "We believe their desire to settle is becoming urgent. If they settle without the benefit of us gathering this data by exhumation, and I can not overemphasize this point, Dr. Jenkins might be able to greatly reduce his obligation to you."

The tears began to flow. "What the hell is wrong with them? Don't Indie feel the least bit sorry? Blinky's dead. I want my damn money, and I want all of it. I deserve justice."

Olden and Leggett exchanged glances. "Betty, we've thought this over at length. We believe it is in your best interest to have Mr. Wilson exhumed," Olden said.

"Exhumed! What if your experts are wrong? Maybe I should settle if I can get over a half mil. A bird in the hand ..."

Leggett took over again. "Ms. Wilson, I agree. Certainly, settlement is something to consider. However, I strongly recommend you not settle unless it is very close to Dr. Jenkins' limits. That is seven hundred-fifty thousand. Still, I would consider reasonable proposals." He took a deep breath. He wondered how the hell he'd gotten in the in the middle of this. "Again, I am not your attorney. I represent the hospital, and......."

Olden jumped out of his chair and waved his arms. "Betty, we know that damn Indie wants to settle right now, before we find the evidence a second autopsy will reveal. Trust me, he is going to do everything possible to avoid an exhumation."

"I don't know."

"Look, Betty." Olden's voice took on a squeak. "Dr. Jenkins is nothing but a dumbass Indian."

Her lips tightened and her eyes squinted. "You're right, Jimmy. My Daddy said that a long time ago. He said Blinky and Indie were nothing but trouble. I shoulda listened to Daddy ..."

Olden held her hand again. "Yes, Betty. Your daddy was a good man. Indie may have a stake in one of those casinos in Mississippi. We need to tap that well for you. Don't settle for anything less than a million. He owes it to you."

Betty paced. "You're so right. I should have listened to Daddy. Sure, I'll tell Gibson I want the new test. It's only fair."

Leggett said, "Good Lord, Ms. Wilson. You can get a fair settlement today. In this business—"

"Don't you understand? This isn't business. This is my Blinky."

"Okay." Leggett scratched his head. "Go ahead, but again, talk to Mr. Taylor about it. I did not give you legal advice here, and don't forget it." He took some notes.

"All I can say is you guys better know what the hell you are doing." She slammed he door, and it flung back open as she stormed out.

Olden shut the door behind her. "What are you trying to do, Jackson? We need to keep the pressure on. I want his license."

"Damn it, Jim. We don't have all the say on this. I think it is in the hospital's best interest to stay the hell out of it. And that, sir, is my legal advice. Jenkins has nothing beyond his insurance and they'll make sure Betty knows it. And what was that crap about a casino?"

"I wanted to give her hope she might get even more."

"She knows Jenkins was her husband's best friend. In the end, some of that loyalty will bleed through, even from the grave. She's got to live here. At the end of the day, her agenda will not be as vindictive as yours. People usually back away when they have nothing else to gain."

"Well, I'm not going to. You make sure they get that exhumation."

"I think Betty will take care of that."

CHAPTER THIRTY SIX

Fish Stories, Rumors, and the Secret Business

SNOOK STOPPED BONES ON ROUNDS. "Hey, man, can you look at my foot? Indie's gone fishing."

"No trial today?"

"Indie called me before he went to the river. He left you a message at the office. Said there was a break for today, and he was gonna take advantage of it."

"A break?"

"Yeah, you know, a day off."

"I see. So what's wrong with your foot?"

He pulled off his shoe. "Gouch."

"It sure looks like the gout. Let's go up to the nursing station. I need to check it."

"Check it? Man, the sheets set it on fire. I sure don't want you to touch it."

"I understand, but I at least need to check the pulse in your foot. Can you come over to the office?"

"All hell, Doc. Don't make me go over there. I gotta work."

"We're supposed to check you before we treat you. I won't charge you; just come on by."

"I ain't worried about my bill. Hey, Doc, you know what the word is in the hospital?"

"What's that?"

"Betty Wilson says she still wants a million dollars."

"A million dollars? Indie ain't got that kind of money."

"I know. They say Olden told her she's worth it and more."

"Good Lord. Let me ask you something, Snook. You know the street. You think a jury would give Betty that kind of money?"

"Nah, Doc. Betty's just one of them people digging for gold."

"Why is Olden aggravating this so bad?"

"I dunno. Everyone says he wants to get shed of Indie. How come you reckon?"

"Hard to say. Hop up on the table." Bones checked his foot. The big toe was fire engine red hot. "Sure looks like the gout. Hmm. Your pulse is okay. I'll give you a script, but we need to get you to the office and do some blood work."

"Sure."

"And Snook, I wouldn't say anything about this."

"Hell, I've already told half the hospital."

"Snook!"

"The nurses said it looked like gout, too. It don't bother me what they know about my feet."

"Your feet? Oh, yeah, okay. Your feet. Yeah. Well, I have to be in the secret business, Snook. I'm not allowed to tell."

"Okay, but it don't bother me."

After supper, Bones put in a call. "Hey, Ms. Jenkins, is Indie there?"

"Sure, I'll get him. Everything okay?"

"Yes, ma'am. How do you think he's doing?"

"He's smoking too much, but not bad. He went fishing today."

Indie came to the phone. "Bones, how are you, boy?"

"Good. How'd you do?"

"Got a couple crappies. Didn't land a pike like that one you caught, though. Anything new?"

"Uh, yeah. I hear Betty's back to wanting a million."

"Doesn't surprise me. Where'd ya hear that?"

"Oh, my, Indie. I can't tell you. A patient said it; we're in the secret business, you know."

"Yeah, that's okay."

"They say Olden has something new."

"What do you think it is?"

"I don't know. Tag's never liked me meddling, but this time might be different. Call Brad in Atlanta. I don't think anyone's going to find a way to settle right now, but don't do it under any circumstances, at least for a few days."

"That shouldn't be hard. Tag wants to settle, but she's not about to vote for a million. I ain't got it, anyway. I'll call him tomorrow. Hell, I don't think any jury would go for such as that."

"Betty's about to get my blood up. If she backs you in a corner I'm about ready to dig up some dirt on her."

Indie laughed. "That's the white, Anglo Saxon savage coming out in you Bones, but I'm about to the same point. She makes it hard to be civilized, huh?"

"Yes, sir. Oh, well, better call Brad Keith. You need to keep him in the loop. He'll be the cat to negotiate your rate when this is all over."

"Mr. Keith? There is a Dr. Jenkins on line two. Something about a fishing trip?"

"Oh, good." Keith picked up the phone. "Indie? When we going back to Hatteras?"

"Next time the blues run, I'm gonna call you."

"Hope so."

"Rumor mill says Betty Wilson's gonna hold out for a million."

"No dice, Doc. If they try to get you to sign something like that, I'll come up there myself. You can't go for that."

"No worry. I'm sure Tag agrees. You know what, Brad? I'd like some time. I hope they don't offer anything reasonable for a week or so. Bones thinks we need to see what evidence turns up."

"You want me to talk to Tag?"

"About the case? Yeah. Not about Bones, though. Tag's crawled his butt a couple times for getting too involved. I need to take the boy back down to the river one day."

"Whatever. I'll talk to her. I won't mention your buddy. I wouldn't worry about it settling any time soon. Tag's kept me in the loop. All indications are Betty Wilson's not ready to be reasonable. I doubt she ever will be with Olden pushing her. I've seen mid-trial settlements end many of these, but this one's gonna go on a while."

"I agree. Let's go to Hatteras when this is over."

"Will do."

"Lucille, Brad Keith in Atlanta. How's the Harvey County case?"

"Oh, about usual, Brad. Always a fight, you know."

"I heard from Indie. He wants to go fishing sometime."

"Yeah, well, he's one great big fish story, that's for sure."

"He's heard Wilson wants a million."

"Harvey County is nothing but a rumor mill. I have to go by the facts, Brad. I haven't made it this far chasing fish stories and rumors."

"I know, Lucille. And you have a damn fine track record."

"Well, don't worry. If they want a million dollars there still plenty of fight left in me. I'll never go for that."

"I agree. Indie says he hopes it doesn't settle for a while."

"Really? Why? doctors almost always want out."

"He wants to see what evidence turns up."

"Hm. Okay, but I don't see any movement anyway."

"When we go on that trip, I'm gonna send you some of those blue fish. We're gonna get you hooked on 'em someday."

"Maybe, but you and Indie'll have to go to that pier by yourself. I grew up in the country and I'm not ever going to clean fish again."

"We'll clean 'em for you."

"Good. Send me some."

"Yes, ma'am."

CHAPTER THIRTY SEVEN

Cut the Gig

FRIDAY MORNING. TAG CALLED GIBSON TAYLOR. "Gib, can you meet before court?"

"Sure. Where?"

"Somewhere we can talk in private."

"We'd have to go all the way to Raleigh to get any privacy around here."

"That's the truth. I got us a back room by the breakfast bar."

"Okay."

"What'll you have, sir?" the waitress asked.

"Western Omelet, hold the cheese."

"And you, ma'am?"

"The Continental."

The waitress took up the menus. She looked at Gibson for a minute. "You here about Indie?"

Gibson sat silently.

"Well sir, everyone knows Betty Wilson is a bitch."

"I'll take it under advisement."

The waitress left, and Gibson laughed out loud. "So much for a private room. What's on your mind?"

"Sure you guys don't want to settle this thing?" Tag asked.

"You know I always prefer that."

"Of course." Tag said, and nodded.

"We've almost always found the middle ground, but I've had trouble with this one."

"We all have," she replied. "I need a few days. The trial is nowhere near over anyway, and we're too far apart on the dollars anyway."

"We already know that. What's on your mind?"

"I don't know. My gut says something will break. I think our interests will align better then."

"What are you talking about?"

The waitress brought their order. They waited until she left.

"I got a strange call from Jackson Leggett last night," Tag said.

"Damn, so did I."

"He sure is interested in this all of a sudden. What's Leggett got to do with this?"

"I don't know. At jury selection he said they didn't have dog in the fight. In fact, in our discussions, stated they only wanted to be kept informed. Now though, he seems to have developed a peculiar interest. He expressed concern about how much influence Mr. Olden has on Ms. Wilson." Gibson took a bite of his omelet.

"Inappropriate at best."

"When he talked to me it was almost like he was trying to negotiate for Indie."

"Bless his heart. What did he say?" Tag sipped on her coffee.

"He said Betty had asked for their advice and he wanted me to know he had discouraged that. Said he had kept extensive notes. When this is all over, he wants to be sure it is clear he did his best not to interfere."

"What's that all about?" Tag asked.

"I don't know." Gibson took a sip of water to quench his lips. "Maybe he just wants to cover his ass. Lucille, let me ask you something. What would you say if we came up with a million for Betty, but you didn't have to cough up but half of it?"

"Fine. We'll go home. Who's the benefactor?"

"I feel the hospital should be in it."

"Do you have enough evidence to name them?" she asked.

"My gut says we might. We just need to hold off a while."

"I'd love to find another well to tap," Tag said.

"It's not exactly a well, but give me a few days. Maybe we can cut the gig."

"Cut the gig?"

"Uh, yeah, the gig. Those boys are jamming every night in the lounge. You ought to take in a session."

"You've gone?"

"Oh, yeah, just once for a little while. Don't worry. I haven't heard anyone talk about the case."

"I might do it."

"See you in court."

Taggert went by the room before she left for court. She dialed Brad Keith.

"Brad. I had an interesting meeting with Gibson Taylor."

"What did he say?"

"He's thinking about naming the hospital."

"The more invites to the party, the better."

"Another twist; he invited me to the jam session Bones and all those boys have in the lounge."

"I believe I'd go."

"Brad, you've been around that music some, right?"

"Sure."

"What does the phrase 'cut the gig' mean to you?"

"Oh, that just means someone can play their instrument at the level required, as in: 'He can cut the mandolin gig with the pros.'"

"I see."

"Good luck."

"Thanks. Not much going to break for a while, though," she said.

"How do you know?"

"Maybe just woman's intuition. But I'll tell you, Brad, for some reason Gibson Taylor has the same hunch."

"Hold your cards."

"Will do."

CHAPTER THIRTY EIGHT

Jam Session—Take Three

MOST OF THE REST OF THE WEEK was more scientific testimony. Indie thought it was too much of a bore to have much impact, and Bones suspected he was right. Other matters intervened and caused delays. Judge Hamrick had to see Dr. Cecil with a gall stone attack. One of the jurors was caught talking about the case at the Harvey Methodist, and the trial was held up to clear a replacement.

Tag had a death in the family, and Judge Hamrick granted a delay for her to deal with that. She was grateful for it. At times Harvey County was hard for her to understand, though. When the holidays drew nigh, Hamrick sent everyone home for Thanksgiving, and told them they would reconvene after the New Year. When Tag complained and asked why, he said, "I want to spend the holidays with my family."

She told Indie she had never run into such a thing. He just laughed. "It's like I try to tell Bones. No point to get in a hurry in Harvey County." Indie loved Christmas more than anyone, and was glad for the break. "The only thing I hate is we're gonna come up on the anniversary of Blinky's death," he told Bones. "I hoped it would be over before then."

After the New Year, the case cranked up again. Throughout it all, whenever there was a session in court, it was followed up with a jam session at the Holiday Inn that night. Indie said music was the only thing that made sense at times. Indie and Bones never missed unless they were on call, and Moose came to all of them. The Warbler did most of the lead singing, and Snook usually played the bass, though others filled in at times. Darrell was in a flat-pick mood, and brought his old D18. Elisa Reyes seldom failed to get there. At the last one, she sang *"In the Sweet by and By."* They had never heard it in Spanish.

At some point in the past, Indie had organized most of his tunes into a notebook. There were hundreds of them. He had divided the songs into general categories such as **SONGS ABOUT PARENTS, WANDERING AWAY,** or **GENERAL ROWDY TUNES.**

Indie got out his fiddle on Friday night, and rosined up his bow. Someone had invited the Cherokee Maiden from Waxhaw and she and Indie twin-fiddled *"Lost Indian"* and the *"Shuffle."*

"I wish that B.G.'d come back, through," Indie said. "He was a player."

"Yep," Moose said. "I've got him on the look-out for a flat head for me."

Indie bowed through *"Old Joe Clark"* and then got into *"Whiskey Before Breakfast."* Throughout the trial he seldom got into the **SONGS ABOUT DEATH** section in his notebook while at the Holiday Inn sessions, though they did play some of those at the cabin.

Someone called for *"Catfish John"* and Darrell kicked it off. *"Mama said, don't go near that river, don't be hanging round old Catfish John."*

"Don't go near that river ... Hey, Indie, you're 'bout like *Catfish John,*" Bones said.

"Yeah. Your mama don't want you hanging 'round me."

They drifted into the *"Railroad and Mines"* part of the catalogue and Indie always had to do a few off the **PRISONER AND OUTLAW** list. He sang *"Shackles and Chains"* so sad Elisa began to cry. "It's all right, sweetie, I'm fine." Indie patted her on the shoulder. "Guys, I'm gonna call it a day. I gotta turn in early."

"You okay?" Bones asked.

"Yeah, but it's our anniversary. I promised Ms. Jenkins I'd get home."

"Wish you could stay."

"I ain't a dumb man, Bones." Indie smiled.

The session took a break when Gibson Taylor showed up. He lay out a familiar Calton case. Sure enough, it was B.G.'s Herringbone.

"Lord have mercy man, how much did it set you back?" Moose asked.

"I wish I could say it was mine. B.G. and I barter a bit; I just have it on loan."

"Flat-pick one," Darrell said. "I'll twin you."

They kicked off *"Black Mountain Rag."*

Darrell matched him note for note. "Mighty fine, Mr. Taylor. That's good picking for a lawyer."

"Thanks. I dug the harmony part. Cool. Hey, guys, I invited Ms. Taggert. I hope that's okay."

Elsia spoke up. "She here to help Mr. Indie?"

"Yes, Elisa, she is one of us," Bones replied.

Tag showed up at ten. Elisa greeted her. "You welcome to Holiday Inn. It Friday. We sing all night."

"Oh, thanks, an hour or so will do, though."

"Tag? What you doing here?" Bones asked. "I thought you were a rock 'n roll fan."

"It's like you say, Bones. The Beatles were just bluegrass without a banjo. McCartney loved Monroe."

The smoke grew thicker. Snook had some home brew out in his car and he and Moose went out a couple times. Gibson put his Herringbone in the case to take a break. "How 'bout that synthetic mandolin, Bones? I'd love to see one of those. They might be the wave of the future."

"It's not up for sale yet, Gib. Just a prototype for now. I ain't had a good enough offer."

"I'll bet that thing'll cut the gig."

Tag moved closer.

"I hear these carbon synthetics last forever. If you don't get it out of the case, it's hard to assess its value. What do you think it's worth?" Gibson said.

"Oh, I don't know, maybe—"

"Incoming." Snook signaled a warning.

It was Jim Olden. No one had ever seen him at a jam session. In fact, the only time most people saw him at the hospital was for a photo op; he was never seen near sick people. His picture was in the Harvey Herald every so often; the last time was with a silver shovel to break ground for a new laundry building.

He was decked out in a leather vest and some fringed moccasins. His checkered flannel shirt still had a price tag. His red hair curled out from under a stiff cowboy hat perched on top of his head.

"Hey, boss, that bandanna looks like it's gonna choke you," Snook said. "Matches your hair good, though," he muttered.

Olden tipped his hat to Tag and the Cherokee Maiden and then looked at Bones and Indie. "Gentlemen, I am so glad to see you are inclusive. The ladies make for a much better experience. Do you know *'Cripple Creek'?*"

"Never heard it," Moose deadpanned.

Olden turned to the Cherokee Maiden. "Young lady, I would love to hear you play your violin."

"Yes, sir, what would you like to hear?"

"Why, I'd think as long as you're playing, it should not make any difference what song you might choose."

She broke into *"Maiden's Prayer."* Olden watched her every move. Dark hair and eyes, lovely Native American cheekbones and skin tone. God, Olden thought, *she looks like she's just stepped off some Mediterranean beach.* The top three buttons on her paisley shirt were unfastened enough to flatter, but not too revealing. She wore some subtle fragrance, which wasn't the essence of Old Spice and chewing tobacco that permeated most jam sessions. She was an impressive young woman; the kind of girl fiddler who would inject pandemonium into any jam session. Twenty-two, beyond cute, talented. Olden was smitten.

Moose turned to the Maiden. "Hey, kid, let me hear you sing *'Mother's Not Dead.'*"

"Oh, Moose, that one makes me cry," Cherokee protested.

"Well, now, then you don't have to play it," Olden said.

Snook rolled his eyes.

"It's all right, sir, I can get through it," she said. She began a sad rendition. *"Mother's not dead, she's only a-sleepin'. Just patiently waiting for Jesus to come..."* Tears welled up.

Olden offered her a handkerchief. He turned to Snook. "Molesby, why do they persist in torturing that poor child?" He observed for another minute. "You know, she's looking right at me when she sings. Oh, my," Olden said.

"Right on, boss. I agree." Snook turned to Bones and flashed an okay sign.

Uh-oh, Bones thought.

When the tune ended, everyone laughed. Olden was indignant. Snookers suppressed a chuckle and turned around to walk away for fear he might laugh at the boss.

Olden took the Cherokee Maiden by the arm. "Young lady, let me escort you out of here. Would you care for a drink?"

Dang it, Olden, you are an old fool, Bones thought.

Olden put an arm around her waist, and they went out in the hall. Bones pulled Snook aside. "Dang it, Snook, now no one's gonna get hurt here, are they? I want to hook Olden, but not at the Cherokee Maiden's expense."

"It's cool, Bones. You worry too much."

"Maybe we've gone over the line. I don't want her compromised. She doesn't need to have to change her name."

"She's a black belt in karate. Olden tries anything and she'll kill him. She's just gonna do a little surveillance," Snook said.

"I hope you're right."

Olden stopped in the hall. "Young lady, you should not be in the company of these ruffians. I'm afraid I know all of them."

"Oh, I've been around them, and I agree. Why they have to talk about that case so much, I don't know."

"The case? They are not supposed to talk about the case," Olden said.

"The mandolin, sir?" she replied.

"Huh?"

"The Mandolin Case. They keep talking about a synthetic mandolin in a coffin case. I've never seen them act so strange." Cherokee flipped her long hair around her neck and across her back. "Bones keep saying the case is closed, and he's not going to get the mandolin outta that coffin case. It makes no sense to me."

"Coffin case?" Olden asked.

"Yes, sir. Why are they so worked up?" she asked.

"Has Dr. Jenkins been here tonight?"

"Yes, sir, but he had to go home. Said he felt so bad he wanted to crawl in the grave with his friend Blinky. Dr. Bones told Dr. Jenkins to cheer up, the mandolin was going to stay in the case, and Mr. Blinky was staying in the grave." She paused. "Then he said he was closing the deal with the Gibson mandolin on Wednesday. I thought Bones would never trade his Gibson."

"Wednesday?" Olden asked.

"Yes, sir. I'm sure he said Wednesday. Why would he sell his Gibson?" the Maiden asked innocently.

"Well, dear. Now don't you worry. I can get us a suite, and you can relax a while. I need to make a phone call."

"Oh, no sir, I promised I'd go back to play. They'll come looking for me. Will you be here tomorrow night?" Cherokee asked.

"Yes, dear. I can get us a room. I'll bring you a key tomorrow."

"Oh, thank you. It is Jimmy, isn't it?"

"Jimmy is correct. And they call you the Cherokee Maiden?"

"Yes, but you can call me Darla." She kissed him on the cheek. "Just don't tell them. I'm not one to kiss and tell, you know."

"Oh, neither am I, Darla. I'll see you tomorrow night. Ten o'clock okay?"

"Sure, Jimmy." She gave his waist a playful pinch. "Ten is fine. I look forward to it."

Jim Olden went out to the pay phone and called Jackson Leggett. "Jackson, this is Jim. We have to proceed with the exhumation first thing in the morning. They plan to close a deal with Gibson Taylor Wednesday. Meet me at my office. We need to get on this. I've got plans for tomorrow night. We don't have any more time to waste."

"I don't know, Jimmy. I'd do whatever it takes to get this son of a bitch to settle, I tell you."

"Leggett, you forget who pays the bills."

"Okay. Whatever. I won't forget."

The Cherokee Maiden returned to the jam.

"Are you okay?" Bones asked.

"That man sure is interested in your mandolin. He wanted to see some other things, but I forgot to tell him I'm going home in the morning. When he asks, tell him I'm from Little Washington."

"I will."

"Why did Snook want me to tell him you were selling your Gibson?"

"Just playing a joke on him."

"Well, I think he'd pay a bunch for it if you did. He liked that synthetic one, too. He says he has a lot of money."

"Appreciate the info, Cherokee. Anything else?"

"Yeah. When he asks where I went, tell him you haven't seen Darla today."

"Why do you want me to tell him that?"

"I just want you to watch his reaction."

"Okay."

"See you at MerleFest this year. Tell Kate I said hello."

"Will do. Play hard."

Bones breathed a sigh of relief. He shouldered his case. "Gotta call it a night, boys." Moose and Warb wanted to play a few more, and Gib stayed behind, too.

Tag followed him out the door and down the hall. "Okay, Bones. What's going on?"

"I'm just tired, that all. I can't play all night any more. Too old."

"No, I mean what's all this about synthetic mandolins? Just what gig are you cutting? And who was that woman? Why was Jim Olden here?"

"Looked ridiculous, didn't he?"

"Bones!"

"Meet me at the Waffle House, one bell. Let me call Kate and tell her what I'm up to. News in Harvey County travels fast, you know."

"Good grief, Bones. I'm young enough to be your daughter," she said.

"All the more reason for me to call home, Tag. You know these small towns."

"Okay, Waffle House. One bell, as you say."

"Yes, ma'am."

CHAPTER THIRTY NINE

Consensus at the Waffle House

BONES LOOKED OVER THE MENU. "Pork chops and eggs, over easy. Coffee, make it high test. Large O.J., too. Can I get you anything, Tag?"

"Coffee and whole wheat toast, no butter."

The waitress took her order, shook her head—"Honey, you'll starve to death if you don't eat no more than that."—and waddled back toward the grill.

Better to die slender, Tag thought. "Okay, so what's all this talk about coffin cases? And when did Gibson Taylor take up bluegrass music?"

"I think he's been a player a long time."

"You were not talking about music."

"Sure I was. And I've never known the hospital to have a bit of interest in mandolins, have you?"

"Why do they keep surfacing in this?"

"I'm not sure."

The waitress brought their orders.

"Man, I love their pork chops, Tag. Want part of one? I haven't touched it."

"Quit changing the subject. What have you got to do with this?"

"Me? It ain't got nothing to do with me."

Tag shifted in her chair and looked him straight in the eye. "Bones, let me make this clear. This isn't your case. You tamper with it and you'll pay the price. I'm on the rate committee, you know."

"Ah, come on, Tag. Hey, what if you save the day? Seems to me you can't lose. Indie wins, you get the credit. He loses, it ain't your fault. I'll take the blame if you want."

"So it was you?"

"Well, not exactly. I don't know who engineered it. I'm guessing it was Gibson Taylor."

"So help me God if this case goes bad I'm not going to protect you whatsoever. I am not putting my reputation on the line for some crazy strategy of yours."

"It is crazy, you're right about that."

"Why do you say that?"

"Shhh. You're too loud, Tag. We're riding the highway home. Like General Jackson said: Hold your fire 'til you see the whites of their eyes. Let me talk to you again Wednesday." Bones downed the last of his coffee. "Like the song says, *'Hold whatcha got, I'm a-coming home, baby.'*"

"I have no idea what you are talking about."

"Aw, heck, Tag, I'm just a dreamer. *'Hold to a Dream,'* you know."

"And what is the dream?"

"I don't know."

"Bones!"

"Really, I don't know. I've got a theory, though."

"Oh, never mind." Tag sat back in her seat and brushed her bangs out of the way. "Of all the meddling doctors I have ever met, Bones you are the worst. Most won't even return my phone calls. They just say handle it."

"That's terrible. I can't imagine asking you to try to solve it all by yourself. It must be mighty lonesome."

"Solitude might not be a bad thing. Next time I draw one like you, I think I'll take a vacation."

"You know, Tag, I agree with you on this music thing. Those Beatles were the best, huh?"

"Hush, Bones."

CHAPTER FORTY

Exhumed

DAWN BROKE WEDNESDAY. Bones could not sleep, and put on the morning coffee. Kate came down the stairs to check on him. "You okay?"

"Yeah, I guess so. I'm gonna work on my mandolin some before I go to the office."

"On a Wednesday?"

"Yeah, I've missed a bunch. I won't make a habit of it." Bones noodled through a few bars of *"Some Old Day,"* then put it down to go get the paper.

Warm today for winter. Some drizzle, too. Good, Bones thought.

Indie got up early and cooked omelets for him and Ms. Jenkins. He went out to smoke after breakfast.

Snook slept in.

An hour went by. Bones could not concentrate on the paper. He put it down and picked up his mandolin again. The phone rang. It was Snook. "Good God-a-mighty, Bones. You ain't gonna believe what's happened this morning!?"

"What's that, Snook?"

"Donna took Ranger Dog out for his morning walk, and they's out there digging up Blinky Wilson."

"You're kidding!"

"Nope. Jimmy Olden was out there 'cause Donna said Ranger went right up and started to growl at him."

"Ranger ain't partial to him either, huh?"

"Nope. Man, is this gonna be the talk at the hospital."

"Good gracious, Snook, Blinky deserves his privacy. Can't y'all let him be in peace?"

"C'mon, Doc. A bunch of people were out there. It's gonna be all over town."

"At least try to hold off a few hours."

"How come?"

"Just trust me."

"Well, okay. If you say so."

Bones finished hospital rounds and dropped by Pathology. "Hey, y'all, Dr. Mortimer around? I promised I'd bring him Darrell's new gospel tape. Lord-a-mercy, it's good."

Jeannie, the chief tech, was at the desk. She looked away.

"What's the matter with you, Jeannie? You love gospel music. You look like you've seen a ghost. Aren't you used to dead people by now?"

She scrunched up her neck, looked back over her shoulder and contorted her face. Jim Olden came around the corner.

"Mr. Olden. What are you doing here? I've never seen you down here in Pathology. You seen Dr. Mortimer? He wanted Darrell's new tape. You wanta buy one? Man, it is excellent."

Olden handed Bones five bucks. "You and your music. You and that Dr. Jenkins are just alike."

"Well, thanks for the compliment, Jim. Where's Mortimer? I gotta get to the office."

"He has an important autopsy going on. I expect he'll be finished soon."

"Autopsy? You must have gone up on the rates. I never knew Seymour to have much interest in autopsy work. What's going on?"

"It's confidential."

"Okay, whatever. See you around."

The doors to the morgue swung open. Seymour Mortimer came out. "Mr. Olden. Can I see you in my office for a minute?"

"Yes."

"Hey, Seymour. You want one of Darrell's new gospel tapes?" Bones asked.

"Sure."

"I'll leave one in your box."

"Okay. Thanks."

Olden took a seat across from Seymour Mortimer's desk. Mortimer studied some papers for a moment. "Let's see here, Jim. Yes, the paperwork is in order," Mortimer said. "Gibson Taylor had Betty sign the consent form so I have permission to bring you up to speed." Olden squirmed in his seat. Mortimer looked up. "God, you're as nervous as an expectant father. Y'all sure are close, aren't you?"

"Yes. Ms. Wilson has relied on my advice for some time."

"Damn, Jim. I don't see why this matters to you."

"I am doing my best to protect the hospital's interest here, Seymour."

"Whatever. Let's see. I understand you wanted the results on this lipid-bound Fentanyl level."

"That is correct. I understand it is the definitive test in the event of sudden death secondary to Fentanyl."

"That's right, it is." Seymour coughed. "But, there's only one problem."

"What's that?"

"I don't know why they wanted this thing. It's only a valid test for about a week after the patient dies. After that the lipid undergoes necrosis."

"What does that mean?"

"Necrosis. It goes away. Melts. Lipid is fat. He's been in the grave almost a year now, so there isn't any fatty tissue left to analyze. Blinky didn't have much fat to start with."

"What? Well, hell, do it anyway." Olden got up and walked around to Mortimer's side of the table. "You don't understand, Morty. I have to have this test. Do it!"

"Jimmy, I'd love to help you out, but I'm telling you, man, no pathologist in the country could. It's a great test, but it has to be done in the first week after death. That's all there is to it."

Olden walked back to his chair and slumped into his seat.

Mortimer went on. "Now, this other study they've ordered; it is valid. At least you'll get some answers there."

"What other test?"

"The bone marrow normeperidine level."

"Who ordered that?"

"Hmm. Gibson Taylor, I guess. He's Betty's attorney. Let me check the papers. Yeah, right, here it is. Taylor signed off on it. Let's see. Hey, don't feel bad. He ordered the lipid-bound study, too. He must not have known the difference, either."

"What did you call that other test?"

"The normeperidine level?"

"Yeah. What does that show?"

"Normeperidine. It's a metabolite. Being a synthetic, it is pretty well permanent in the bone marrow after death. It'll tell you for a fact if the man had any Demerol."

"Demerol?"

"Yeah. Why else would you order a normeperidine level? It's metabolite of Demerol. We already assayed it; should have you a result in a day or two. Three days tops. We send them out to T.T.I. That Roger Turner up there is an ace. Arrogant S.O.B., though. Call him if you don't believe me."

Olden turned pale. He put his head in his hands, and then looked up. "There is no Demerol in this case, Seymour."

"Well, if there is, this'll show it. Very accurate. Are you sure you're okay,

Jim?"

"Yeah, yeah. Yeah, I'm okay I guess I am, anyway. I'm not sure. I need to get back to the office."

"I'll give you a buzz when it comes in."

Olden waved a hand on the way out the door.

CHAPTER FORTY ONE

Hospital Named

SEYMOUR MORTIMER HAD AN ANSWER for Gibson Taylor in forty-eight hours. "Mr. Taylor, this is Dr. Seymour Mortimer. I have your results, at least for one of your questions."

"How's that?"

"I'm not sure why there has been so much confusion as to the lipid-bound Fentanyl level."

"Beg your pardon?"

"There was no way to do the assay. No lipids."

"Hm. I guess I'll have to go with my free Fentanyl level. What about the normeperidine level?"

"Yes, sir, it's positive. No question."

"How accurate is it?"

"Oh, ninety-nine. It is a very definitive study."

"When did he get it?"

"Hard to say. A patient will metabolize the drug when they are alive, but at death whatever is in the body stays as a residual. Being a synthetic, it doesn't go away. All you can say is he had it in the last week of his life, most likely in the last few days before he died. I can't get it any closer than that."

"Can anyone?"

"I don't think so. A tox man like Roger Turner might be able to narrow it down some, but not much. The technology is excellent, but it isn't that good."

"Remarkable. Can you fax it over?"

"Hate to co-operate with the enemy, Mr. Taylor, but that's the law."

"Oh, and one more thing."

"Yes?"

"Would you notify Mr. Olden? He has expressed his concern. Betty Wilson signed a release; he has our permission to have the results."

"Sure. I'll make sure he gets the results."

"Thanks."

Gibson hung up and called Tag. "Lucille. I have good news."

"And?"

"We are going to add the hospital to our complaint."

"When did this come about?"

"Today."

"Why the change of heart?"

"Mr. Blinky Wilson has a residual of normeperidine in his bone marrow. The pathologist says this is ninety-nine percent conclusive he had Demerol sometime in the last week of his life—most likely it was in the last few days before his death."

"Demerol? Are you sure?"

"Yes."

"Damn."

"Lucille? Lucille? Are you there?"

"Uh ... yes, Gibson, yes. How did you come to this conclusion?"

"We had Blinky Wilson exhumed on a hunch. It seems it was a good one."

"Damn. Well, thanks for letting me know. I need to call my client."

"Very well. I'll be in touch."

"Dr. Jenkins, this is Lucille Taggert."

"You sure are formal today. What's up?"

"Blinky Wilson."

"Old Blink?"

"Yes, old Blink. Old Blink has a residual of Demerol in his bone marrow."

"Well, I'll be."

"How did Bones know?"

"I don't know."

"Do you think Blinky got it somewhere else?"

"Not likely. Bones took care of him one year when me and Ms. Jenkins went to the beach. Otherwise Blink never saw anyone but me and sometimes Sharma when he was in the hospital. I didn't keep Demerol in my office. Neither did Bones."

"Who do you think ordered it?" Tag asked as she picked up a copy of Blinky's chart. "I've been over it. Sharma never ordered Demerol. I don't see anywhere the record looks altered. Nothing scratched out. Everything else matches up and all the orders are in a logical sequence. Where did he get it?"

"I dunno. I don't know what to make of it."

"Do me a favor, Indie. Call Bones."

"You sure? He's a good boy, but he can be awful meddlesome."

"Call him."

"Yes, ma'am."

Indie put in the call. "I guess you heard the news."

"Yep. I wish I could have seen Olden. Snook said he didn't know if the man was gonna cry or cuss, but he sure was pissed off," Bones replied.

"Does Snook know why?"

"I don't think so. I hated to leave him in the dark but it had to be that way."

"What do you think Olden's got to do with this?"

"I don't know, other than he hates your guts. Everyone knows that. Betty Wilson don't care for you, either."

"No kidding, and Olden's sleeping with her."

"Lord have mercy, What a nightmare."

"You got time to go over and talk to Tag with me?"

"Sure."

Tag was watching the Rolling Stones on television. She turned it off when they walked in. "Bones? How did you know? Where did the Demerol come from and who gave it to him?"

"I'm not sure. I have some theories. The science will be hard to explain to the jury. Dang, I wish we had a witness. Nobody's talking."

Gibson Taylor interrupted them with a phone call. "Betty Wilson is here with me. I have advised her to file against the hospital as a second party in the litigation. She wants to ask you something."

"Fine, Gib, but let me go on record right now. We are in no way bargaining for testimony, and we will not abide by being portrayed as such later. Ms. Wilson needs to understand this is not a trade, got it?"

"Yes, ma'am. I've already talked to her. She understands."

Betty Wilson came to the phone. "Ms. Taggert, this is taking some adjustment for me. I want you to ask Indie one thing, and I want him to swear on it."

"Sure, Ms. Wilson, what's that?"

"Ask Indie if he gave Blinky any Demerol and forgot to write it down," Betty asked.

Tag relayed the message.

"Nope. Swear to God. He got some fifteen years ago and it gave him the heebie-jeebies. He said to never to give him any more and I didn't. I don't know where he got it," Indie replied.

Tag passed it on to Betty.

Betty thought back. "Was that when Blinky said it was like ants were crawling all over him?"

Tag translated.

"Yep." Indie remembered it well. "It took two shots of Vistaril, one of Kenlog, and a Valium to get him down."

Tag recounted those events to Ms. Wilson.

Betty recalled that night. Indie was telling the truth.

"Anything else, Ms. Wilson?" Tag asked.

"Nope," Betty replied.

"Indie?"

Indie paused for a minute and then broke into a grin. Tag hurried to cover the receiver with her hand.

"Yeah," Indie said. "Tell Betty that mole on her left boob is a nice one."

Tag punched him in the ribs. She laughed and then put the phone back to her ear. "Ms. Wilson? Indie said no, he couldn't think of anything else."

"Okay," Betty said. "Let me give the phone back to Mr. Taylor."

"Tag? Okay, sounds like we've covered it. I have advised Ms. Wilson to amend our suit. We have not proven anything yet, but we are going to sue the hospital," Gibson said.

"Tell her I agree with your judgment," Tag replied.

"We'll be in touch soon with the paperwork. Oh, Tag. When we did our background check, we found Indie had some Native American heritage. Is he Navajo?"

"I don't have any idea. I'll ask him."

"Look forward to hearing from you, Gib." Tag hung up. "Indie, do you have some ancestors who are Navajo?"

Bones answered before Indie could speak. "No, ma'am. He's got a little Choctaw, though."

"I asked Indie."

"Bones is right. It's Choctaw on my mama's side."

"Gibson thought it was Navajo."

"I dunno why he would think that," Bones said.

Tag squinted, and twisted her lips into a scowl. She looked him right in the eye.

"I don't know no Navajo, Tag. I swear I don't."

CHAPTER FORTY TWO

Loyalty Realigned

"NOW BETTY, JUST CALM DOWN. This is some kind of mistake. We've got the situation under control, sweetheart."

"Don't you sweetheart me, you fool." Betty paced around Olden's office. "Janie says this is a problem."

"Who?" Olden asked.

Betty Wilson spit out the words. "The beauty operator. Janie. She's the one who told me to hire Gibson Taylor to start with." Betty thought back to the days when they composed the letter to Gibson. "Boy, did she turn out to be right. She said to let you handle it alone would be a conflict of interest. Besides that, it would have been stupid."

"Well, tell Janie not to be talking about the case. Our experts are working on it, Betty. They believe this Demerol theory is bogus; just a smokescreen. It'll blow over."

'Well, it better. Janie says this could get the case against Indie thrown out."

"Oh, not a chance. Not a chance in the world. Don't worry. It won't be thrown out."

"Damn right it won't be. Mr. Taylor wants to name the hospital, and you know what? I'm going to let him."

"Now, Betty, be reasonable. We've been through a lot together. Where's your loyalty?"

"Loyalty? Where's yours? Damn it, Jimmy. You promised me a million dollars, and I'm going to get it one way or another. If that means Gibson Taylor gets it out of your pile of bricks, then so be it."

Olden tried to put an arm around her shoulder, and she pushed him away. "I'll see in you in court." Betty stomped out.

"Damn it, Leggett. They can't add us on in the middle of a trial. You better get down there to the courthouse and find a way to block this thing."

"Jim, I told you we were too entangled in this. We should have been hands off. I tried—"

"Go try harder."

Leggett and Taylor met Judge Hamrick in his chambers.

Gibson spoke first. "Your Honor, we have additional information and request an amendment to our complaint."

"And what is that, Mr. Taylor?"

"Our experts have irrefutable evidence Mr. Wilson received several doses of Demerol, and it contributed to his death. Dr. Jenkins did not order it. We have every reason to believe it was given in error at Harvey Memorial Hospital. They have contributory negligence here."

Leggett interjected, "Your Honor, there is not a shred of evidence in Mr. Taylor's assertion."

"Do you have any documentation, Mr. Taylor?"

"Yes." He handed the judge a copy of the pathology report.

Hamrick read the report and turned to Leggett. "Well, counselor, it's right here in black and white. Demerol."

"Yes, but there is no evidence this happened in the hospital."

"Then where did he get it?"

"Well, we don't ... uh, I'm not certain, but that should be up to Mr. Taylor to prove."

"Isn't that what he is trying to do?"

"Well, yes, but he has to have probable cause."

Hamrick read the paper again. "It looks like he does."

"Now, Judge, we didn't have any say in jury selection."

"I suppose that does present a procedural dilemma."

Taylor spoke again. "Sir, if I may. Here is the documentation. I gave Mr. Leggett the jury list and an opportunity to offer any suggestions. We always consult a local attorney for jury selection." He lay the paper on the judge's desk. "Mr. Leggett was satisfied and signed off."

"But Judge, we did not realize we were going to be added at the time, and—" Leggett protested.

"Is this your signature, Leggett?"

"Well, yes, sir, but—"

"Hell, you had an opportunity to object to anyone on the list."

"But, Judge, you can't...."

"I what? Can't? Leggett, it is my courtroom. I can do any damn thing I want in my kingdom, and don't forget it. However, you are correct on one point. We will have to suspend this trial. I will give you time for depositions and discovery. Mr. Taylor, we will reconvene in ninety days."

"Ninety days?"

"Sixty is customary, but I have some surgery scheduled, and I can't put it off any longer. Ninety days. After depositions, if the evidence is not sufficient, you'll have to drop the hospital's having any responsibility in the case. If the evidence is what it seems, this would have to undergo the scrutiny of the jury."

"But, sir..." Leggett protested.

"Sorry. We'll sort through it. I am a judge, not a despot. It'll have to be heard out. If I don't, Taggert would have grounds for appeal. I'll have a mistrial sure as hell."

When Lucille Taggert heard the news, it was just another day at the office. She had seen the best theories unravel right before the jury's eyes. Still, even the stoic Tag could not hide her elation. "Bones," she said. "I got to hand it to you. How did you know Demerol was involved?"

"Wheatie Willis has few redeeming qualities, but he is an expert on the euphoria of Demerol. I never doubted he didn't get his drug," Bones said.

"Proving Mr. Wilson got it is a different matter, though. Now we have the bone marrow result, though ... Do you think this Wheatie would testify?"

"Yeah, but he's a junkie. They might dismantle him before the first morning recess. Might even be able to turn it against us and try to make it look like we paid him to testify. I wish we could find a more reliable witness."

"Who?"

"So far, no luck. My ace green card is out of the country and no one else is talking."

"Green card?"

"Yeah. Green card. Diosas. You know, 'Sex for Citizenship.'"

"Okay, okay. And where is she?"

"Somewhere in Russia."

"Damn. Bones, you have great ideas, but get me some people. Abstraction won't cut it with jurors."

"Yes, ma'am. Somehow we will."

Indie might have gotten into the Jim Beam if it weren't for Tag being around. He lit a cigarette and blew some smoke out the window. "Not that he was too high on my loyalty list to start, but Olden's done plummeted right off my radar."

"Maybe he's overplayed his hand. You gotta watch him, though. That S.O.B would sell you down the river in a heartbeat to make a dollar," Bones said.

"You ain't telling me anything I don't already know."

Tag spoke up. "I have to agree. He doesn't understand the long-term implications of his behavior. If the medical staff realizes the reward for years of service is a bunch of lies when the chips are down, they'll seek out other options."

Indie blew some smoke rings toward the ceiling. "One of my patients said I know something I ain't telling. He's right. One of these days, I'm gonna write all this crap down."

Tag shook her head. "I can't say I blame you. At least the case moved in the right direction today. But, it isn't over yet."

"Hell, Tag. Olden'll tell lies today to cover the lies he plans to tell tomorrow to dodge everyone next week. He's a pro." Indie put out his cigarette. "I'm just glad to get ninety days to go fishing."

"Ninety days. Dang, if this thing ain't slow as molasses," Bones said.

"Patience, my boy. How 'bout driving me home?" Indie got up and started toward the door, then turned back. "Tag, I appreciate you believing in me."

"Well, Indie, I've learned one thing in this one. You should always believe in a man who can conquer the fiddle. That thing is a beast."

They laughed. Tag was turning into a bluegrasser.

CHAPTER FORTY THREE

Settlement Refused

JIM OLDEN PAGED HIS SECRETARY. "Get Jackson Leggett on the phone."

"Yes, sir."

"Jackson, better get over here. Betty's gone crazy."

"What's up?" Leggett asked.

"Damn if Gibson Taylor hasn't convinced her to add us on. This always happens when the doctor doesn't have enough assets," Olden said.

"I told you we should have let this settle. Damn."

"Well, get over here, we got to get this under control," Olden said.

"What the hell is going on here, Jim? This Demerol thing just doesn't make sense. I can't see where the hospital should have had any exposure."

"You need to be sure we don't."

Leggett arrived and walked straight into Olden's office.

"Hold my calls," Olden said. He closed the door.

"Judge Hamrick agreed with Taylor,"Leggett said. "We have ninety days to get a handle on this."

"Ninety days?" Olden flung his newspaper in the trash. "We had him by the balls and you let go."

"Jim, are you crazy? I'm happy we bought some time. We can't proceed right now. Most clients are glad for any reprieve they can get."

"I expect you to secure our release. We can't lose sight of Jenkins. He is the one at fault here. Greedy S.O.B. Don't let him get away. Nail him now." Olden looked out the window. "Do you realize what it took to build all this?"

"Yes, Jim. Yes, I know." Leggett sat down and tugged at his ear. "I don't know what it is about that doctor that gets under your skin so bad, but you better forget about him and start worrying about the hospital. I'm afraid in ninety days, we'll be in this thing."

"This Demerol theory doesn't add up. And I reviewed the record again; there is no mention of it anywhere," Olden said.

"I agree. It makes no sense, but I understand Taggert has an expert who will testify it is a fact that Demerol killed Blinky Wilson."

"We need to find a way to discredit him."

"Regardless, this will inject doubt into the jury; the last thing we want to do."

"You think it will?"

"You can count on it."

"Yeah, but Gibson Taylor can't push the theory too hard. He knows he will get something out of Jenkins. He won't let up on him," Olden said.

"Maybe. Still, I think we should try to get out of this thing. Let me call Gibson to float a settlement. You know Jenkins wants out. Maybe we should contribute a little." Leggett chewed on his pencil. "Dr. Jenkins was damn good on the stand. I'm afraid the jury isn't going to go for a full court press on him."

"Damn it, Jackson. How the hell did you drop the ball on this?" Olden asked.

Leggertt looked at Olden with an expression close to scorn. "Just let me handle it. If we can get out, we should."

"Well, I am not going to lose to that savage. I want us out, and I want us out now, and I want Indie to pay."

"We might not get everything the way we want, Jim. Did anyone talk to Sharma?"

"Yes. He is positive." Olden stood up and slammed his hand against the wall. "Sharma was the doctor that night. I asked him. He did not order any Demerol. There was no damn Demerol!" Olden sat down again, and was quiet for a moment. He took a few deep breaths. He picked up the phone and handed it to Leggett. "See what Gibson has to say," he whispered.

"Gibson, Jackson Leggett here. How are the wife and kids?"

"Fine."

"And your father?" Leggett asked.

"Oh he's doing well, also. Retired in St. Croix. Plays golf and poker. Once a competitor, always a competitor, you know," Gibson said.

"Yes, well, we have reviewed this Demerol theory at length. There is not a shred of evidence any Demerol is in the case."

"I disagree."

"Yes, well, uh ... at the same time, Mr. Olden is afraid the thing will get so muddled up no one will understand, and the jury will get hung up. He doesn't feel like Ms. Wilson should go away empty-handed. It would be bad public relations for all involved."

Gibson chuckled. "You gotta admire him for sticking by Betty. Is he afraid she'll broadcast the details of his sex life?"

Leggett looked across the desk and cast an eye Olden's way. "Yes, Gibson. I agree. I admire Jim for his loyalty under the circumstances. Let's get together and talk about some numbers."

"Fair enough. Meet me at the Magnolia for supper. Six p.m. You buy."

"See you then." Leggett hung up the phone. "Now, Jimmy, we have an out but you have to leave this to me. I'm to meet Gibson at the Magnolia, six p.m."

"Well, you better do good."

The Magnolia was the only fancy restaurant in Harvey County. It was at the Holiday Inn, and was only open for the evening meal. There were but a few scattered patrons. Leggett got a table near the back with a nice view of the pool, and waited on Gibson Taylor.

"Good to see you, Gibson. Have a seat." Leggett pulled out a chair for

Taylor.

"Not exactly cosmopolitan, huh?"

"Yes, well, when the Holiday Inn has the best restaurant in town ..."

The waitress came to take their order.

"I'm not that hungry. I think I'll just have a glass of tea and a salad." Gibson said.

Leggett ordered the Delmonico steak. He opened. "About settlement, Gibson. We know Betty's number has hovered around a mil, but of course she's being unrealistic. With this confusion injected, I think more along the lines of three-quarters is indicated."

The waitress brought their drinks.

"I understand." Gibson sipped his tea and listened.

Leggett went on. "Well, now. We believe Dr. Jenkins would be happy at five-hundred grand. We are prepared to throw in two-fifty as a matter of good faith. I think three-quarters will cut a deal. This thing could drag on forever, and we'll eat up enough in expenses that we'll wish we'd gone home early."

The waitress brought their order. They ate in silence. Gibson recalled the waltz numbers at the jam session. He finally spoke. "Three-quarters might do it. I can't say what cut Tag will bid. I'll have to run it by her."

"Sure, sure, Gib. No problem. Take your time. Get back with me in a day or two. Care for dessert?" Leggett asked.

"No thanks, not hungry."

Gibson returned to headquarters to call. "Tag. We need to talk. I had dinner with Jackson Leggett tonight."

"What did he say?"

"It seems the hospital has softened up a bit. They will contribute, but only two hundred and fifty grand," Gibson said.

"Two-fifty! Forget it! No way, Gib. With this Demerol the hospital will be out on toward a half mil."

"I thought that's what you'd say."

She clarified her position. "We had a conference today. Indie is confident Demerol is in the mix. He won't go past three-fifty. If they can't make up the difference we can't cut a deal."

"Leggett says Betty will break at three-quarters. You want me to check and see if the hospital will go for four hundred?"

"Sure. Make my day. If Olden has anything to say about it, they'll turn it down, though."

"I'll get back with you."

It wasn't but fifteen minutes and Taylor was back on the phone. "No point to lose sleep over it. The answer is a flat no."

"Oh, well, he had his chance. See you in three months."

"It's about what I expected. If Indie will settle for something reasonable, we'll give it every consideration. Olden might be dumb enough to go for the checkered flag," Gibson said.

"Yep. And it'll be a mistake. He's trying to play cutthroat, but he doesn't have the game."

Gibson Taylor suspected she had a good hand. "I'll be in touch."

"Yes, sir."

CHAPTER FORTY FOUR

Stats and Lies

BONES SWUNG OPEN THE DOOR to the cabin. The screen door squeaked on its hinges, then slammed shut. "Indie? Indie? You home?"

"Hey, boy. Come on in."

"How's Olden taking all this?"

"Mad as hell. Snook said he damn near fired Leggett for not getting them out.

"Gotta love loyalty." Bones laughed.

"Ninety days, Bones, old boy. I don't see how it could have come at a better time."

Bones smiled. "Yeah, it was time for a break."

"Yep. It was time to tend to the roses. I gotta get ready for the cook-out."

It was vintage Indie. Here he was up to his ears in trouble, and he had his mind on the cook-out. Every year he put it on at the cabin for his elderly patients. He invited each one over eighty years of age. The whole band would come and cook on the grill and play music. Indie loved it. As each woman came in, Indie would pin a rose on her and kiss her on the cheek. He would fiddle any request they wanted.

"Indie, you're okay. Here you are worried about your patients' party. Most folks would be worried about saving their ass."

"I'm gonna be old before long. I hope someone will remember me."

"No one's ever gonna forget you, pal."

The reprieve was short-lived, but Indie made the best of every minute. He said it was the best spring he could recall in years.

Indie called Bones at the office. "Hey, bud. They're finally gonna reconvene next week."

"God, these lawyers sure know how to drag things out. I believe I'll get one to plan my funeral."

"It's already hot and it's only May. It's gonna make for a miserable summer."

"Regular damn Hades, huh?"

"I thought summertime was second only to spring for you."

"It usually is. Awh, I ain't gonna let this change nothing. It's only a thing. I hate it might foul up your golf."

"It's too hot, anyway. I wasn't gonna go back to it 'til fall."

"Tag wants to bring McBride back. Can you get hold of him? Is he good to go?"

'Sure. He loves the beach. I can get him a condo lined up."

Tag called Indie Sunday night. "Okay. Indie, your expert Bones found is due up tomorrow afternoon," Tag said. "I gotta give him credit; he was as advertised before. I've talked to him about this Demerol thing, and he's equally impressive on this issue."

"Thanks. I'll call him, too."

"Good luck, Indie."

"Thanks."

"So how was the beach, Larry?" Indie asked.

"Great. Wonderful. The fishing isn't as great this time of year, but I loved the condo."

"Couldn't have you back in town and not get you the best accommodations. Bones knew some golf guy down there."

"Tell him thanks. It was first class."

"Will do. Tag says you're on for tomorrow."

"Yep. Gonna try to make her real happy."

"Good man."

Tag inspected Dr. McBride before his testimony. "Good. I like the lab coat better, Doctor. You can't come across as a high-dollar hotshot, even if you are."

"I haven't worn one in years."

"You will today. You look very professional. The last thing the jury wants is some bluegrass rogue like Indie."

"I beg your pardon!" Indie pretended to be indignant.

"Just teasing."

"I like the gray in the temples, too. Quite distinguished."

"Hey, Tag," Indie asked, what should I do about my gray? Reckon I ought to touch it up?"

"It's too late to change it now, Indie. Everybody in the county knows you. It'd look like a cover-up," Tag replied.

Indie laughed.

Tag put McBride on the stand. She warmed up with some questions to reinforce his previous Fentanyl testimony and reconnect him with the jury. He might as well been a crop-duster pilot on a lazy summer afternoon. They were cream puffs, and he spouted off answers with ease, but then again went so deep into the stats Tag began to worry the jury might get lost. Old man Watson's eyes wandered aimlessly.

Tag feared losing the jury's attention, and decided to get right to the point. "So, Dr. McBride. Did Blinky Wilson receive any doses of Demerol at his death?"

"Oh, yes, ma'am, I am certain of that."

"How confident are you?"

"This is very reliable technology. Ninety-nine point eight percent certain," McBride said.

"And you have no doubt?"

"No doubt. None at all."

Tag produced a sheaf of papers. "These records have been entered into discovery. They are the medication invoices from Dr. Jenkins' office for the two years prior to Dr. Wilson's death. No Demerol. Dr. McBride?"

"I find these accurate. There is no evidence Mr. Wilson had any Demerol as an outpatient."

"Your witness, Mr. Leggett."

Leggett stalked around for a moment, and then began to fire his questions. "Dr. McBride, you say this is ninety-nine percent certain. Is that correct?"

"Yes, sir. Gas spectrograph technology is quite accurate."

"But is it not true, sir, that you can not date the exact time this Demerol was given to him?"

"We can not give the jury an exact time, no sir."

"What window of time is possible, Doctor?"

"With current methodology, it can be narrowed to two weeks, but…"

"Two weeks! Sir, do you mean to tell me this man was in the hospital less than forty-eight hours of those two weeks, and there is no mention of Demerol anywhere in his hospital chart, and now, more than a year later, you claim *these records are* inaccurate? It is well documented, sir." He handed the jury a copy of the medication entries from the hospital. "There is no Demerol in the record. Is it not possible that Blinky Wilson received this medication somewhere other than in the hospital? In fact, is it not likely? Perhaps Dr. Jenkins gave this to him in his office. Everyone knows Blinky Wilson had a substance-abuse problem. So does Dr. Jenkins."

"Objection!" Tag protested.

"Sustained."

Indie scratched out a note to Tag. *You don't diss dead people.*

Tag smiled. Indie was right. Leggett came off as mean-spirited.

Tag intervened. "Dr. McBride is an expert witness in toxicology. We can call witnesses to the stand, but the office records speak for themselves. Dr. Jenkins did not have any Demerol in his office."

"But it is true, is it not, that it could have been given to him at another office?"

"Well sir, the matter has been researched at length," McBride answered in a calm monotone. "Other than one visit to Dr. James Robertson four years ago, Mr. Wilson did not see any other physicians. My understanding is Blinky Wilson was one to stay with the same physician. Ms. Wilson could be sworn in on that matter. I'm certain she would agree. As Ms. Taggert said, I am an expert witness in toxicology, not office notes. However, the defense can produce several witnesses who can speak to the authenticity of these records."

Bones passed Tag a note. *The old pilot can still dog-fight.*

Tag nodded.

McBride resumed. "Years ago Blinky Wilson had an allergic reaction to Demerol. I am not certain why this was not noted in the hospital record."

"Objection. Inadmissible. No documentation of allergic reaction has been entered into discovery," Leggett complained.

"Sustained."

Bones passed Tag a note. *Missed the target that time.* She shrugged her shoulders.

Jackson Leggett returned to the attack. "Again, though, Dr. McBride, there is zero proof any human being gave Blinky Wilson Demerol at any time during his last hospital stay. Is that correct? How do you propose he got it? Down in the cafeteria? By osmosis, perhaps? If it wasn't written down, it wasn't done, and there is no evidence of this whatsoever. Just how do you propose he could have gotten this medication? Magic?" Leggett asked.

"Well, Blinky Wilson did have Demerol in his system. The total dose was somewhere in the two to three-hundred-milligram range. Ninety-nine-point eight percent confidence level. Someone had to have given it to him."

"Someone? Who?" Leggett asked.

Suddenly it hit Bones. *Leggett was out of the loop. Olden had not clued him in.*

"We aren't certain at this point. For all I know, they could be in Russia, but we'll see," McBride replied.

Leggett didn't flinch. Olden turned grayer than Bones' woolly mop of hair. Bones hoped it had sunk into the jury's subconscious.

McBride took a seat, and Leggett called their stat man to the stand.

If one were a numbers freak, Dr. Rollins could be a persuasive fellow. He was a bony little guy with red, scaly skin, a bow tie, black-rimmed glasses, and a seersucker suit. Indie passed Bones a note. *My Barney's got more meat on him than that cat.*

Tag let him have a little rope. He continued his presentation, and his confidence seemed to grow.

Son, Bones thought, *you're gonna get hammered.*

Tag began her counter. "Dr Rollins, you're a man of numbers. A ninety-nine percent confidence level seems fairly high to me."

Rollins lectured. "The sensitivity of this assay is reasonably acceptable. However, the positive predictive value is less reliable. All assays have their limitations, of course, and the normeperidine level is no exception."

"But ninety-nine point eight percent?"

"It can still be inaccurate. The study is only ninety-nine percent accurate if the p-level is less than point oh-five percent." He then proceeded through a maze of statistical analysis. No one on Team Indie followed his logic.

"Dr. Rollins, let's go back to your statement as to positive predictive value."

"Yes."

"Would you restate that, sir? I'm not certain I understood."

"Surely. Even though the confidence level is ninety-nine percent, the positive predictive value for a normeperidine level is only sixty-three percent. One can not state with certainty this man got the Demerol while he was in the hospital. Human behavior is best interpreted by proper statistical analysis."

"Positive predictive value. Are you sure?" Tag asked.

Rollins seemed to waver. He took off his glasses and polished them with a handkerchief, then put them back on. "Uh ... yes."

Tag pushed on. "I'm certain the jury understands this particular statistic is only valuable in the study of a large population of healthy patients who have a low probability of having a given condition. In fact, this particular statistic is only valid in patients who are alive. It is not a valid tool in a dead body. Dr. McBride is well versed in this."

Tag turned to the jury. "So, members of the jury, I submit to you the suggestion that Demerol is not causative in Mr. Wilson's death is false." She projected onto the screen in block letters—GAS SPECTROGRAPH NORMEPERIDINE LEVEL: 943 NANOGRAMS. She again addressed Rollins. "Sir, is there any doubt? Normeperidine is the metabolite of Demerol. Did Mr. Wilson receive any Demerol? Any at all? I would suggest you not quote positive predictive value here."

Rollins hesitated.

"It's okay. You can tell the jury. I know you know the answer." Tag put one hand on her hip. "You can take your time. I have plenty."

"Well, uh, it, yes, it would, perhaps it would seem possible. As we have discussed, we all know no test has one hundred percent accuracy."

"I think the jury can live with ninety-nine point eight, don't you?"

Rollins sat silently.

"Now, sir, I'm certain you realize you have understated reality. Dr. McBride says Mr. Wilson would indeed have had to receive Demerol in the dosage range of two- to three-hundred milligrams, and the odds that this is not accurate are about one in one point three million. Excellent technology. No known false positives, no drug interactions. We'll be happy for you to review the literature at your leisure."

Rollins was out of answers.

Gibson Taylor watched all that, and then got his turn. He had Rollins sit down, and called Dr. McBride back to the stand.

'Dr. McBride, you were a fighter pilot, correct?"

"Yes, sir."

"I understand you were shot down in Vietnam."

"That is correct."

"And you were offered an option for preferential treatment?" Gibson asked.

"Yes, sir."

"But you declined. Why was that?"

"Sir, we communicated in code. Tapped on the walls. They knew I was the instigator. The enemy never did break the code. They would have given me better treatment, at least for a while, if I'd given it up. It would have broken everyone's spirit. I couldn't do it."

"What did you do?"

"They beat me hard. I finally gave them a bogus code. After a few months they got suspicious. I got beaten again. I guess they would have killed me, but we were rescued."

"And you chose not to give in, even though you knew the consequences?"

"Yes, sir."

"And why was that?" Gibson asked.

"Loyalty, integrity."

"I take it you are not much of one to shade the truth for personal gain."

"No, sir. After those S.O.B's tried to break my legs, you lawyers don't scare me too much," McBride said.

Taylor smiled. "No further questions. If the Russians ever get after us, I hope you are there for us, sir." Gibson looked Bones right in the eye as he went by.

Taylor did not bother to ask Rollins even a single question.

Bones was elated at the conference after court had adjourned. "Dadburn, Tag. You took Rollins apart. Where the heck did you learn all about stats?"

"My brother is chair of the department at Princeton. You're a big Twain fan. What was it he said? 'There are lies, damn lies, and then there are statistics.'"

"Well, that Rollins was a loser. He never did give you a straight answer. When the jury deliberates, once it gets down to a yes or no, they have to conclude somehow Blinky Wilson was given some Demerol. Once they do, if we can prove who did it—"

"That's the nagging question, and it's a big one." Tag studied her notes for a moment. "Tell you what, guys, I'm going to retire for the evening. I want to study today's testimony."

Bones reached for his coat. "That Tag is something else, isn't she, Indie? She never gets ahead of herself, does she?"

"These things are never over 'til they're over. She flat ripped the bowtie right off Orville Redinbocker there," Indie said. "Knocked him right outta the box."

"Yeah, how 'bout that line about human experience is best interpreted by proper statistical analysis?"

They both doubled up with laughter.

"That cat almost makes me want to take up smoking cigarettes just to be a little more human," Bones said.

Indie lit up a cigar. "Cohiba?"

"No, thanks. You know what, Indie? I think Gibson is onto the Russian deal somehow. If I just had a human being to connect the dots ..."

"You're right, Bones. Taylor'll bet on a human rather than a bunch of numbers every time. At the end of the day, the poker player's gut will trump every time."

"Yep. I interpreted his faith in McBride the same way."

"It was powerful, but no one knows how a jury will interpret data and science. It's hard to say 'til the vote comes in. Tag did a good day's work, but I could still lose."

"Man, I hate for you to get this close and not take it to the house."

Indie puffed on his cigar and blew some smoke rings. "I ain't worried, Bones. It's just a thing."

CHAPTER FORTY FIVE

Mason Marley's; A Visit from Jim Olden

WHEATIE WILLIS TOOK A BREAK. He was proud of his work on Mason's hedges. They were the neatest ones on the River. They were like a green fortress that surrounded Mason's white frame cottage. Wheatie said they were like one of those moats to a castle he saw on TV. He also kept the grass trimmed and even edged the walkway leading to the front door. Mason said green was pastoral. Wheatie didn't know what that was, but he knew it made Mason happy. Mason also kept roses around back, though not as many as Indie. Her confinement to the wheelchair made it hard for her to tend to them, but Atsa was good to water them.

Atsa came out to inspect. A low wind whistled around and tousled her long gray hair. She signaled her approval, and motioned for Wheatie to come back in the house.

"Are you finished up, Wheatie?" Mason asked.

"Yes, ma'am. I think Atsa is satisfied."

"If Atsa is happy, then I'm happy."

The screen door slammed shut. Atsa came in and kissed Mason on top of the head.

Mason tapped her wheelchair with her cane a few times. Atsa smiled and went to the kitchen.

"I believe I'll go finish up the grass, Mason. I'm glad Atsa likes the shrubs."

"Yes, Lord. You wouldn't want to be on her bad side, Wheat."

"Yes, ma'am."

"Wheatie, let me ask you something. If me and Ms. Atsa needed for you to act like you had a stroke, could you do it?"

"I'd do anything for you, Ms. Mason. You know that. Why would you want me to do that?"

"You know Snookers pretty well, don't you?"

"Yes, ma'am."

"He told me to be expecting a visitor and they were up to no good. Said it would best to pretend you'd had a stroke. Can you slur your speech?"

"Heck, Ms. Mason. A bottle of Thunderbird would do that."

"I mean without the wine."

"I guess."

"Show me."

"Gawdda mighley MIZZZ Mayyshunnnnn."

"Great. We will put you in the play next year. Tell you what Wheatie. If Atsa tells you the enemy has gotten into our castle, you act like you've had a stroke."

"How will I know, Ms. Mason? Most no one but you can understand Ms. Atsa."

"Listen for the ancient tones."

Wheatie scratched his head. "Okay, Ms. Mason. Sure. Uh, I'm gonna go mow the grass."

"Okay."

A black Cadillac pulled in the drive.

"Is this the place?" Olden asked.

"Yes, sir," Snookers said.

"You wait here." Olden walked up the gravel drive and onto the porch. He rapped on the screen door. "Ms. Marley? Anybody home?"

Atsa came to the door. Olden waited. Atsa stood silent in the way.

Mason rolled to the door. "Can I help you, sir?"

Olden took off his hat and brushed back his hair. "Yes, ma'am. Is Ms.

Marley here?"

"Yes, I'm Mason Marley." She tapped her cane a few times. Atsa stepped aside. "May I ask who's calling?"

"Oh, yes. Jim Olden. C.E.O. at Harvey Memorial. We are doing some community public relations work."

"Come in. Have a seat."

Mason wheeled into the den. "What brings you out to the country?"

"Oh, just some P.R. work, Ms. Marley. Good to see you." Olden extended his hand and touched her palm. Marley gave him an unenthusiastic shake. "Is that Wheatie Willis doing your yard work?" he asked.

"Yes, sir."

"I need to talk to him. Our yard man at the hospital resigned. Does Mr. Willis do any larger contracts?"

"My goodness. Up 'til a month ago, he would have jumped at the chance. After his stroke, I don't see how he could do it. We try to give him a little work, you know."

"He had a stroke?"

"Yes, sir. He was at the coast fishing when it happened. They flew him to Sandhills. It's such a shame. He was about to get himself turned around," Mason explained.

"Well, that is a shame. How did it affect him?"

"Oh, it was very strange. Dr. Jenkins called it amnesia. He can remember today just fine, but even a few days back is foggy for him." Mason coughed. "Excuse me. I've got a frog in my throat." She rapped her cane on her chair. Atsa brought some water. "Can I get you anything?"

"No, but thanks. Okay if I speak to this Wheatie?"

"Sure." She tapped on her chair again, spoke in broken English and gestured with her hands. "Ms. Atsa. You ... go ... find Wheatie. Mr. Olden wishes to speak to him." She tapped again. "You'll have to excuse her. Her English is terrible. Why, she doesn't make much more sense than Wheatie does. The poor boy is so garbled up no one can understand a word he says."

Atsa brushed away a tear. "I go." She tapped on Mason's wheelchair.

"She says she thank you for your concern for Mr. Wheatie and she'll fetch him. I should warn you. He is very difficult to understand. The stroke affected his speech. Slurred, you know."

"Well, that is too bad." Olden stopped to admire the picture on the wall. "Who's the young lady, Ms. Marley?"

"Oh, that was my cousin around the time of W.W. Two."

"Pretty girl. Does she live around here?"

"No, she's died."

"That's too bad. Quite attractive."

Atsa came back in the room and took the picture down. She sprayed it with Windex, rubbed it with a cloth, and took it into the kitchen.

"Well, I suppose I'll be on my way. I'll speak to Mr. Willis on the way out."

"Oh, before you go, Mr. Olden, you wanted to ask about public relations?"

"Public relations? Oh, yes, yes. Yes, Ms. Marley. The Board wants us to do an extensive survey. How does the hospital look in the public eye?"

"Oh, quite good, Mr. Olden. The medical staff is well respected. You know, it's funny you ask. The beauty operator was in the other day and she said it: "You can't help but love old Indie.""

"Does he have a problem with women?"

"Oh, no. He's a sweetheart. He's like everybody's daddy, and very loyal to his wife. Did you know, one time Betty Wilson tried to get him to sleep with her at the country club?"

"No, I wasn't aware of that." Olden's ears turned red. "I see. Well, I'll go out and speak to Wheatie, and then be on my way."

"If he goes to work for you, he still has to do my yard," Mason said. Mason called for Atsa. She signed to her, and then wrote a note. Atsa left to get Wheatie.

"Sure I can't get you anything to drink, Mr. Olden?"

"No, no. I must be on my way. What's taking her so long?" Olden got up and began to pace.

A low guttural moan echoed.

"God, what was that?" Olden asked.

"What?" asked Mason.

"That noise?"

"Noise? I think it was just the wind, sir."

"I guess. My Lord, it sounded awful."

"Yes. It comes in off the river here quite often."

In a minute Atsa arrived with Wheatie Willis at her side. Mason rolled toward the kitchen. "If you would excuse me for a minute, Mr. Olden." She tapped her wheelchair. "Atsa?" She tapped her chair. "We'll let you gentlemen talk." Atsa followed her out of the room.

Olden spoke with Willis a minute. Wheatie's speech was garbled, and Olden grew impatient. "You get your damn Indian friend to tell Marley I left." He went out to the driveway and climbed back in his Cadillac where Snookers waited.

"Drive me home, Molesby."

"Yes, sir."

"That Willis is in bad shape."

"Yeah, I heard he had a stroke. Too bad."

"Well, Molesby, you can't count on house painters or yard men. Unreliable."

Snook drove on.

"Damn." Olden muttered.

"Sir?"

"I wish I'd known Willis had a stroke. Leggett finagled Hamrick to give us the whole damn summer off to figure out what to do...."

"Dang, boss. If I'd a known you needed to know I'da told you. How come it matters?"

"Oh, uh well, uh ... you see, our yard man at the hospital didn't fulfill his contract. Leggett was going to hold him to it, but...Hell, we could have wrapped this up if Leggett had done his homework... Little S.O.B. leaves it to me to figure out everthing..."

"Sir, you have important things to do. You shouldn't have to worry about who the yard man is..."

"The yard man?"

"Yes. Didn't you say Leggett was gonna have to look into why he broke his contract?"

"The yard man? Oh uh, yes. Yes, the yard man.... Oh well, never mind. It doesn't matter."

"Sorry, Mr. Olden. You're right. You can't trust a yard man. They shouldn't have made you worry about it."

"Damn right, Snookers. Right. Yes, that's right. Well, we'll get it squared away by fall. Could you help us some with the mowers?"

"Yes sir. Wheatie sure can't. No doubt, Wheatie ain't worth a damn to anybody anymore. At least before his stroke he could tell some great stories. Now it ain't nothing but gobble-de-goop." Snookers drove on. "This Caddy is some good wheels, Mr. Olden."

Olden called Leggett as soon as got back to the office. "Jackson, Olden here. Damn it, with what I pay you, you could do a decent background check."

"What are you talking about?"

"Wheatie Willis."

"Willis? He hasn't had a decent job in years. I am certain he can be bought. He'll be on board after one summer of mowing the grass."

"For God's sake, Leggett, the man can't talk! He's had a stroke!"

"You're kidding!"

"Nope. You need to go back to Hamrick and see if he'll cancel the delay."

"Jimmy, you must make up your mind. I got you a reprieve for three months when I told him your aunt in New Bern was dying. I can't just go tell him there's been a miracle."

"You know what I hate the most about this?"

"What's that?"

"Now that damn Indian will be down on the river fishing and won't think a thing about it. I will have to worry about this all summer. Dammit."

"Sorry, Jim."

Willis finished up the yard. Atsa went to inspect, and then came back in the house. Mason called out through the window. "Atsa says they look wonderful, Wheatie. Come on inside."

Mason went to the pantry and retrieved a bottle of Oban. "What did Mr. Olden have to say?"

"I did just like you said, Ms. Mason. We couldn't carry on nary no conversation. I figure it's this durn stroke," Wheatie said.

"You reckon?"

"Yeah, I tried to tell him what happened to me, but he said he couldn't understand a damn word I said, and then he laughed. Nice man, huh?"

"Compassionate, sure enough, Wheatie. Here's something for you." She handed him a bottle of Oban.

"Miss Mason! That's your best."

"Well, don't gulp it, then, Wheatie. If you just have to get drunk, go with your Thunderbird. This is for sipping,"

"Yes, ma'am. Thanks." Wheatie cradled the bottle of fine Scotch in his arms like he was to carry home a baby. "I'll be back in a couple of weeks." Wheatie stopped on the front porch and turned around. "Miss Mason, you think Indie will be okay?"

"Yes, I do. You struck a lick for him today."

"You think I'll have to go down to the courthouse? It makes me nervous. I'll go if it'll help Mr. Indie, though."

"You might not have to testify."

"I hope not. Me and the missus just got everything all good, and they'll turn me inside out. I don't think she'll give me too many more chances."

"Don't worry, Wheatie. If you do testify, you can credit Indie with your recovery from your stroke. Mr. Olden won't know what to think."

"Whenever I'm in the hospital Indie's the only one who knows how to treat me."

"Yeah, you can't get by without your Demerol in the hospital, huh, Wheatie?"

"No, ma'am. And I remember that one day when that little foreign girl didn't give it to me, it pissed me off. You know, Olden's girlfriend."

"That's what I hear, Wheatie. That's what I hear. I wouldn't tell anyone, though."

"Yes, ma'am."

CHAPTER FORTY SIX

Cabin in the Pines

"HEY, MS. JENKINS. INDIE AROUND? Thought he might want to pick a little tonight," Bones asked.

"No, he went to the cabin. I was glad to see Friday get here. I don't think he could have taken another day of court. I'm worried about him. I don't think I've ever seen him so serious," Ms. Jenkins said.

"I missed today. I had to see some patients. But I talked to him at lunch. He seemed okay. Nothing went wrong this afternoon, did it?"

"No, I think he's just worn out. It's been a long week."

"He wouldn't hurt himself, would he?"

"Of course not. Well, not on purpose, anyway. But he is drinking too much. He always does in the fall. I can't believe they've let this drag on so long. They say in the beauty shop that it's Mr. Olden's fault."

"I don't know. Sometimes the system throws up more roadblocks than a police manhunt, though."

"I sure wish you'd go check on him."

"Sure, Ms. Jenkins. I'd be glad to. I'll call you when I get back."

"Thank you so much, Bones. Your wife doing well?"

"Yes, ma'am."

"Well, good. If he wants to stay out there tonight please call me, and I don't care how late it is."

"Yes, ma'am."

The moon was full, and Bones took the low road down by the river. It was a shortcut and full of potholes, gravel, and ruts. Everyone called the route *Old Rough and Rocky.*

People used the low route when they wanted to slide in unnoticed or didn't want to drive through the State Park. Indie was most likely half drunk, and Bones did not want to spook him.

The road was so bad when he got down to the last five hundred yards he parked and walked on foot under the moonlight. There was a strange car in the drive. Then he tripped and fell.

What a gosh-awful noise. Tree branch. Dang, this road is horrible.

The branches and twigs went off like firecrackers under his feet as he tiptoed along. That car looked familiar. A new silver Impala. Where had he seen it? What the heck was it doing down in the woods? Most everyone came in on the low road by truck or four-wheel drive. Bones knew everyone in the local music crowd, and it didn't belong to any of them. Indie's '47 Chief motorcycle rested up against the house, so he was here, but who else was?

They had to have come by way of the longer high road. Oklahoma plates. Way out of state. Who was this? *Dadburn that Indie. He better not be down here with no woman.* Indie swore he gave that up after the French foreign exchange student years ago. It took Ms. Jenkins a long time to get over it, and Bones was in no mood to mediate with her on that kind of issue. *Dangnation, what in the world am I going to tell her?* One window cast a light. Bones eased up to it. He pulled up and looked just over the sill.

Oklahoma plates. Damn. *Wait a minute. He was supposed to be out of town. What in the hell is he doing here? What is Indie thinking?* Bones ducked down. What am I doing here? *What the hell am I thinking, getting mixed up with that crazy Indie?* He eased back up on the window sill, grabbed it with his fingertips, and, like Kilroy, pulled up and again peered inside. There was Indie with his fiddle, and the two were jamming away. He slid back to the ground. They were engrossed in the music, and Bones went unnoticed.

What to do? Maybe just go home. Lord have mercy, even a sober Indie was in no position to negotiate with B.G. The man was a trained negotiator—and Bones had a notion it was not just in bluegrass instruments. *What a mismatch. Shoot, I've got to listen in. If B.G. was to paint him in a corner, maybe Tag could cry foul.*

Around back there was an out-of-service stovepipe that used to be hooked up to the old wood heater. Unless Indie had fixed it, it would serve as a perfect conduit for any conversation in the room.

Bones eased around back. The stovepipe was still propped up on top of the well house, just as it had been for years. Bones was glad Indie had not gotten around to any home repairs. He bent down, put his ear to the end of the pipe, and listened.

They were playing *"Cotton Patch Rag."* Indie rendered it mighty fine and B.G. was an excellent guitar man. He backed Indie up and chunked out some smooth Texas chord-walking- type progressions on his old Herringbone Martin. He wished he'd brought his mandolin. Bones' foot went to tapping. He was caught up in the moment, and then realized he was stomping the dry leaves. They didn't hear him. Maybe they were just going to play. Bones debated joining in, but did not want to 'fess up he came by to check on Indie, so he decided after one more he'd go.

The music stopped. B.G. started talking. Bones listened.

"Oh, my, Indie, now that was extra good."

"You played the finest flat-pick guitar I've heard since Doc Watson was in town. How 'bout another home brew?"

"I'd better leave it at one. Didn't you say there was a shorter way back out of here?"

"You don't want to go that old pig path. The ruts and branches will tear up that Chevy of yours. Someone might figure where you'd been tonight. You're welcome to spend the night. Don't know when the sheets were washed, though," Indie offered.

"Better not. Appreciate it, but I don't need to push my luck. I'm only in town a few hours. Headed out for Sandhills tonight. Got business early in the morning. I reckon I'd better split after another one."

"You mean another brew or another tune?" Indie asked.

"Better stick with the tunes. D.U.I.s and my business don't mix so good."

"Well, I'm gonna have one more before I turn in. I'm staying here tonight;

I'm too old to get that motorbike outta here in the dark. I don't reckon a third beer would hurt old Indie since I ain't gotta drive."

At least he was not drunk. Bones started to think about leaving when B.G. said, "Indie, I wish there was some way to get you out. My man has tried hard, but Ms. Wilson is adamant that everyone contribute. He has to be loyal to her, you know."

Oh no. They were talking about the case.

"Awh, hell, B.G., it's okay, I understand," Indie replied.

No, it isn't, Bones thought. *What are you saying? Lord, Indie, you didn't do anything wrong. You could get out altogether.*

"Look, I think they can split you out for a hundred-fifty grand. Man, I've run the best intelligence on this case for Gib we've ever have. We believe a historic verdict is in the works. The Navajo says you don't need to be there at curtain call."

"I appreciate that. I just don't think one-fifty will cut the gig with Betty. She's still mad as hell. As long as I stay under two-fifty, I can avoid the rate hike in my insurance fee structure. How 'bout two forty-nine?"

What the hell kinda negotiation is this? Damn, Indie, you sure you've only had three drinks? Bones was upset, but under the circumstances, had no choice but to be quiet and listen.

"Now, look here, Indie. Our contacts think we know Betty's mind as well as anyone. If Taylor comes in over two hundred, our intelligence says she'll be satisfied. Hell, if it weren't for the fact that the law requires a fifty-fifty split at the end, I'd tell you to stay in and see it to the end. It's just too dangerous, man."

"I understand. I ain't got half of several mil. There is one favor I'd like to ask of you."

"Sure, Indie, what?"

"I want my settlement to benefit Blink's grandchildren. Betty getting all that money bothers me. She don't need it, and besides, she should get a pile from the hospital. Maybe we could do some kind of scholarship for the boys. A couple hundred grand would send both of 'em anywhere they want to go, and they are smart as little whips. She's been estranged from them a while, and I know she wants a way to get 'em back. Immogene heard it at the beauty shop."

"Will do, Indie. I don't see a problem with that at all."

"Thanks. It'd make me feel better about it."

"Now you know, Indie, we still project you could escape this thing."

"Too big a risk."

"I agree. It is low probability, but I just want you to have all the facts. I tell you, the last thing I want is for the hospital to take a tumble and you to get buried in the rubble."

"Yeah, I ain't much in favor of that, either." Indie laughed.

"Of course Physician's Liability could take the hit better than you, but if it got over your limits it could break the bank for you."

"It wouldn't take much."

"The crazy thing is it's in the hospital's best interest to get out, too. Olden just can't see it."

"He's ABCDA."

B.G. laughed. "A Board Certified Dumb Ass, right?"

"Yep."

"If it wasn't for that substitute juror they brought in I might say take a chance."

"I shoulda known she was a ringer."

"Honest to God, Indie. We didn't know she was out to get you for your drinking."

"It's okay. We missed it too. Bones found out and pitched a fit, but she was already in."

Dang right I did.

"He might be a bit naïve, but he's a good boy."

Shucks, Indie.

"Gibson says the nice guys are the ones he worries about." BG thought a minute. "So, how did y'all find out about the juror?"

"Snookers ran into her at the liquor store. Judge Hamick wouldn't boot her, though. Bones was tore down for days. He knew it was going to be a problem."

Damn right. That woman is a hypocrite.

"Of course, Gibson will have to run it by your attorney, but I feel Betty will want out, too."

"I think she'll go for it," Indie replied.

"I agree."

Bones heard them stand up. There was silence like they shook hands.

Dang. I gotta get outta here.

"B.G., I gotta ask you: This ain't illegal, me and you talking, that is? I mean, you're not a lawyer, so I guess it's okay," Indie said.

"There ain't no law against looking at a Martin guitar on a moonlit night is there, Indie?"

"I guess not."

"At least the Cherokee Maiden wasn't violated," Indie said.

Thank goodness for that.

Bones heard them walking to the door. "Can you believe that Olden?" Indie asked.

"That girl could not have one bit of interest in that old man." B.G. shook his head. "I ain't a lawyer, but me and you gotta be like the CIA, brother."

"Yep. Friends can be enemies and enemies can be friends," Indie replied. "Hm. Two hundred, it is. Let's see if we can live with it."

If Indie could, Bones guessed he had to. It still didn't seem fair.

"Deal." They changed their minds. "How 'bout let's play one more good'un?" B.G. asked.

"Sure, what'll it be?"

"I like 'Cherokee Shuffle?'"

"Maybe 'Lost Indian?'" Indie countered. Both men laughed, and they commenced to playing. Indie fiddled it good. Bones listened to a few bars, and then decided it best to leave. He snuck back to the Scout, and crawled out old Rough and Rocky with the headlights off.

Once back out on the blacktop, he turned his headlights on and headed home.

He stopped by Indie's. Ms. Jenkins came to the door.

"How is he, Bones?"

"Fine, Ms. Jenkins. Sleeping like a baby. I tucked him in before I left."

"Thank you so much." She turned to go back in. "I appreciate you checking on him. Now I can rest."

"Yes, ma'am."

CHAPTER FORTY SEVEN

High Ball/Low Ball

BONES STRUMMED A TUNE ON HIS OFFICE Martin on Monday morning. Both Bones and Indie had a an office guitar; when the power went out, elderly patients often got scared. The music always calmed them down.

"Dr. Bones, Snookers Molesby is on line one and says it's urgent."

Snook and Bones had a code; urgent for a golf game, imperative for medical, and emergency for music.

Bones placed the Martin in the case, and crooked his neck to hold the phone in place. "What's up, Snook? You on for the choose-up Wednesday?"

"Naw, man, we gotta bail on our regular gig. Hospital business. Olden wants to play the club."

"Jeez, count me out. The only thing that cat ever does at the club is swim in Speedos to try to pick up women, or play senior bingo on Friday nights. He's no golfer."

"Olden wanted me to get you. This is gonna be a drag. Don't make me go alone."

"Good Lord ..."

"He said no business allowed, it was just golf; at least if that's what you call it."

"Man, don't drag me into it. I have to see him enough at the hospital."

"C'mon, Bones. You ain't gonna make me go alone are you?"

"The things I do for you. The man can't break a hundred."

"Thanks, Bones. I knew I could count on you."

"Wait a minute, Snook. I didn't say I'd—"

"See you there. Bring your one iron. The wind is supposed to be up."

"You're the only cat in town who can hit a one iron; I sure can't."

"We might get a shower."

"Okay, I'll bring my rain gear."

"No, bring the one iron. You know what Trevino said: 'If it's lightning, hold the one iron over your head—even God can't hit a one iron.'"

"I'll pack the rain gear. What's the tee time?"

"Nine-fifteen."

"See you."

Wednesday morning saw an early drizzle but the rain slowed and the sun began to peek through clouds. Snook and Bones got to the clubhouse a half hour early to hit a few balls.

"So what's the story on the golf game?"

"Hate to tell you, Doc, but we'll be on opposite teams. The good news for you is I gotta play with Olden."

"It's the burden you have to carry. The boss knows you're the best player at the hospital. So, who's he got me paired with?"

"Jackson Leggett."

"Leggett! That's it, brother, I'm out. I forgot, but I promised Kate I'd take her to the mall in Richmond. Sorry, I'm all booked up." Bones put his club back in the bag and began to take off his glove.

"Come on, Bones. I promised Mr. Olden."

"I gave up those six-hour rounds years ago, Snook. This is gonna be a long day. I'm afraid to ask, but what kind of game does Leggett play?"

"'Last Cheater's Waltz,' Bones, and he can't break a hundred, either."

"Mercy, Snook. If it were anybody but you I'd bolt."

"It is me, though. Remember? You got a high school state championship trophy at home 'cause I shot sixty-eight the last day."

"I guess, Snook. So, what game are we gonna play?"

"High ball-low ball. Mr. Olden said he wanted it to keep everyone in the game. It's okay by me; harder game for him to cheat at."

"High ball-low ball? Shoot, Snook, you're at least three shots a side better than me. I might as well go ahead and concede the low ball to you now."

"Don't worry, Doc. I told Olden it would be unfair to you without three a side on the low ball. He said that was okay."

"Magnanimous S.O.B., huh? You gonna rent him some clubs?"

"I reckon."

"Snook, I feel like I'm part of a Black Sox scandal here."

"Yeah, well, Shoeless Joe was just a country boy who did his best. You're a country doctor; you do the same."

"You know, I've always thought Joe was innocent, but he never made his way back to the big time. In the end he ran a liquor store in Greenville, South Carolina."

"You'll be okay. You don't need to apply for a liquor license yet."

Olden and Leggett arrived at the last minute and went to the first tee without so much as a warm-up shot.

"Good morning, Dr. Bones, so glad to see you." Jim Olden shook Bones' hand like somewhere between a used-car salesman and a bad tent evangelist.

Bones smiled. "About to clear off, huh?"

Olden took control. "Indeed it is, Bones. Let us see, now, Mr. Molesby here is our resident golf expert. What game shall we arrange today, sir? Keep in mind that we must play fair. We are all family, you know."

"Mr. Molesby?" Bones cast a glance in Snook's direction, but looked away before he laughed. No one ever heard Olden call Snook Mr. Molesby.

"Let's see, the only game I can think of that might be fair would be high ball-low ball," Snook replied.

"And what is that?" Leggett asked.

"It's a great game, 'cause it keeps everyone in it. Straight up wouldn't be fair, but in high ball-low ball the team gets one point for having the low score, and one point for not having the high score."

"Better than cutthroat, I guess," Bones said. "Okay, Snook. Fair enough, but I can't quite hang with you; the low ball is a lost cause."

Olden weighed in. "Now gentlemen, we want to play fair. I have a reputation to protect, you know. It seems to me for it to be even, we should allow Dr. Bones three shots a side."

"Hm.......Okay, Mr. Olden. If you and Snookers say it's fair, I'll take you at your word. High ball-low ball it is. Three shots a side off the low for us. Okay, I'm in. Sort of like the CIA," Bones muttered.

Olden conceded the honor and the game was on. Leggett teed up first. Bones later told Indie Leggett made a gawdawful lunge on the first swing, and gouged a weak slice about 150 yards into the right rough. Bones hit his standard trap hook, about two-forty into the left cut, but was okay.

As bad as Bones' team looked, Snook was even worse off. Olden whiffed his first shot, then air-mailed the second ball out of bounds. The high ball was conceded before they left the first tee. Snookers cracked his tee ball 270, and straight down the pipeline. It was one of those Arnie-like trajectories, akin to a jet airplane that just avoided the end of the tee box on take-off. The ball cheated the wind, ascended into the horizon, and then fell dead center in the fairway. Snook birdied, and Bones made par. The teams were all even.

The front nine was a slow bore. Snook slouched over a club in the middle of the fairway, smoked cigarettes, and waited on his partner to catch up. Olden and Leggett saw a lot of the course that was unfamiliar to Bones and Snook, but somehow both of them turned in a questionable 48, just over bogey golf. Bones scrambled to an ugly 40. Snook carded an even par 37, and the match was all square. Olden offered lunch on the hospital ticket.

Olden excused himself for a moment, and Leggett lay his cards on the table. "You know, Bones, I like this high ball-low ball game. Very fair. Hard for anyone to get hurt too much, don't you think?"

"I guess. Better than cut-throat, I reckon."

Snook excused himself to go smoke.

"Agreed, agreed. You know, Bones. It's a lot like legal high-low agreements, huh?" Leggett asked.

"Jeez, Mr. Leggett, I've never heard of that. What's that?"

Leggett laughed. "Well, Bones, when all parties wish to be fair, and know that juries are not sophisticated enough to understand these cases, it is often a solution that protects the doctor from devastation. We are concerned for your friend, Dr. Jenkins. Yes, I know he has been an adversary of Olden's for years, but Jim does not wish to see Dr. Jenkins humiliated."

"I don't get how a high-low would help Indie."

"Very simple, Bones. We are all gentlemen, and experts in these matters. In complex cases, we can decide on a low, say a half million, and a high, perhaps of one. We all agree ahead of time. Then, no one gets hurt, and the patient's family is guaranteed a settlement. After all, juries can not be trusted, you know. If they return a judgment of several million, it will be limited to one, they just don't know it. By the same token, if the jury doesn't get it and stiffs the family, at least the loved ones don't go home empty-handed. We'll have to split it fifty-fifty at the end anyway, but we'll all know what we'll be out before the jury does," Leggett explained.

"I don't know, Mr. Leggett. That's all interesting, but are we supposed to be talking about this? Besides, I'm only a country doctor, and Indie's friend. I don't have any say so."

"Understood, Bones. Understood. Still, as his friend, don't you think you owe it to him to make sure he understands the concept?" Leggett asked.

"Yeah, I guess so, Mr. Leggett."

Snook finished his smoke and took a seat.

Olden returned to the table. "Now, no business allowed today, gentlemen."

The back nine was more of the same; Leggett and Olden looked more like they were killing snakes with shovels and wielding weed whackers than playing golf. Snook was close to his average game, but off his feed a bit. Bones played his usual par/bogey/occasional birdie golf. By the last hole the match was dead even.

Olden and Leggett hit a couple worm-burner tee shots, and Snook powered another beauty. Bones was up last. The wind was at their back, and he managed a high power fade that rode the wind and came up only ten yards short of Snook's ball.

By then Snook and Bones had set out on foot, and left Olden and Leggett to ride alone. They trudged up the hill, and Snook glanced over at Bones. "Nice power fade, there. Not your usual game."

"I can learn some new shots."

"I reckon. Martin Taylor still in St. Croix?"

"Yep."

"You ever fly?"

"Nope."

"Doesn't Taylor hit a power fade?"

"I dunno."

"Sure you ain't been flying?"

"Positive, ever since I saw that CIA documentary, I'm scared of small planes."

By the time the boys caught up with them, Snookers and Bones were at the 150 yard marker. Snook puffed on his cigarette and waited.

"Snook, ole buddy, I gotta get you off those things one of these days." Bones pulled out a seven, hit it only fair, and thinned it pin high and left.

"I know, you're right. One of these days, I'm gonna give 'em up," Snook replied.

"I know you've done it a bunch of times."

Snook put out his smoke, walked a few paces, and surveyed his ball. "Whaddaya think from here, Bones, eight?"

"Maybe for me, Snook. I scraped my seven a bit, you better hit nine. The wind's at your back; you don't have to step on it."

Snook pushed to the wrong side of the green. He left himself a downhill, side-hill, right-to-left putt he did not prefer.

Olden and Leggett made it to the dance floor in four each. Olden lagged to a few feet and knocked it away. "In the leather, boys, I'm good for a double."

You can't argue with the boss, and no one objected. Leggett three-putted, and the high ball point went to team Olden. It was left to Bones and Snook.

Snook was away. He tapped it down the hill. The ball rolled so slow you could read the TITLEIST as it went by. It touched the hole, but lipped out.

Bones bore down and rolled his putt in. It won the low ball, and the match dead even.

Snook took the pencil from behind his ear, ciphered to be sure of the score, and then handed Olden and Leggett the card. "Team captains need to sign, but it's a done deal. All slick, gentlemen, good match."

Olden and Leggett signed.

After a few drinks at the nineteenth hole, they seemed anxious to leave. Olden headed for the car, and Leggett stopped to remind Bones of the deal. "Enjoyed the game, Bones. Good play. I like it when a man plays fair and is aware of all his options," Leggett said. "Give Jenkins my best."

"Okay, Mr. Leggett, I will, but just as a friend. I don't know nothing 'bout all this legal stuff."

"Good. Good." He patted Bones on the shoulder.

CHAPTER FORTY EIGHT

Post-Game Wrap Up

BONES AND SNOOK PUT THEIR CLUBS in the trunk, and sat in the parking lot and waved at Olden and Leggett as they drove off.

"In spite of the company we kept, I enjoyed the game, Snook."

"Mercy, can you believe those cats? If I couldn't play any better than that, I'd have to concentrate on my bowling. Damn. Let's go over to the B-&-B."

They stopped at the counter to order. "What do you want?" Bones asked.

"How 'bout a bacon Swiss cheeseburger basket and a Coke?"

"Sure. Hey, Lou, we'll have a couple Swiss CB baskets."

"Sure enough, Doc."

"On me, Snook, I learn something about the game every time we tee it up." Bones slid Lou a twenty.

"Professional courtesy today, Doc." Lou handed the money back.

"Come on, Lou. You can't run a profitable establishment like that."

"It ain't on me, Doc. Indie covered it. He said he hoped you boys played good. He's betting on you in the Member-Member."

"I see. We were slick."

They got their order and found a table.

"That was some kinda golf today, don't you think?"

"I don't know if I'd call it that." Snook reached for the ketchup. "I'm glad

Olden didn't ask for any swing advice."

"What would you tell him?"

"Take two weeks off and quit. Whadda you tell a man with a swing like that?"

"I gotta ask. Did you miss that last putt on purpose?"

"Hell, no, Bones. I ain't never gonna lay down on ya."

"It doesn't matter to me, but if I hadn't made mine, team Olden woulda won. I've never known you to throw a game."

"You forgot, Bones. You didn't have to make it. That was a stroke hole—unless you'd three-putted, the game was over. It just worked out even, that's all. But to tell you the truth, it was a hard game to get into it; that warn't golf today."

Snook ordered a second cheeseburger. He looked up. "Well, hell, Bones. I ain't worried about them tri-gly-ciderides. You gotta die of something." He smothered his fries with ketchup. "Like Indie says—one of the four food groups." He hollered for Lou to bring another bottle. "Hey, Doc, what was that they said about helping Indie?"

"Huh?"

"Leggett. I heard him say he wanted to help Indie."

"I don't know what he was talking about."

"I bet Mr. Olden didn't, either. He'd be pissed if he knew that little fellow was gonna do anything for Indie."

"I don't think I'd spread that around, Snook."

"Yeah, I wouldn't want Mr. Olden to get mad at him. He didn't seem that bad to me."

"Yeah. I better split. I'll try to hit a few balls before the Member-Member."

"See ya, Doc."

Bones went by the office to make a call. "Tag? Anything going on?"

"What are you up to, Bones?"

"Oh, nothing."

"Yes, you are."

"Well, I played golf today. I thought I better tell you about it."

"Who did you play with?"

"It wasn't my fault."

"Who was it, Bones?"

"Snook asked me to play. He arranged it all."

"Who?"

"Snookers Molesby. You met him at the jam session. He works in maintenance at the hospital."

"The hospital?"

"Well ... uh, Tag ... I didn't know it was gonna be Olden and Leggett ..."

Tag was silent.

"I got roped into it, Tag. Honest to goodness."

"What did they say?"

"Well, ... uh ... have you ever heard of one of these high-low settlement arrangements?"

"Good God almighty, Bones. Surely you didn't!"

"You'da been proud of me, Tag. I didn't tell him a thing. I told 'em I was a county doctor and I didn't know anything about it and ..."

"Bones?"

"Yes, ma'am?"

"You get your ass over here to the Holiday Inn right now. We need to talk."

"Yes, ma'am."

CHAPTER FORTY NINE

Cold Feet

BONES RAN INTO INDIE in the doctor's lounge the next morning. "Well, don't you look spiffy?"

Indie had on his best gray suit. He wore his black polished shoes.

"Not exactly your brogans, Indie. What's the occasion?"

Indie's eyes were moist. "It's been a year and a half; they've won the war of attrition. I want out."

"I think Olden has played out every stall card he's got. I heard Judge Hamrick is sick of it."

"Don't matter. Olden'll maneuver some way to delay it again. I'm ready to be done with it. Nothing's gonna bring Blinky back."

Bones looked again. "I'm sorry, Indie. I think you wore the gray one at the funeral."

"Yep. I wanted to honor him today."

"What's on tap at court?"

Indie nodded his head toward the room next door. "Let's go outside."

"Sure." They walked out to the parking lot. "You know, Bones, look at the trees. They're just plum bare. I just don't care for the fall. Me, I love the springtime."

"Me, too, Indie."

"I gotta get this over. Come spring I want to be down to the cabin and tending to my roses."

"I understand. Well, you better not go to the cabin in that suit, Indie. Ms. Jenkins'll get on you."

"No kidding. I'm ready for life to get back to normal, at least as close at it can without Blinky. You know me, I go by gestalt. I think this thing is gonna settle soon."

"Man, I wish I could come today. What's on tap?"

"Some expert. Tag says we got another good one."

'Who's that?"

"Roger Turner."

"The M.D. PhD cat?"

"Yep."

"They say he's one of the best in the state. How'd she get him?"

"I don't know, but she has high hopes."

"Call me at lunch."

"Will do."

"Good luck."

Roger Turner took the stand. He was a blocky linebacker sort of guy with a close crew cut, black-rimmed glasses, a white shirt, and a pencil protector in his left pocket. He would have passed for one of those NASA scientists in Mission Control. Jim Olden took one look, and turned white.

Tag went right to the heart of the matter. "Dr. Turner. Your credentials, sir?"

"M.D. PhD. I have been the chief toxicologist at Tobacco Triangle Institute for seventeen years. We are a reference laboratory for these sorts of cases. Most of our work is in the southeast, but we have clients all over the world."

"Do you know Dr. Larry McBride?"

"Yes, very well. He's a cowboy, but the man is the best toxicologist in Texas. His word is his bond."

"And have you read his deposition as to Mr. Blinky Wilson and the issue of Demerol?"

"Yes, I have."

"Your opinion, sir?"

"McBride is right on target. There is a ninety-nine point eight percent chance Mr. Wilson had residual metabolite of normeperidine in his bone marrow."

"Meaning?"

"The man got some doses of Demerol in the last week of his life."

"Did it cause his death?"

"There is a very high probability it was a major factor."

The room went quiet.

"Your witness, Mr. Leggett."

Leggett wandered around for a moment. "Dr. Turner, do you have any prior knowledge of this case?"

"No."

"Are you sure? No one called you about it?"

"We get calls all the time with theoretical questions. I do not recall any specific questions as to Mr. Wilson. It is a common name, though. My first knowledge of his case was from the call from Ms. Taggert."

"We find the State Coroner's office to be of integrity. I am certain you agree a free fentanyl level was reasonable study at the time of autopsy."

"We have been doing the lipid-bound assay at T.T.I. for almost three years. Let's see, this death was close to two years ago. I do not think the State had ill intent and Boyles is a good man but in my opinion he was a bit late to embrace the technology. The free fentanyl level is an outdated test. As McBride said, the lipid-bound assay is a superior study at the event of sudden death."

"Do people get confused about when to use it?"

"Of course. One time I got a call from a layman who wanted to use the test on a patient who had been dead for months. Can you imagine that? How could you have any lipids after being in the grave six months? All that is left is bone by then."

Betty Wilson began to cry.

"I'm sorry. I didn't mean to be disrespectful to the deceased, but it is a ridiculous concept."

Olden left the courtroom.

"Gibson. We need to meet."

"Sure, Lucille. What's on your mind?"

She motioned for Gibson to come inside Indie's makeshift courthouse conference room and closed the door. "The hospital tried to float a high-low."

"You're kidding! When did they call you?"

"They ran it through one of our contacts."

"What did you say?"

"I sent back a message. 'No dice.'"

"They must be desperate."

"I agree. We're still willing to settle, but the price just dropped."

"I understand."

"I'll give one-fifty," Tag said.

"Two-fifty."

Tag paused then said, "Two hundred."

"Okay."

"Talk to your client."

"She's getting cold feet. I think she might take it."

"Good."

Indie called Bones at lunch. "Hey, boy, you ain't gonna believe what kinda day we're having." Indie proceeded to recount the entire testimony.

"Hot damn, Indie. You oughta be able to get out altogether."

"Well, I wouldn't go that far. The man said that it was a high probability that Demerol was a major factor."

"What did Tag say?"

"She wants to strike. We think we can get out for a token."

"Gosh, Indie. Maybe you ought to hold out. You didn't do anything."

"Life ain't fair, Bones. Can you come over after work? Tag has a conference planned."

"Are you sure she wants me?"

"I told her if me and you could play music I wouldn't drink as much."

"Anything else?"

"Yeah. Let her handle it. She's gonna do the right thing."

"I'll be there."

Indie was late for the meeting, but only fifteen minutes or so. He'd had a nip, but was far from drunk.

"When bluegrass folks dress like that, it's a sign, Tag," Bones commented.

She agreed.

Indie stood at the door for inspection. In his right hand, he cradled some flowers still wrapped in paper and boxed. He looked like he was headed out on a date.

"You going to town?" Tag smoothed his lapel, and straightened out the crooked tie. "You look nice, what's the occasion?"

Indie glanced Bones' way. He was embarrassed, but enjoyed the attention, too. "I'm ready. I want to talk to Betty. All this has gone on, and no one will let me speak to her. It's time."

"Okay, Indie, but let's talk it over a minute. Tell me why."

"These things take so long; it gives you time to think. I hate what happened to Blink. There's no way that jury's gonna go home without giving Betty something, and I'm scared they might not understand what happened. They have two grand-young'uns. Maybe we can set up a scholarship for the boys in Blinky's honor. A couple hundred grand would take care of 'em, and I'd still have insurance and not risk my license. I have to keep going. I take care of a lot of folks."

Tag smiled. "I think you're doing the right thing. I've talked to Gibson. I think Betty is getting cold feet."

"What'll you think the company will say?"

"Oh, they'll be pleased to get out of a death case for two hundred grand. We'll make it up. I hate to see you get hit at all. But, from the company's perspective, two hundred is reasonable."

"Bones, what do you think?" Indie asked.

"If Betty's got cold feet, there is a part of me that's like to hold 'em to the fire. But I'm not gonna stand in the way. Tag's the boss. Like the song says, 'It's done come time to not know nothing 'bout what you done to do me wrong.'"

Tag laughed. "Bones, you're more circuitous than their experts. Thanks for clearing all that up. Indie?"

"I say we move."

"I'll call Gibson. Let's see if we can meet with Ms. Wilson before anyone interferes."

CHAPTER FIFTY

Peace Offering

TAG MADE THE CALL. "Gibson, Lucille here. Dr. Jenkins is ready to settle."

"Is he serious or just kicking tires?"

Tag glanced at Indie. He held tight to his box of flowers like a teenager waiting on his first prom date. "He's serious, Gib. You know I'm always straight with you. Let's talk."

"I'll get Betty and bring her over."

"Meet us at our room at the Holiday Inn."

"Will do."

"Hey, Tag. You want me to leave?" Bones asked.

She smiled. "No. You've come this far, no use in testing my luck now."

Gibson Taylor and Betty Wilson were there in fifteen minutes. Tag checked the hallway for any signs of the hospital team. She closed and latched the door.

Tag was most gracious, and could have passed for a suburban house-wife hosting a dinner party. She offered Ms. Wilson some water, and Betty seemed to relax. Indie still had on his gray suit and Tag had made him put on the tie. The fish didn't quite match, but she gave in because he felt more comfortable with it on than the burgundy one she had picked out.

Betty and Gibson sat at the table. Indie sat in the easy chair in the corner. Bones took a seat on the couch. Tag moved her papers from the desk to the table.

She then got right to the business at hand. "Ms. Wilson, first of all, I want to say we are sorry for the loss of your husband. Everyone involved in this should never forget that. Doing right by him should be our highest priority."

"Yep, Blink should be number one on everyone's loyalty list," Bones interjected.

Tag motioned for him to hush, then went on. "Dr. Jenkins came to me today and we discussed his desire to settle. As you know, I called Mr. Taylor to arrange this conference. It is customary for the attorney to outline these proposals, but Indie wanted to do so himself. If you are agreeable, I am going to let him do so."

"That's fine," Betty said.

Indie walked across the room and lay the flowers on a nearby nightstand. He took a chair and slid it over to Betty's table, then sat across from her and began to speak. "Betty, I uh, well, God Almighty, I'm sorry Blink's gone, I swear to God I am. I promise you, I still don't understand exactly what happened. Before the lawsuit ever started I went over it with Sharma a dozen times, and he didn't, either. I looked at it from every angle you can imagine, and it just doesn't seem to be the Fentanyl ... At any rate, I'm sorry." Indie got out his handkerchief and blew his nose. "For the last month I've wanted to somehow try to make it right. I can't bring him back, but it seemed like to me the best thing would be to do something to honor his memory. We all know how much he loved those two grandsons." He didn't mention Betty had all but run them off. "I know how much you miss them...and, well...I'd like to start a college trust fund for them in Blinky's honor. I'll tell 'em it was all your idea."

Ms. Wilson began to tear up.

"Betty, now you know I ain't got this kind of money, but Tag's insurance company here will give two hundred thousand dollars. With that the boys will be able to get any kind of education they want and have some left over at that." He walked over to the sink to clean off his glasses, and came back to sit down. "I've always heard that in Japan if something goes wrong, the doc bows and offers what he can, all a matter of honor, you know, and then folks put their hard feelings aside. Me and Blink was best friends and we all got to live here when this is over." Indie bit his lip.

Betty sat silent for a moment, and then responded. "I'm ready to be done with all this. Can I talk it over with Mr. Taylor for just a minute?"

"Sure."

"We have the executive suite next door, Ms. Wilson. Y'all can borrow it." Tag offered.

"We'll be back shortly," Gibson said.

They waited for what seemed an eternity, but in reality was all of five minutes. Gibson let Betty have the floor.

"Indie, you're right about one thing. You were his best friend. Without you, I guess he would not have been here as long as he was, especially after his heart attack. I think he would like the idea of a scholarship for the boys. I accept your offer. I'd like to put this behind us." She hesitated, and then gave Indie a hug.

And just like that, at least for Indie, it was over. No fireworks, no banners, no headlines. But, at the same time, it was over.

"Hold on a minute, Betty, I got a little something for you." Indie picked up the roses from the table where he had put them down. They were in a long box marked **EAST VIRGINIA MEDICAL SUPPLY**. He opened the box and handed them to her.

"Well, Indie, they are beautiful." Betty took a deep breath. "They smell wonderful." She held them up. "Just gorgeous. Where did you get them?"

"Oh, I know folks who grow them."

Gibson spoke up. "If you would, Tag, I'd like to keep this agreement under wraps until I can get the paperwork done. Of course, once it's signed we'll admit it into evidence. I'd rather the hospital not know until it's official, if that's okay."

"Fair enough, Gib. We'll get in done in short order, though," she said.

Indie reached out and shook Gibson Taylor's hand. "Mr. Taylor, I'm glad we can shake on a deal. I thank you for not setting out to destroy me."

"It wouldn't have been the truth," Gibson replied.

"Well, thanks still."

Betty and Gibson left, Betty clutching her roses.

There might not have been any fireworks, but it was Fourth of July for Indie.

"Hey, Indie," Bones said. "Let's go pick a few. I brought my double-aught Martin. It's perfect for backing up fiddle tunes."

"Sure 'nuff, Bones." He put his arm around Tag's shoulder, "Thanks for sticking by me. Bones said you were a good'un. He was right. I'm glad it's a done deal. Y'all come out to one of our shows sometime."

"Will do," Tag replied. She walked the two to the door to bid them good-night, and pecked Indie on the cheek. "I'm glad it's over for you."

Indie turned red. "Now, Ms. Tag, we better keep that between us."

Tag laughed. "Don't worry, Indie. We're in the confidential business." She watched them walk down the hall, and went back into the room for the night.

CHAPTER FIFTY ONE

Good Golly Miss Molly

IN A FEW DAYS, INDIE WAS BACK at the office. It wasn't even winter yet, but all he could talk about was getting back to the cabin to tend to his roses.

Bones was happy to get back to patient care, too. Thursday was a nice, simple Family Doctor day. High blood pressure, diabetes, moles, the usual stuff. It was the kind of day that brought a doctor back like a well-struck drive on number eighteen after a marginal round of golf. He placed his stethoscope on the desk, and turned off his Dictaphone.

He was all but out the door when Peg buzzed him. "Dr. Bones, a patient just walked in and wants to see you. Do you want to stay, or should I send her to the ER?"

"Who is it?"

"Just a kid. Molly Saucony. She says her nerves are shot, and it won't take but a minute."

"Molly Saucony? Who's that?"

"You know, Molly Tenbrooks. She got married April before last and moved up north after the wedding."

"Dang, I'm so bad to forget those married names. What's Molly doing in town?"

"I don't know. She seems upset."

"Maybe you better send her back. I hope the kid's marriage ain't on the ropes."

Peg put her in room one. Everybody but Bones, Peg, and the patient had left for the day.

Bones opened the door to the exam room. "Hey kid, whatcha up to?"

"Visiting mama."

"Did you go on and get your L.P.N.?"

"Yes, sir, but I got out of healthcare. I'm an assistant manager at Radio Shack."

"Shucks. I was hoping you might come home and look after me in the nursing home someday."

She began to cry.

"Hey, there. I was just teasing." He handed her a Kleenex. "Why the tears? Jonathan is treating you okay, isn't he?"

"Oh, yes, sir. It ain't nothing like that, but I can't eat, can't sleep. I've gotta tell you something I shoulda told you before I left town."

"It's okay, Molly. I ain't gonna tell. What in the world is wrong?"

She dabbed her tears. "I'm so ashamed. I shoulda told."

Bones put a hand on her shoulder. "Let me tell ya, Molly, I've heard it all twice."

She began to calm down. "It was Mr. Olden. I was only seventeen and he tried to ... well, you know ..." She began to cry again.

Bones stuck his head out the door, looked at Peg, and held up all ten fingers to indicate another ten minutes. Peg flashed an okay sign. He went back in and closed the door.

"He tried to rape me."

It was all he could do to hear her through the sobs. *Sorry sumbitch.* "Jeez, Molly, it wasn't your fault. For God's sake, seventeen. What the hell's wrong with him?"

"I went to therapy, and I'm okay now, at least until I have to go over it again."

"Well, Molly, I'm glad you're better. That kind of thing never goes away, but if you got stronger, that's good. I didn't know it happened. I sure am sorry."

"My therapist taught me how to empower myself, Doc. I've thought about it a lot, and I think I can help you."

"I don't understand, Molly. I'm fine. What are you driving at?"

"I was working the floor the night Blinky Wilson died."

"Wait a minute, Molly. You can't get involved. It'll dredge up too much. You wouldn't believe what lengths they might go to try to discredit you. You don't owe anyone a thing. You need to know nothing. Besides, Indie's out. You just need to go home, kid."

"I know too much, and they know that I know," she said. "You wouldn't believe what they write when someone does a reference check on me for a job. I'm better off in the long run if it goes public." She dabbed her eyes with the Kleenex. "You remember how I was working the pharmacy as a courier when I got out of high school? I got my C.N.A. right about then, and I got to work the floor some. Right before Mr. Blinky died, Mr. Olden promoted me. I went to the floor full-time, and worked with Maria Diosas. About a month before my wedding, Maria told me she'd given some Demerol doses to the wrong patient. She knew she'd done it, but she was sorry. Not long after that, Mr. Olden paid for her trip to help take care of her grandparents in Russia. He got her through that Federal program for foreign health workers and then shipped her away just like that."

"I'll bet he did."

"She was gonna be a bridesmaid, but he saw to it she was gone."

"I'm not surprised."

"One day, the battery on my Volkswagen went dead, and Mr. Olden gave me a ride home. That's where he, well, he would have ... but Daddy came home about that time...and..."

Thank God, Bones thought.

"...and...well, he didn't, but I'm sure he would have."

"I know, Molly. It's okay."

She teared up again. "He's got some kind of problem."

"I'm afraid you're right, kid."

"When Jonathan and I got married, Mr. Olden said if I talked I'd never get a job again. He said he'd tell everyone I came to his office and closed the door and wanted to give him ... uh, well, he makes me sick. We decided to leave town. I thought I'd never come back, but I heard what was going on. I just couldn't let Dr. Jenkins be done wrong. He was always nice to me; used to loan out his motorcycle to me and Johnny."

"Does Olden know you're here?"

"No, sir."

"Then we need to get you out of here. You need to go home. You're a nice kid. You don't need any part of this. Indie's okay, I promise."

"No, sir." She straightened up in the chair. "My therapist taught me to be strong. I'm gonna tell the truth about what happened even if you don't let me."

"Have you talked about this decision with your therapist?"

"Yes, sir, and she thought it best to rely on her advice, and on you, for my strength. I'm gonna do the right thing. Are you gonna help me?"

Bones sat on the exam stool to think. "Tell ya what, Molly. I'd rather you talk to a lady about this before you decide. Her name is Lucille Taggert, but you can call her Tag. She's the head honcho on Indie's team." He opened the door and motioned for Peg to stay just a few more minutes. Bones found a pair of sunglasses in his desk drawer, and gave them to Molly. "Good Golly, Miss Molly, your eyes are just too puffy. Not becoming of a girl as pretty as you."

Molly checked herself in the mirror. "They ain't that bad."

"Wear 'em. Ask no questions."

"Yes, sir."

Bones picked up the phone to call Tag.

She didn't have to hear much. "I'll be right there to get her."

They waited on Tag. Bones went to get Molly a Coca-Cola. Peg followed him to the break room. "Is she all right, Bones?"

"Oh, yeah, just some of that girl stuff. I'm gonna let her stay with a friend 'til she can get her act together."

Tag arrived in five minutes.

CHAPTER FIFTY TWO

Tag Team

BONES CLOSED UP THE OFFICE, and got to the Holiday Inn in short order. He arrived at Tag's headquarters and knocked on the door. As soon as he walked in, he knew Tag had connected with Molly. The two were piled up on the bed, and both wore sunglasses. They were eating popcorn and drinking Co-Colas. Tag was a huge Beatles fan, and an old Fab Four newsreel flickered on the TV screen.

"Hey, Doc, didja know that Ms. Tag here met Paul McCartney before he played with Wings?" Molly asked.

"Pretty amazing for a twenty-eight-year-old woman, Molly," Bones replied.

Tag lowered her sunglasses. "Bones, don't forget. I saved your buddy's ass and I might have to save yours someday. And, also, I am chair of the rate committee next year."

"Yes, ma'am."

Molly went on. "Them Beatles was pretty good musicians, weren't they?"

"You reckon? Yeah, some things transcend time, huh?" Bones watched as McCartney stepped off the plane.

"Yes, sir, sure 'nuff." Molly was transfixed by the footage of screaming teenagers as the boys walked down the off ramp and waved at the crowd. "Amazing, I can't believe everyone went that nutty."

"Molly, you'd had to have been there. Tell you what. I gotta catch up with Ms. Tag about some stuff. You okay to watch this for a while?"

"Sure, Doc. This is great."

Tag and Bones walked down to the end of the hall.

"Okay, Tag, tell me straight up: Is Molly up to all this? She might be a grown woman, but she's a kid to me. I just don't want her to get hurt, and my highest loyalty has to be to her as a patient first, and a witness second. Besides, Indie is out. It ain't my fight now. You're a woman, what's your take on it?"

"I don't want to use her, either. But, but you have to realize she doesn't want you to be paternalistic. She feels like she owes it to herself to have the truth told. Getting through the process validates her. She even called her therapist, and put us on a conference call. It has her blessings."

"Brave young 'un, is all I got to say."

"We need to let her talk to Gibson. If we were still in, I'd say go for it, but he'll have to interview her. It's his call." She brushed her hair back. "I wish we had run into her a few weeks ago."

"I know, Tag, but you gotta admit with the information we had at the time Indie did the right thing."

"Oh, no doubt. Besides that, you never know how these things are going to go. I'm confident she's telling the truth, but they could still break her down."

"I worry about it, too. You pretty sure she'll be okay?"

"Yeah; she is very strong. And even more important, it has her therapist's blessing. If Olden ever trapped another young lady, Molly will have a hard time getting over it."

"I hope we're doing the right thing."

"I think we are. Besides, Gibson won't let them get too rough. He's got a daughter. He'll protect her."

"I bet Indie would try to talk her out of it if he was still in."

"Well, the papers aren't signed yet, so technically he is. I'm glad he's out, though. You never know how a jury will see it. He's done the right thing. Better to be out. I worried Indie was gonna have a heart attack with all those cigarettes."

"Yeah, I worried over him, too."

"And by the way, you do need to educate the young lady."

"How's that?"

"For the girl to be your patient, and a music fan, and not know of the Beatles is unthinkable."

Bones laughed. "I'll make amends, Tag, I promise."

CHAPTER FIFTY THREE

Go For It

BONES TOOK FRIDAY AFTERNOON OFF, and went to meet with Tag.

"Where's Molly?"

"She's with Gibson Taylor."

"Dang. I wish I'd been able to go with her."

Tag put the charts and graphs aside. "Bones, you just can't let this one go, can you?"

"Too many friends in it. How come we aren't there with her?"

"The three of us met this morning. I'm going to meet with Leggett this afternoon. If that goes like we think it will, then she'll become more Gibson's witness than ours. He wanted to interview her some more and be sure she understood what she could be getting into."

"I don't understand."

"Indie is out; the hospital just doesn't know it yet, remember? Gibson asked us to not disclose until we have to. Indie hasn't signed yet."

"Oh, yeah."

"Besides that, you know her medical history. I need you there. Gibson and I both thought it is still possible we might decide she's not up to this."

"I'm afraid they'll treat her like a dog."

"I share your concern. Gibson's seen all these tactics before. He'll know how to handle it with the utmost sensitivity."

"I guess so, Tag, but I can't help but worry. Sometimes the one who tries to tell the truth comes out as the bad guy. I don't want them to railroad her."

"Don't be so nervous. Gibson told me after we talk to Leggett and Olden if you said it was not in Molly's best interest he would drop her off the list. He thinks he can get the job done without her."

"Are you kidding?"

"No. He'll let it be your call."

"Damn."

Soon Gibson was back with Molly in tow. Molly had a broad smile, and appeared unconcerned.

"Well, Bones," Gibson said, "I must say your friend turns out to be quite a surprise. She could turn the hospital on its ear. I suspect after her testimony Indie might opt to back out. All the settlement documents are ready, but he hasn't signed yet, you know."

"He is owed informed consent, Bones," Tag said.

"I suppose so. You want me to talk to him?"

"I'll take care of it," Tag said.

Bones turned to Molly. "Now, Ms. Molly, you sure you're okay with all this? You can still go back home if you want to."

"I'm fine, Dr. Bones. Mr. Taylor here is really cool. He reminds me of my daddy. I might go back to school and be a lawyer."

Bones gave her a hug.

Tag set out the agenda. "Two p.m. today, conference room B. Molly, we'll put you into hiding for now. She's going to stay with her mom."

"See you guys later," Molly said.

"Be good, kid." Bones replied.

"Bones, are you free?" Tag asked.

"I'm off the rest of the day. I'm happy to help if I can."

"I'll probably need you."

"How's that?"

"As good a witness as the girl might be, Gibson has some reservations. He does not want to use her if it is against your judgment. He's afraid they'll tear her apart."

"Yeah, it worries me, too."

"Same 'ere. We'll test the water without her there, and then talk it over."

"Okay."

"Just don't speak unless I ask you a question. I have a feeling you will help the cause."

"Yes, ma'am."

They met at Tag's suite at 2:0' PM at the Holiday Inn. Jackson Leggett and Olden got there early.

"What is this all about, Ms. Taggert?" Olden asked.

"I don't know. A patient of Dr. Bones' wanted us to interview her. Bones wanted us to talk it over. He's not sure she is relevant."

"Well, let's make it quick. I have a hospital to run."

"Yes, sir."

Gibson Taylor looked at his watch. "Where the hell is Bones? I don't have all day."

He arrived ten minutes late. "Sorry guys, I went to check on Indie."

"Is Dr. Jenkins coming?" Olden asked.

"No. He told me to let him know if there was anything new, but he was too tired today."

"Okay," Leggett said, "let's go ahead."

Gibson opened. "Gentlemen, we need to open the discovery process as to a new witness in the matter of Wilson vs. Dr. Henry Jenkins, and Harvey Memorial Hospital. That witness is Ms. Molly Tenbrooks Saucony, L.P.N." He fiddled with the recorder. "Wait a minute. This thing was on pause. Here we go. Let me state that again." He repeated himself.

Bones watched Olden. He had a confident smirk. *Somehow he had gotten wind of her arrival,* he thought. Jackson Leggett fiddled with some papers, but was calm. Tag sat quiet.

Olden smiled and said, "Yes, indeed, Gibson."

Gibson went through the whole saga. "This Molly is now an L.P.N. She says she was a C.N.A. on the floor the night in question, and she found out Wheatie Willis had not gotten his Demerol. A Maria Diosas confessed she had given it to the wrong patient, to Blinky Wilson, in fact, and then he coded and died."

"Any questions, Ms. Taggert?" Taylor asked.

"No. Dr. Jenkins was not there that night. Proceed." She took some notes.

Leggett and Olden huddled for moment. "Can you excuse us just a minute?" Leggett asked.

"Sure," Gibson said.

They stepped to the back of the room. Olden handed Leggett some more papers and whispered in his ear, then they returned to the table.

"Of course, Mr. Taylor, I'm certain you realize these events were now almost two years ago. We have concerns as to a witness who would come forward at such a late date. It would seem the most reliable witness on this matter would be Miss Diosas. We feel this testimony should not be entered into evidence without her corroboration. Have you obtained her statement?" Leggett asked.

"No, she is currently out of the country. I have no doubt that Judge Hamrick will rule in our favor to allow Miss Molly's testimony," Gibson said.

"I have my doubts, but we'll take it to him and see," Leggett replied.

"Okay." Taylor turned off the tape recorder and got up to pour a glass of water. "Tag, Bones?"

"No, thanks."

"Gentlemen?"

"I believe I will." Olden's lips were dry, and he reached for a glass.

Leggett pulled out some papers. "Oh, yes. One other thing, Taylor. As to Miss Tenbrook's credibility, we have some serious issues. She was a friend of Dr. Jenkins, and would be a biased witness. We understand she enjoyed riding his motorcycle at times. I believe there are a number of people in town who recall Dr. Jenkins and his relationships with motorcycles and young women."

Olden interrupted. "Let's see, there was that French foreign exchange student, as I recall."

Tag grabbed Bones' arm. It was good Molly didn't have to hear all this.

Olden smiled.

Bones scribbled a note in small letters. *He's not smiling, he's just baring his teeth.* Tag elbowed him in the ribs.

"We are positive Molly had no relationship other than platonic with Dr. Jenkins." Gibson said. "Defamation is not in your best interest."

"Whatever relationship she had with Dr. Jenkins can be explored in more depth later, but we do have other information as to the girl's sexual history. Administration had to deal with this matter before Ms. Tenbrooks left town." Leggett produced a document from Personnel. "She was caught in the broom closet in Endoscopy with the Jonathan boy while he was employed there."

"Hell, she married him." Bones sputtered the words.

Tag grasped his elbow.

Leggett went on. "We would prefer not to explore such history. I'm sure it is in this girl's best interest for us to let this drop. We don't wish to be forced to damage her reputation." Leggett reached for the water pitcher. He seemed satisfied.

Tag shuffled through her papers, and scribbled some notes. Everyone waited. "Dr. Bones. I believe you were Molly's physician, is that correct?"

"Yes, ma'am, half raised her."

"I need to ask you a few questions. I am sure Mr. Leggett or Mr. Olden might want to ask some also. Is that okay?"

"Not a problem."

Olden looked at Leggett in bewilderment, then whispered, "What is this?"

Tag continued, "Bones, how long have you known Molly?"

"Shoot fire, Tag. I've looked after that child since day one. The only folks who have known her longer than me are her mama and daddy. I was her doctor in the newborn nursery. Now you talking 'bout a cute young'un, she had a head full of soft hair that stood straight up; looked like a little downy chick, she did. Now those were some days. I used to do circumcisions in the nursery; oh, now not Miss Molly, of course. We had an old Flatt and Scruggs tape in there and I played *'Your Love is Like a Flower'* while I did the procedure, but that was before the days of E.M.L.A. anesthesia cream, and I was worried I might give bad memories to the little fellows 'bout bluegrass music, so we switched to classical ... Oh, man, I sure was glad when the anesthesia techniques got better, and—"

"Bones, Bones! Please! We haven't all night. Please, stay focused." Tag waved her pen in the air.

"Yes, ma'am."

"So, you've been her doctor since birth. I assume you saw her through grade school, junior high, and so on."

"Yes, ma'am. Sent her a high school graduation present."

"And did you know of any sexual indiscretion of your patient during that time?"

"No, ma'am, and I think she'da told me of anything she was worried about."

"Did you do her marriage physical?"

The light bulb came on. Bones knew where Tag was headed. "Tag, I can't talk about some things, even with you."

"Dr. Bones, I have come to know you well. I'm certain you would not share your patient's personal history without permission. Is that correct?"

"Yes, ma'am."

Tag produced a document with Molly's signature granting permission to discuss her medical history. She handed Bones a copy of the marriage physical. "What were your findings at that time, Dr. Bones?"

Damn, this doesn't seem right. "Gee, Tag, are you sure she wants me to discuss this? I mean, it is awfully personal to her, and it sure doesn't seem related to whether or nor Blinky Wilson got a shot of Demerol that killed him."

"You can call her if you want."

"I'll have to. Can I go next door? I need to talk to her in private."

"Sure," Tag said.

Bones went to the adjoining room. Olden excused himself and went to the restroom.

They waited. Bones finally returned and sat down.

"Everything okay, Bones?" Tag asked.

Bones looked right at Jim Olden. "Okay, guys, I guess you win. But I tell you what. Whatever is said here stays here. One of you hurts Molly, and I'll hire Roy Davidson to chase you all over Harvey County. Yeah, I did her marriage physical, and it ain't nobody's business, but I'm a hundred percent certain any allegations of sexual activity by this girl prior to her marriage physical are false. I hope you're happy."

Jackson Leggett responded. "Doctor, can a medical exam establish such a fact with any degree of certainty?"

Bones looked him right in the eye. "It's one thing for y'all to wrestle with a bunch of old men, but it's another to go after a little girl." He got up and paced. "Tell you what, Mr. Leggett. I'm certain, so why don't you just take me over to the courthouse and contest my credibility? I'm gonna go down there and stand up for her. You'll just have to convince the county I'm a bum." He held back the curse words. "You know, Leggett, in all negotiations there is some common ground. I suspect we are in agreement on one issue here."

"And what is that?"

"Molly was one of those kids who wasn't sexually active until she married, but she was threatened at one time. It's in her chart at the office. The incident was right there in her house. Thank God her dad came home early from work. Otherwise..." Bones sat back down. He turned and glared straight at Olden. "I can go over that part of her file. I would hate to have to subpoena that, wouldn't you?"

Olden froze.

No one could say anything.

Gibson Taylor took a few more notes.

Tag watched Olden's eyes. They sank back in his head as if he was shot.

Gibson looked around. "Unless anyone has anything else to say, I think this meeting is over."

Tag stared at Leggett. "I expect an answer in an hour."

"What answer?"

"Leggett, I don't know who is more of a dumb man, you or Olden, but you better figure it out fast."

Tag and Bones went back to her Holiday Inn and stopped to get a cup of coffee. "Bones, I gotta admit you're growing on me. Your intuition was great. I led you down the path, but you followed as I hoped you might. That end was a hundred percent spontaneous. I'm glad you had it in your record about the night at her house."

"I didn't. I bluffed 'em."

"Damn, Bones." She spilled her coffee and mopped it up with a napkin. "What were you thinking?"

"I just learned about that from Molly when she came in the other night. You can always bluff a liar, 'cause he's scared to death about what cards the truth might hold. Olden won't go there."

They went to headquarters and waited. The phone rang in a half hour. Tag answered. She kept a straight face and responded in brief. "Yes. No. We will not do that ... No way."

"What are they saying, Tag. What are they saying?" Bones paced and scratched his head.

She waved her left hand to motion for him to sit down, and then covered the receiver. "Ssssh!!!" She spoke back into the phone. "I understand. Yes." She hung up. "Damn boy, you don't have a bit of poker face, do you?"

"What'd they say?"

"They'll allow Molly's testimony. Even better, they feel to expose her sexual history would not be compatible with the hospital's image Mr. Olden wishes to portray. They said to tell you they will not invade your patient's privacy."

"Hot damn, I reckon not!" Bones leapt into the air, and hit his head on the ceiling fan.

"Calm down, Bones." Tag laughed.

"I want to talk to Molly. I think she ought to take them S.O.Bs to the wire."

Tag wrote some notes. "You slammed shut the only end run strategy they had on her, Bones. With their exit route closed, we think she is up to the journey, too."

Bones ran into Gibson Taylor in the lobby when he left Tag's. "Hey, Gib. Man, I got to rattling on today, and forgot to ask about your thoughts. I'm sorry. I was just so wrapped up about that kid, I forgot."

"Not a problem, Bones. Got a present for you." He reached in his coat pocket, and produced two Cohiba cigars. "Consider it a peace pipe of sorts. One is for you, and one is for Indie. Tell him I want to hear that '*Cherokee Shuffle*' after this is all over."

"Well, thanks, Gib. Indie loves a fine cigar. I might have to break down and smoke one with him."

"I'm gonna appeal to Tag to give him a break on his rate bump next year."

"You guys always were about the truth."

"Well, don't tell anyone. I am a lawyer, you know."

"I promise, Gib. We're jamming tonight at the Cabin. Come on by. No business allowed."

"Better not, Bones. I've got a case to prosecute. In these big ones, you have to be extra careful to avoid impropriety."

"I understand. Good luck."

"Thanks."

CHAPTER FIFTY FOUR

A Deal's a Deal

MRS. JENKINS ANSWERED THE PHONE.

"Mrs. Jenkins? Bones here. Is Indie around?"

"Oh, no. He's down at the cabin."

"Is he okay?"

"Oh, my, yes. Ever since they released him he's a new man. Hasn't had another word to say about it."

"Reckon he'd mind if I came down?"

"Heavens no. He'd love to see you. Make sure to take your mandolin. He went to fiddle and I think he's gonna fish some, too."

"Okay."

"Thank you for everything you did for him. He really is a good man. Sometimes he just hides it from folks."

"He is that and more."

Bones took the high road to the cabin. Indie was just a-fiddlin' away. Bones rapped on the door, and Indie broke into the *"Mandolin March."*

"Come on in here, Bones, old boy, and get that mandolin outta the case."

"There's something I need to tell you, Indie."

The music screeched to a halt. "Nobody broke their word, did they?" Indie asked.

"Oh, no, nothing like that. I wish you'd been there today, Indie. Little

Molly Tenbrooks showed up, and man does she have a story to tell. I got a feeling she's gonna lay the hospital to waste. Olden was behind the whole thing."

"Hell, Bones, you trying out for rocket science?"

"I'm telling ya, Indie, I think you could get out all together now."

Indie fiddled a few bars of *"Broken Promises,"* then stopped. "Nope. Gave my word. Besides, Betty's gonna call it the 'Betty Wilson and Dr. Henry Indie Jenkins Scholarship Fund.' I shook hands on it and I'm sticking by it. Besides, she's gonna tell everyone I gave the money for it myself. Can you imagine that? Betty Wilson done gonna turn Indie into a damn hero."

"Dang, Indie. You're a good man. But Betty'll turn on you in a skinny minute."

"Yeah, I know. But maybe this time I got her where she can't diss me for the rest of my life. What would her grandchildren say? I've kilt her with kindness. Besides that, I promised Gibson Taylor, too. I gave him my word. I can't back out of it."

"Oh, speaking of Gibson, he sent this. Here." Bones handed him the cigar. "I don't think he'd hold you to it."

"The Navajo will."

"Damn, Indie. You got some scruples."

"Hell, I want them to remember I keep my word. It's a Navajo honor thing, you know." Indie put away his fiddle and rested his case on the sofa. "Too bad the hospital didn't understand."

"No kidding."

"Lie once, and you're stained forever. An attorney like Gibson Taylor never ever forgets."

"I think the hospital is about to learn that lesson."

"Yep, and he's got 'em by the balls forever-more." Indie lit a smoke. "You know Tag real good, don't ya, Bones? She's okay with it, ain't she?"

"Tag won't squank Taylor, either. They'll have to go up against Gibson in a case before we do."

"God, I would hope so. As for me, I'm retired from the litigation business."

"Yeah, Tag's got more gigs than us bluegrassers. Something's always gonna go wrong in the doctor business. Somebody's gotta do it, I reckon, but I'll stick with medicine and bluegrass on the weekends."

"Get out your mandolin. How 'bout singing '*When the Roses Bloom in Dixieland*'?"

"Lord, Indie. I'm a terrible singer."

"Don't matter. Kick it off."

"You like it in G?"

"That works."

They played an hour.

"Hey, Indie. Ms. Jenkins said you were going fishing today."

"Yeah, boy. Wanna go?"

"You still got my rod down here?"

"It's on the screen porch."

"I'll go get it."

"Well, you better bring a life jacket, too. You remember that time you got that big ole pike on the hook?"

CHAPTER FIFTY FIVE

From Russia with Love

TAG AND INDIE MET WITH Gibson Taylor before Molly's testimony.

Gibson handed the paperwork to Indie.

Indie got out his pen.

Gibson took one last look. "Indie, you never know how these things are gonna go. After her testimony, I don't know—"

"It's okay, Gibson. You've been fair. I have no regrets."

"Tag?" Gibson asked.

"I agree with Indie. His word is his bond."

Indie signed.

"I'll give it to Judge Hamrick. He'll pass it onto the jury," Gibson said.

They shook hands.

Molly took the stand. She wore a nice business suit and looked five years older.

You think she'll be okay?" Bones asked.

Tag nodded. "I told them they better treat her like a lady."

Molly took the stand, and Gibson began. "Ms. Saucony, do you recall where you were on the night of Mr. Blinky Wilson's death?"

"I'll never forget. I was a C.N.A. on the floor. It was terrible."

"And for the record, a C.N.A. is?"

"Oh, certified nursing assistant."

"Okay, go on."

"We were short-staffed. We had a near-code. There were a lot of people to look after. Maria had only been an L.P.N. a few weeks. She was scared. We needed an R.N. that night."

"You mentioned Maria. Is this the same person as Maria Diosas?"

"Yes."

"And what did she have to do with Blinky Wilson's death?"

"She gave him the Demerol."

"Demerol?"

"Yes. She said she got mixed up. It was for a man named Wheatie Willis. Maria's English was not that good, and she got confused. She gave it to Blinky Wilson instead."

The room was silent.

"Where is Ms. Diosas now?"

"Mr. Olden had her sent to her grandparents. He said he would come for her later."

"Objection!"

"Overruled."

"Why did he do that?"

"She said he didn't want anyone to know what happened."

"Objection!"

"Overruled."

"So let me sure we have this right. Mr. Olden knew she had given the wrong medicine to Mr. Wilson and asked her not to talk about it. In fact, he even sent her to Russia to be certain no one found out. Is that correct?"

"Yes, sir."

"Your witness, Mr. Leggett."

Leggett began. "Ms. Saucony, you allege Mr. Wilson was given the wrong medication. This was nearly two years ago. How can you remember back that far?"

"You don't forget a day like that, sir. The man died."

"What did you do when you went home?"

"I cried."

"And the next day?" Leggett asked.

"I cried then, too."

"And the next?"

"I'm not sure."

"So you can remember one day but not the next?"

"Well, yes, sir, but there is a reason."

"And that is?"

"No one died that next day." Molly sat straight; her head moved as she followed Leggett from side to side. She took a deep breath and thought before each answer. She did not flinch, but smiled at old man Watson who stayed awake for the entire testimony.

Leggett attacked. "You allege this was Demerol. How are you so sure? There is nothing in the record about Demerol." He held up Blinky's chart. "Are you saying your memory is better than everyone who worked the floor that night? No one else recalls any Demerol given to Blinky Wilson."

"Oh, it was Demerol, I'm sure. Maria cried over it for days. After that, she worked down in Mr. Olden's office a few weeks, and then she left."

"Perhaps we should depose her."

"Now, sir, you know as well as I do she's in Russia. Mr. Olden had her sent to her grandparent's right after Mr. Blinky died. He told her she had to go so he could get things cleaned up here so he could marry her. She's still waiting."

"Child, Mr. Olden is married. I think you have an overactive imagination," Leggett said.

"No, sir, and I think some people lie."

"Objection!"

"Sustained." Judge Hamrick coughed away a laugh.

"So, you have no record, except the recollection of a nurse who is out of the country. What is your training, Ms. Saucony?"

"I have an L.P.N., sir. I was a nursing assistant back then."

"And does this qualify you as an expert in narcotics?" Leggett asked.

"No, sir."

"So you have no way of knowing the medicine was Demerol, do you? For that matter, you could not look at a bottle and determine if it was Demerol or something else, could you? Perhaps it was Fentanyl and you drew it up yourself. Was it Fentanyl? That's what he died of. Maybe you gave it to him. I think you want to blame a nurse in Russia for your error; a nurse who can not defend herself." Leggett's voice grew louder. "Perhaps you administered the Fentanyl yourself!"

"No sir. I didn't give it, and—it—was—Demerol." Molly stuck to her guns.

"Almost two years later and you expect us to believe you can be so sure? Really. This is just to help Dr. Jenkins, isn't it? You are friends, aren't you?"

Gibson Taylor jumped up. "Objection!"

"Overruled, you can answer."

"Dr. Jenkins loaned me and Johnny his motorcycle sometimes, but other than that, no."

Taylor called a conference, and went up to the judge's bench with Leggett. "Jackson. I'm only gonna warn you once. You start that crap and I'll kick your legal ass and have Olden thrown in the Harvey County jail with the rapists. Got it?" He stared at Leggett.

That was the end of that.

Leggett resumed. "So you claim you have superior knowledge to everyone else in this case. No one seems to know anything about Demerol but you, child."

"One person does. Wheatie Willis."

Olden shifted in his seat.

"And how would you know Mr. Willis?" Leggett asked.

"He trims my dad's hedges."

Olden and Leggett held a brief conference.

"Let's see," Leggett asked. "I believe Mr. Willis has had a stroke, isn't that correct?"

"Oh, no sir. He's fine. As a matter of fact, Mr. Olden wanted him to cut the grass at the hospital. He knows Mr. Willis is reliable; you can ask him. Mr. Wheatie is the picture of health, 'cept he's hooked on Demerol," Molly explained.

Olden turned to Leggett, started to speak, and then mumbled to himself.

Gibson spoke. "We would like to call Mr. Wheatie Willis to the stand. Jackson, he is a new witness, do you need time to prepare?"

Jackson Leggett asked for a break. He and Olden whispered out in the hall.

Molly walked by with Gibson Taylor and flashed a grin and the okay sign to Bones.

"Dang a mercy," Bones said. "That kid was plum fabulous. The son of a bit— er, son of a gun didn't shake her one iota."

"Yep," Tag said. "I wish you could have seen Mr. Olden's face when he realized Wheatie Willis could talk. I can't wait to see what Gibson Taylor does with Wheatie. Even if his testimony doesn't help, Molly laid it to 'em."

"I bet he'll do good," Bones said.

Wheatie put his hand on the Bible.

Bones had never seen him in a coat and tie.

"Mr. Willis," Gibson Taylor began, "I understand you didn't get your Demerol on the night in question. Tell us about that."

"Mr. Taylor, when my neuralgia spells flair up if I don't get my Demerol they get plum out of control. I get the shakes and the dry heaves. I gotta have it."

"So what did you do?"

"I went up the road to Fuqay. They know me good there, too, and they treated me and got me straightened out." Wheatie reached in his pocket and retrieved a copy of his discharge summary, and handed it Mr. Taylor. "Y'all can keep it. I got a copy at home anyway."

"And do you keep copies of anything else, Mr. Willis?"

"Yes, sir." Wheatie got out his wallet, where he kept a tattered record of his formal complaint. "I kept this here complaining form. I'm glad I done it, 'cause Bones says the hospital lost it. I made a copy for him, too."

Several heads at the table turned to look at Bones. He looked up at the ceiling and then buried his face in a medical journal he'd brought to read.

Taylor took the papers and entered them into the record.

"I believe I'd make me a copy of that. It's hard to keep up with papers. They can get lost you know," Wheatie advised.

"Will do, Mr. Willis. Let me ask you, who gave your Demerol to Blinky Wilson?"

"Well, I can't remember her name, but I recall what she looked like. Dark hair and eyes, Lawd, that skin what looked like cinnamon toast ... it was that Columbian nurse."

Leggett and Olden were both pale and sweaty. "Your witness, Mr. Leggett," Gibson said.

Leggett and Olden huddled at the table. Olden whispered to Leggett. "I swear to God, Jackson. The man couldn't talk a lick when I was out there at Mason Marley's. Damn."

"Mr. Leggett. *Leggett.* Your witness, *sir*," the judge said.

"Uh, yes, sir. Yes, sir. Now let's see, Mr Willis," Leggett began. "What do you do for a living?"

"I do shrubs. Mow grass. Sometimes I paint."

"Paint?"

"Yeah. Houses. I ain't no artist."

"And I understand you have a substance-abuse problem."

"Huh?"

"Do you drink?"

"Yeah, I drink too much."

"Were you drinking in the hospital? We have witnesses who say you were."

"No, sir, I needed my Demerol, but Demerol and Thunderbird don't mix. One time I did 'em both and Bones had me in the 'tensive care unit fer three days over it. He crawled my ass good. I don't mix 'em no more."

"Mr. Willis, please refrain from the profanities," the judge admonished.

"Yes, sir. They told me not to cuss. Sorry."

Leggett resumed. "And you want us to believe you can be positive you didn't get a specific medication yet you can't remember the name of your nurse?"

"Well, I sure remember what she looked like. That woman had the best set of legs I ever laid eyes on. In a way, it ain't no surprise Mr. Olden was screwing her."

"Objection!"

"Sustained. Mr. Willis, please try to restrain yourself."

Wheatie didn't know how to lie, and the jury laughed at every quip. Olden turned red. Leggett got Wheatie off the stand.

Bones walked Wheatie out to the courthouse steps. "Hey, Wheat. Thanks."

"Not a problem, Bones. You saved my life once and Indie has a buncha times. I warn't gonna let 'em blame Indie over a damn lie."

"Come on in and see me. I'd like to get you off that Demerol some day. It'd be on the house."

"Might do it, Doc."

Bones turned and went back to the courtroom.

After Leggett and Olden huddled again, Leggett called for a meeting in Judge Hamrick's chambers.

Once they were all in the room and the door closed behind them, Leggett all but shouted, "Your Honor, we move the second-hand testimony be stricken from the record. One can not enter hearsay from someone in Russia."

"Your Honor, we can bring Ms. Diosas' testimony directly to the courtroom for your review," Taylor said.

"Is she here?" Judge Hamrick asked.

Gibson Taylor looked at his watch. "No sir, but we can contact her right away." He glanced at the time again. "However, we have to touch base with her in the next few minutes. I request permission to put our witness back on the stand."

"But, Judge. How can we know it is this Diosas girl? They could put anyone on the phone. We object."

"We won't put her on the telephone, your Honor. If you are not convinced of the authenticity, you may strike it immediately. You'll know it is her."

"Hmm, I don't see how a few minutes could hurt. Okay."

"But, Judge. This sounds like a damn séance," Leggett protested.

"If it is not acceptable, I'll strike it." The judge slammed his hand on the desk. "You have ten minutes."

"Your Honor, if we can prove here in the chambers beyond all doubt this is Miss Diosas, will you allow the jury to see the evidence?"

"I suppose so. The clock is ticking."

"Your Honor, Mr. Olden has requested permission to be present," Leggett said.

"Mr. Taylor has all grounds to object."

"We'll allow it, you Honor. He is the only one who can confirm her authenticity," Taylor said. "If Olden comes in, we request Molly also be allowed. We think Molly might be able to help prove to the court who Maria is."

"Leggett?" Hamrick asked.

"Okay."

"Very well. Bring them in," Wilson consented.

Olden arrived. Molly brought in a cardboard box. They again shut the door.

"What do you have there, young lady?" Hamrick asked.

Molly opened the box. "If you'll let me hook up to your computer, we can get dial up access with the Internet." She slowly dragged out twenty-five feet of telephone cord and the modem.

"What is that thing?" Judge Hamrick asked.

"Sir, this is the brand new modem. It will connect your computer to the World Wide Web. Let's see. You've got the right stuff here, Your Honor. I.B.M. P.C. That'll do it."

"With this modem, Molly can dial up her friend in Russia. Moscow just went on the Internet. Mr. Olden will know it is her," Gibson said.

"I object, your Honor, this is unproven technology. I think ..."

"I'll decide, Leggett. It is my courtroom. You may proceed, Mr. Taylor."

"Yes, sir. Fire it up, Molly." In a moment she was at log-in.

"Tell me about this." The judge looked at the machine over his glasses.

"Yes, sir. Do you use e-mail?" Molly asked. "I learned it working for Radio Shack."

"Not yet, but I have heard of it. How does it work?"

"You can write back and forth on it."

"Anywhere?" Hamrick asked, intrigued.

"With much of the world you can. It is just getting started in Russia. Maria works nights at the Moscow Lomonosov University library; they have e-mail ability there. She checks her e-mail on her break at the top of the hour." Molly looked at her watch. "We should be able to get her now. Hey, y'all, here it is! 'From Russia with Love.' Wanna see the e-mail she sent me the other day?"

"Tell her who is in the room, Molly. She is owed informed consent," Gibson said.

"Yes, sir." She typed a message. In a moment, there was a return.

"Just to be certain, your Honor, let Mr. Leggett ask a few questions as to her identity," Taylor said.

Leggett fired a few queries about Harvey County and the hospital. "What country were you living in before the United States?"

Maria: Columbia.

Leggett (via Molly): "I thought you were from Russia."

Maria: No, that was my grandparents.

Leggett (via Molly): "What time is it there right now?"

Maria: Ten o'clock. Twenty-two hundred military.

Leggett (via Molly): "When you were Mr. Olden's secretary, how did he start his day?"

Maria: He wanted his coffee and the Harvey Herald.

Leggett (via Molly): "And how does Mr. Olden like his coffee?"

Maria: Two creams, one sugar, or take it black.

Taylor looked at Olden. "She's getting them right." Olden nodded. Then Taylor said, "Ask her something personal."

Leggett (via Molly): "What is Mr. Olden's middle name?"

Olden stood up. "Gentlemen, I think this could be her. Can we break for just a moment?"

The answer came back right away. Maria: Rufus.

Molly: How did you know it was Rufus?

Maria: Out in the garden, under the willow tree; Jimmy will tell you.

Olden coughed. "Uh, your Honor, I think ... this may very well be the girl, but, uh ..."

"It seems it must be her, your Honor," Taylor said.

"We object," Leggett said. "This person could have been coached. For all we know, they have a cribsheet right in front of her. This is not acceptable."

"It seems a legitimate concern, Mr. Leggett. Taylor, this is very interesting, but you have no proof this is Miss Diosas," Judge Hamrick responded.

"Oh, yes, we do, your Honor," Molly said. "It'll take a couple minutes to get it, but I can ask her to send her picture. I can print it out if you want."

"Proceed."

The picture downloaded and the printer labored away. First there was the rooster weather vane from Jim Olden's farm house. Then the big oak tree branches that hovered over the tin roof came into view. There she was. The hair, the eyes, the smile. Olden shifted around in his seat. The paper scrolled to her bare chest, curled out of the printer, and fell to the floor.

Judge Hamrick retrieved it. "Young lady, we'll not allow such in my courtroom. What are you trying to prove?"

"We will not introduce the photos in the courtroom, your Honor. We just want Mr. Olden to confirm or deny that this is Miss Diosas," Mr. Taylor said.

The judge studied the photo. He handed it to Olden. "Jimmy?"

"Uh, I'm not . . . let's see, uh . . ."

"Remember, you are subject to perjury."

Olden took a closer look. "Yes, your Honor. I do believe that is Miss Diosas." He cradled his head in his hands. His entire body shook.

"Your honor, we'll leave off the photo shoot, but we can print out the text for the jury in the courtroom. We only ask to let them read it and decide for themselves." Taylor said.

"But, your Honor, this is nothing but electronic hearsay, you can't—"

"We will appeal if this is not admitted," Taylor said.

"I understand," Hamrick replied.

"We feel we have grounds for appeal if it is entered, your Honor," Leggett responded.

The judge pondered the issue for a long moment. "I rule to allow it."

Leggett leaned over the judge's desk. "But, your Honor, this risks a mistrial. There is no precedent—"

"I'll take my chances. It is my courtroom. I have to decide."

"You Honor, may I take the computer into the courtroom?" Molly asked.

"You may, young lady."

Molly set up the computer and printer on a small table in front to the jury. "Excuse me, sir, I need that outlet."

"Sure, sure." Old man Watson got up and fed the power cord to a nearby wall outlet.

Molly ran the phone line to a jack near the bailiff. She powered it up, and the modern miracle of the Internet made its way to the coutroom in Harvey County. It was a first.

Bones turned to Tag. "What the heck is she doing?"

Tag shrugged her shoulders. "Don't know," she whispered.

The judge explained to the jury that in the judge's chambers all parties were convinced the person Molly would be talking to was Maria Diosas. They craned their necks.

Taylor asked Molly to tell Diosas where they were and what was going on. Molly typed in a message. We are in a courtroom. Everyone in the jury can read what you type. What is your name and where are you? The printer clicked and sputtered. As the papers rolled off, Molly read them outloud, and then handed them to Mr. Taylor. Taylor then turned them over to Watson, who passed them on down the line to the other members of the jury.

I am Maria Diosas. I used to work in Harvey Hospital as an L.P.N. I am now typing from the library of Moscow Lomonosov University.

Molly (for Taylor): Tell the jury how you and I have stayed in touch.

Yes, we have been pen pals since I left Harvey County. Now we e-mail.

Molly (for Taylor): Tell them why you left.

Jimmy sent me away after I make mistake. He says he will come for me later. In a moment, Maria sent another message. I am sorry.

Molly continued to read the responses out loud. The jurors began to reach for the papers as quick as they could get them from the one seated next to them.

"Ask her what happened the night Mr. Wilson died," Taylor said. Molly typed.

Maria: I gave the Demerol to the wrong patient. It was an accident.

Taylor (via Molly): Who was it for?

Maria: The one they call Wheatie. I gave it to the wrong one. It was the man they called Blinky. I confused the name. I am so sorry.

Molly: Jesus will forgive you, Maria.

Maria: I wish Jimmy would. Ask when he is going 2 come. I miss him so.

Molly: Yes, I will.

Gibson Taylor addressed the jury. "Ladies and gentlemen of the jury, we can ask any question you like."

They sat in silence.

"Any further questions?" Gibson asked.

No one spoke.

Molly: See U.

Maria: U2.

They recessed for the day.

CHAPTER FIFTY SIX

Fiddling While Rome Burns

THE END WAS AT HAND.

Tag called Indie the next morning. "Indie, I know you're out, but I wouldn't have you miss the finale for anything."

"I've about half wrecked my practice anyway. What's one more day?"

"I'll call Bones, too."

"Thanks. I knew he'd come in handy."

"You're right. He did. I'm still a bit puzzled as to how, but I am confident he did help. Meet me at this conference room you came up with, right after lunch."

Bones went by to visit Indie before heading out to his office. Indie was on the back porch sipping coffee with Ms. Jenkins. "Top of the day to ya, Bones, boy. Ain't it a good one? The sun's bright, and the roses smell so sweet. I pinned one on Ms. Jenkins just this morning. I tell you, Bones, she looks like a school girl. I might change my mind on the office and stay home. Spring'll be here before you know it."

"Hush, Henry." Ms. Jenkins blushed and went back in the house to get some more coffee.

"It sure is a pretty day. You oughta play golf. I'll write you a doctor's excuse."

"Man, I'd love to, but I don't want to have to read it in the paper after all this."

"Come by the office and get me about one. I sure ain't gonna miss it."

"I'm glad you aren't any part of what's going down today. The bookies at the B-&-B are betting four mil."

"I'm glad I folded. Too much of a poker game for a country doc."

"You didn't fold, Indie. You just played your cards right. Bring your fiddle. Might as well pick a few."

"You're getting as contrary as me, son."

When the two arrived at the courthouse, they looked like a couple of tourists. Indie had on a straw hat and a denim shirt that read **MY GRASS IS BLUE** on the back. Bones sported his best Sam Bush Hawaiian red shirt with loud pineapples all over it.

"You need a haircut, boy." Indie watched as the breeze tousled Bones' gray hair.

"Yeah, I'm afraid mama might see me and say I'm looking woolly."

When they walked up the steps Jim Olden turned away and didn't speak.

Of course Indie wouldn't let it go at that. "Top of the day to you, Jimmy. Ever thought about a tour of the Ukraine?"

"Indie," Bones laughed. "Hush up. We don't need a mistrial now. Tag would skin you."

"Yes sir, Master."

They went to the storage room that had served as a conference room.

"I think we ought to name it 'The Indie Jenkins Conference Center,'" Bones said.

"Nah, let's just leave it between the custodian and us. I hope we never need it again, but you never know."

They took out their instruments, and played as they waited. Tag arrived shortly. If she had any regrets she didn't voice them.

Indie bowed away on *"Rag Time Annie."* It was a grand session. He lit into a medley to honor Olden, and Bones backed him up on mandolin. They started out with *"There's No Hiding Place Down Here."*

"How 'bout another for our old pal Jimmy Olden?" Indie tucked his fiddle under his chin. *"Maybe 'I'll Break Out Again Tonight'?* I just love a good prison song." Tag smiled, shut the door, and let him hold court. It was nice to see him so relaxed, and she didn't want anyone to wreck the moment.

The hospital team was somber.

Bones called for *"You Can't do Wrong and Get By,"* but they only got through one verse: The jury had a verdict.

Indie put up his fiddle. "You know what, Bones? That S.O.B's girl killed ole Blink and he ain't a-damn bit sorry for it. I hope the jury speaks loud."

"I've got a notion they will."

They went in to listen to the verdict.

Bones looked at his watch: 3:30. "Tag, this has been going all this time and now they are done in ninety minutes? Whadda you make of it?"

"You never know what a jury thinks 'til it's over, but most often it is a sign they found it to be clear cut. We have found a quick verdict to mean they were in agreement; it's innocent or guilty, and with little doubt."

"Which way?" Bones asked.

The right side of her lip curled to the side. The men thought of it as her Mona Lisa smile. It means "You should know the answer and I ain't gonna tell you." She tousled her hair to the side. "Honestly, Bones, for a doctor ..."

"I guess the question is how much?"

"If this were New York or California, I'd say mega millions. Rural areas tend to be conservative, but that is the only reason I'd hedge my bets," Tag said.

Indie shuffled along with his cane. Bones held his elbow.

Indie said, "You know, Bones, Olden will appeal and maneuver like crazy, but you know something? That son of a bitch doesn't even know he should be sorry. This thing warn't about him. It warn't about me, either. It was about Blinky. How did folks forget that?"

"I don't think they ever knew it." Bones put an arm around Indie's shoulder. "I tell you one thing. I'm proud of you. It's easy to lose sight of that when the world is chasing you, but you never turned your back on him, even after he was in the grave."

"He'd a-done it for me, Bones. It ain't no more complicated than that."

The verdict was read.

The clerk looked like he was going to pass out. A reporter flung the door open and ran out of the courtroom.

Seven million dollars. No one in Harvey County had ever heard tell of that kind of money.

Mr. Olden locked himself in the courthouse bathroom and cried. When Leggett began to fear for his safety, Snookers came and took the door off the hinges, led Olden out to his Cadillac, and drove him home.

CHAPTER FIFTY SEVEN

Back to Normal

AFTER THE TRIAL, INDIE SELDOM talked of it again. Like he'd always done, he came around at Christmas dressed up as Santa to visit all the children in the neighborhood. "Ho, ho, ho. Merry Christmas. Kids, you know the difference between a violin and a fiddle?"

"No, Dr. Indi—I mean, Santa. What is it?"

"One has strings or one has strangs! Ho, ho, ho!! Merry Christmas!!" It wasn't Christmas until Indie came by.

One night at the cabin he had a few drinks and told Bones he knew he couldn't have changed it, but he still hated it happened to Blinky. "I appreciate you sticking by me, Bones. You were right about that loyalty thing. It meant a lot."

Bones almost got brave enough to take a swig of Indie's Jim Beam and tell him how he'd eavesdropped in on him and B.G. at the cabin. But then he'd let it lie. As close as Indie and Bones were, Indie never breathed a word of it, even when he was drunk. Indie must have felt he owed his adversaries the proper discretion.

"You know, Indie, we ought to go visit Mason tomorrow night. She sure did worry over you."

"Sure, let's go."

Bones picked up Indie just before dark-thirty. As they drove down the Lee Highway, Bones had to ask. "Indie, how do you figure Mason knows so much?"

"I dunno."

They turned the final corner to the Marley home stretch at dusk. A car pulled out of the driveway and sped off.

"Hey Indie, what kinda car was that? Looked fancy."

"Hm. Not sure. I can't see so good when the light is low." Bones gave chase for a moment, but Indie suggested they let it go. Bones turned around and went back to Mason's.

They pulled in the driveway. Mason had left the porch light on. The shrubs were as neat as ever.

"Man, who'd ever thought Wheatie would be a star witness like that?" Bones asked.

Indie smiled.

Atsa opened the door for them. Bones shook her hand. She and Indie exchanged a greeting.

Bones clasped Indie's arm. "What did she say?"

"Eyes like eagle."

"How do you understand her?"

"You forget. I'm part Choctaw, and a bit of Cherokee, too. I guess I have some Native American ways left in me."

"Is Atsa Choctaw?"

"I'm not sure, but all Native Americans have a kinship of sorts."

"Lord knows there's a lot I can learn from you."

Mason rolled her wheelchair to the door. "Well, hello, boys."

"Hey, Mason. Who was the visitor?" Bones asked.

"Hm. I think you are confused, son. We haven't had any strangers lately." Mason turned and rolled into the parlor. "Come on in. Two doctors in one day; I am honored."

There was a faint cigar aroma in the air.

"Now Mason, you do stick to one a day after supper like I told you, I hope?" Bones asked.

"Yes, of course. I always follow your advice, except on special occasions, you know," she said. "I must say, you sure can be uptight about rules, though."

Indie smiled. "It's okay to break the rules every once in a while."

Indie went over to her coffee table, and opened the little wooden box that was always there. "These look like the real thing, Mason." The box was chock full of brand new Cuban cigars. The bands were the characteristic gold and black, but the label had the precision white pin dots rather than the herringbone trim of the Dominican imposters. They were Cohibas, and no knock-offs, either.

"Where'd they come from?" Bones asked.

"Now, Bones, I have my ways. I do wish you gentlemen would have one."

"Bless you, Mason," Indie said.

"Would you bring me the box, Indie?"

He took it to Mason, and she handed him two cigars.

Atsa made a gesture to Indie, then tapped Mason on the shoulder several times and spoke in a low voice.

"Atsa would like to light them," Mason said. "She is glad there is peace."

Bones and Indie went out the porch. "You know, Indie, I can't understand a word Atsa says, but I like her. I sure appreciate her looking after Mason. I don't know how she'd get along without her."

Indie sat in the front porch swing to rock, and blew some smoke rings toward the ceiling. "I agree, Bones. I agree."

Life went on unchanged for a couple more years. When Ms. Jenkins passed one fall, Bones thought Indie was gonna crawl in the grave with her, but somehow the old doctor continued on for a while. Indie began to spend a lot of time at the nursing home. He would go over, play his fiddle for the residents, and stay for lunch. "I don't want 'em to forget me over here," he'd say. "I ain't but one heart attack away from being here myself."

As it turned out, it was a stroke that winter. Indie used to tell Bones when

Bill Monroe had his stroke and couldn't play his mandolin anymore he knew it was time to meet his maker, and he figured he'd be about the same with his fiddle.

Bones would visit him in the nursing home every Wednesday, and would cook a few burgers on the little grill Indie kept and then play a few songs. "*Will the Roses Bloom?*" was a favorite.

Sometimes he'd get Bones to pour up a drink of Jim Beam in a Dixie cup while Barney the skeleton stood watch. Indie knew it was against the rules. Bones always thought Indie enjoyed being contrary more than the drink. Indie took his fiddle to the nursing home, but usually left it under the bed. After his stroke, he could never play quite the same.

Every so often the case would come up.

"You know what, Indie, sometimes I think the truth about Blinky came from divine intervention," Bones said.

"Has a way of finding it, huh?"

"I'm glad it came out. It wouldn't have been fair for you to get blamed."

"Didn't matter to me." Indie sang a line of *'I'll Take the Blame.'* His husky voice was garbled after his stroke. He laughed out loud. "Damn, Bones, I'm a worse singer than you." He lay down on the bed and fluffed up his pillow. "I sure am glad we know what happened for Blinky's sake, and for anyone who comes along after him."

"How do you think it got figured out?"

"Like you say, divine intervention, I guess. Tell you what, Bones. Before Uncle Bill died, you know what he'd always say?"

"What's that?"

"Love all, trust few, confide to less, do wrong to none."

"Your Uncle Bill said that?"

"Shakespeare with a twist, Bones. You need to read more."

"I guess so." Bones had to laugh. Where'd Indie come up with all this stuff? Bones tucked him in. "I'll be back next week."

"Good. You bring that mandolin. As I get older, it's gotten to be my favorite of all."

"Yes, sir."

The day of the funeral was a hot one. They called for rain, but it held off.

Everyone in town came. It was short, and more music than anything. Indie always hated it when the preacher went on too long. They did *'You go to My Church, and I'll go to Mine,'* just like Indie had asked for. No one played the fiddle that day, but Indie's spot was left open. All the musicians knew he was there with them. Musicians are like that, especially the bluegrass crowd. They all sweltered. Bones loosened his tie. When the men took off their coats, perspiration had wicked its way up the back of their shirts.

Young girls wore bright sundresses, and several had prints of roses. Somehow the ladies didn't sweat. Many of them shielded their heads with broad-brimmed sunhats. Indie would have liked that. He thought it was classy when women wore hats. Molly announced she was pregnant. Bones wished Indie could have heard the news. Indie had left his '47 Chief motorcycle to Molly in his will.

Martin Taylor was at the back of the church. He and Bones didn't speak; it wouldn't have been proper, but Martin tipped his hat before he took it off as he

walked in the door. Bones signaled a silent salute in return. It was misting at the graveside service. Taylor took shelter under the old oak tree there, and put his hat back on after the service.

Atsa rolled Mason to the funeral, and they sat in the back. Wheatie came up and shook Betty's hand and told her grandsons what a good man Blinky had been.

When Bones got home he was restless. He and Kate went down to the cabin. They took the old rough and rocky road by the river. Bones drove slow, and rolled the window down. It was on toward dusk. The banjo frogs played a chorus.

Kate watered the roses. "Now, Bones, they need about an inch of water a week."

"Yes, ma'am."

"Too much and they'll get a fungus."

"I'll need your help. Indie knew all about the roses."

"He did. Here, just water around the base, not on the leaves."

"Like this?"

"Exactly."

"We can't let the roses go."

"I agree."

They walked down by the river. Indie understood people were human first. He said they wouldn't need doctors in heaven, and there he'd fiddle for eternity. Bones was sure he was at it already. He bet he didn't even need his Jim Beam up there. Or maybe they had an endless supply that wouldn't hurt your liver. Bones didn't know.

He skipped a few flat rocks across a calm spot in the water. Indie always said the river would cure what ails you. Bones took off his shirt and jumped in for a swim.

He broke above the water. There was splash and noise, and then all was quiet again.

"Kate?" Do you hear it?"

"What's that?"

"The wind. It's like Monroe said; the ancient sounds. I can hear Indie's fiddle break on 'The River of Jordan.'"

"Yes, Bones. I do."

"It's gonna be hard without him."

"I know."

An eagle swooped out of the sky and dipped down near the water, then soared skyward and disappeared around the next bend.

Indie was right. There was no finer place than the river.

THE END

Visit Dr. Tom Bibey Online

http://drtombibey.wordpress.com

Find out where he will be signing books
Post stories you know about Indie
Invite him to a conference call with your reading group
Read what others say about his latest stories.

_____

Visit The Mandolin Case Website

http://www.the mandolincase.com

See where the traveling mandolin will be next
Read what others say about The Mandolin Case

_____

Become a Friend of Dr. Tom Bibey on Facebook

Ford, Falcon & McNeil Publishers
Chattanooga

LaVergne, TN USA
28 June 2010
187643LV00002B/24/P